L

THE LIBRARIAN SPIES

THE LIBRARIAN SPIES

Philip and Mary Jane Keeney and
Cold War Espionage

*Rosalee McReynolds and
Louise S. Robbins*

Praeger Security International
Westport, Connecticut • London

Library of Congress Cataloging-in-Publication Data

McReynolds, Rosalee.
   The librarian spies : Philip and Mary Jane Keeney and cold war espionage / Rosalee McReynolds and Louise S. Robbins.
       p. cm.
   Includes bibliographical references and index.
   ISBN 978-0-275-99448-8 (alk. paper)
   1. Keeney, Philip O. (Philip Olin), 1891–1962.   2. Keeney, Mary Jane, b. 1898.
3. Spies—United States—Biography.   4. Communism—United States.
5. Subversive activities—United States—History—20th century.   6. Espionage—United States—History—20th century.   7. Espionage, Soviet—United States—History.   8. Librarians—United States—Biography.   9. Cold War.   I. Robbins, Louise S.   II. Title.
   E743.5.K34M37 2009
   327.12092—dc22
   [B]   2008047571

British Library Cataloguing in Publication Data is available.

Library of Congress Catalog Card Number: 2008047571
ISBN: 978-0-275-99448-8

First published in 2009

Praeger Security International, 88 Post Road West, Westport, CT 06881
An imprint of Greenwood Publishing Group, Inc.
www.praeger.com

Printed in the United States of America

The paper used in this book complies with the
Permanent Paper Standard issued by the National
Information Standards Organization (Z39.48-1984).

10   9   8   7   6   5   4   3   2   1

The authors and publisher gratefully acknowledge permission to reprint the following material:

Portions of Rosalee McReynolds, "Trouble in Big Sky's Ivory Tower: The Montana Tenure Dispute of 1937–1939," *Libraries and Culture* 32 (Spring 1997): 163–190. By permission of the author and the University of Texas Press.

The portrait of Mary Jane Keeney, © *New York Times*. Courtesy of Redux Pictures.

For Rosalee, Eric, and all of Rosalee's family

For the Robbins Family—Robby,
Patrick, Greg, Maura, Cole, and Harper

"Cass Mastern lived for a few years and in that time he learned that the world is all of one piece. He learned that the world is like an enormous spider web and if you touch it, however lightly, at any point, the vibration ripples to the remotest perimeter and the drowsy spider feels the tingle and is drowsy no more but springs out to fling the gossamer coils about you who have touched the web and then inject the black, numbing poison under your hide."

—Robert Penn Warren, *All the King's Men*

CONTENTS

PREFACE

This book was a joint effort. Rosalee McReynolds spent more than fifteen years on it, until her early death. She passed a partially completed manuscript and a veritable deluge of documents on to me. I have labored over the unexpectedly difficult task of making someone else's research my own, forming pictures of events and circumstances that often, but not always, agreed with Rosalee's. It has inevitably been changed with viewing by a new set of eyes and the surfacing of new information. I am grateful for her work and hope that my completion of it has been worthy of her beginning.

I owe special thanks to John Earl Haynes, twentieth-century political historian at the Library of Congress, for remembering my Keeney inquiries and exchanging helpful emails. The Tamiment Library at New York University and the Harry Ransom Humanities Center Library at the University of Texas at Austin both responded in timely fashion to my requests for information. George F. Simmons sent material about his father, G. Finlay Simmons, Philip Keeney's nemesis at Montana. I wish to thank my colleagues and students at the University of Wisconsin-Madison and my patient family for their understanding as I pushed aside other duties to complete this book. A special debt of gratitude is owed to my son, Patrick B. Robbins, for his work on the index.

Louise Robbins, Madison, Wisconsin, 2008

Library history is a small and fledgling discipline. The people in the United States who call themselves library historians can be counted on the fingers of fewer than ten hands. We are spread throughout the country and, consequently, are something of a fragmented group. Nevertheless, I have not lacked for support and assistance from my colleagues as I have written the story of Philip and Mary Jane Keeney, two American librarians blacklisted during the Cold War because of their Communist sympathies. I am especially appreciative of Pat Doran; librarians and archivists at the government documents department of Tulane University Library, the University of Illinois Urbana-Champaign, Berkeley's Bancroft Library, the University of Montana, the University of Chicago, and the University of Michigan; the Federal Bureau of Investigation; Art C. Klehr; and Boys Republic. Numerous people have been subjected to my yakking about the Keeneys in the way others endure snapshots of strangers' grandchildren. Loyola, my employer, provided released time for research and writing. A group of Japanese students, with whom I connected through Andrew Wertheimer, shared my interest in Philip Keeney and found some sources on Keeney's time in Japan. Fellow historians Daniel Ring, Jim Gordon, Wayne Wiegand, Louise Robbins, Joe Kraus, and Ed Holley shared my passion for discovery and were willing to talk and read parts of my work.

Readers who are uncomfortable with sappy tributes may want to skip the next two paragraphs. The first one is devoted to my sister and to my physician. The next one belongs to my husband.

On October 28, 1997, my life changed dramatically when I was diagnosed with malignant ovarian cancer. The doctor who performed my surgery said that, with luck, I might live for two years. I was ready to go home and put my affairs in order. The Keeney project, which had begun ten years earlier, appeared to be equally doomed. Thanks to my sister Judy's determined efforts, I found myself in the care of a doctor with a more optimistic outlook. Dr. Milton Seiler, Jr. is a wonderful oncologist in New Orleans who has never put a time clock on my survival. He has treated my cancer and has kept me amazingly healthy. By all rights, I should be dead even as I am writing these words. I credit Dr. Seiler and his fine staff with keeping me alive.

Ultimately, it is the love and support of my husband Eric Sands that has enabled me to continue work on this book. He has read the manuscript several times and has talked to me about the Keeneys with the same enthusiasm that I have for them. Whenever I feel a little squeamish about my attachment to Philip and Mary Jane—I never met them, after all—he assures me that my biographer's obsession is perfectly normal. He also has nudged me through numerous cases of writer's block. Most importantly, he makes me laugh.

This book is for Eric with deepest affection.

Rosalee McReynolds, 2002

ABBREVIATIONS

AAUP   American Association of University Professors
AFT   American Federation of Teachers
ALA   American Library Association
ARU   American Railway Union
BEW   Board of Economic Warfare, a federal agency
CIA   Central Intelligence Agency
CIE   Civil Information and Education Section of SCAP
COI   Coordinator of Information, forerunner to the OSS
CP   Communist Party
CPUSA   Communist Party USA
FEA   Foreign Economic Administration, successor to BEW
GRU   Glavnoe Razvedyvatelnoe Upravlenie, Soviet military intelligence
HUAC   House Committee on Un-American Activities, commonly called the House Un-American Activities Committee
IPR   Institute for Pacific Relations
KGB   Komitet Gosudarstvennoi Bezopastnossi, the chief security service of the USSR
NSA   National Security Agency
OSS   Office of Strategic Services, forerunner to the CIA
PLC   Progressive Librarians Council
SCAP   Supreme Command Army Pacific
SISS   Senate Internal Security Subcommittee, informal name for the Subcommittee of the Senate Committee on the Judiciary charged with overseeing internal security

Introduction

At the height of the Cold War, a little known junior senator from Wisconsin traveled to Wheeling, West Virginia, to address the local Republican Women's Club. Although Joseph McCarthy had searched for a pivotal issue that would bring him into the public eye, he had yet to distinguish himself during his four years in Congress. But things were going to change that night. He was about to become famous; he would ultimately lend his name to an era and an attitude. As he struck the raw nerve of America's fear of Communism, McCarthy was going to create an "ism" of his own.

On February 9, 1950, the senator stepped up to the podium and declared that the State Department of the United States was a haven for reds and traitors. He claimed to be holding a list of 205 individuals loyal to the Communist Party "who nevertheless are still helping to shape our foreign policy." McCarthy would not identify any people on the list, but he was quite willing to condemn a select group of former State Department employees as Communist sympathizers. The best known was Alger Hiss, a prominent member of the State Department during the Roosevelt administration. Lesser known names on McCarthy's list included John Stewart Service, an authority on China; Julian Wadleigh, an economist; Gustave Duran in the department's Latin American division, and

then there was a Mrs. Mary Jane Kenny, from the Board of Economic Warfare in the State Department, who was named in an FBI report and in a House committee report as a courier for the Communist Party while working for the government. And where do you think Mrs. Kenny is—she is now an editor in the United Nations Document Bureau.[1]

Although his appearance in Wheeling catapulted Joe McCarthy to fame, it also marked a personal crisis for Mary Jane Keeney, the misnamed woman he meant to target. For her, the best thing about the speech was that McCarthy had gotten her name wrong. Unlike McCarthy, the last thing she wanted was more publicity. Mary Jane had gotten enough of that when she and her husband Philip were called before the House Committee on Un-American Activities (familiarly HUAC) in 1949 to account for friendships with suspected Communists, memberships in so-called Communist fronts, and authorship of articles that had been published in leftist periodicals.[2]

Conservative journalists and politicians had seized the occasion to denounce the pair as Communist sympathizers and as spies for the Soviet Union. If the accusations were true, the Keeneys had provided the Soviets with classified information about American defense and economic policies that could alter the balance of power between these rival nations. If false, the Keeneys had been shamefully wronged by their own government, for they had quickly toppled from their comfortable lives into grief and poverty. And they were hardly alone. Philip and Mary Jane Keeney were but two of the many people whose lives were turned upside down by the fierce anti-Communism that permeated the second half of the twentieth century. But, unlike many others, they were not innocent victims of guilt by association. Although we may never know exactly what information the Keeneys gathered to share with their Soviet handlers, it is clear from our vantage point that Philip and Mary Jane were spies.

Formal charges of espionage were never brought against the Keeneys. The reasons for this are not clear, but in similar cases the government chose not to prosecute, even when it had a strong circumstantial case, because doing so would require introducing sensitive information into the public record. It also meant divulging the methods used by the government to obtain its evidence, methods that were not always orthodox nor legal. Freedom from prosecution did not mean, however, that suspected spies got away scot-free. There were other ways of punishing them: through surveillance, through harassment, through blacklisting. Mary Jane Keeney asserted that her career and that of her husband had been destroyed by their foes by design.[3]

The Keeneys' ordeal continued long after they were called before HUAC and after Joseph McCarthy denounced Mary Jane in his Wheeling, West Virginia, speech. In September 1950, having corrected his erroneous version of Mary Jane's name, McCarthy cited her as an investor in Washington, D.C., radio station WQQW, which he accused of broadcasting pro-Communist propaganda. Two years later, she and Philip were summoned by a Senate committee and questioned about their involvement with the Institute of Pacific Relations, an organization of Far Eastern specialists who had allegedly tried to foster a pro-Communist American policy toward China. During the course of those hearings, Mary Jane was asked to name any State Department employees who helped her to get a job at the United Nations, and when she refused to comply she was charged with contempt of Congress.[4]

The Keeneys frequently took the Fifth Amendment when asked uncomfortable questions. In other instances, they refuted insinuations that they were disloyal to the United States. They flatly denied having ever been Communist Party members, but that was something of a technicality. They were professed leftists with strong sympathies toward the Soviet Union, an indelible stain during the Cold War, when most Americans lived in terror of Soviet aggression. The couple soon would find that they were unemployable and that they would have to rely on friends even for a place to live. They would be forbidden passports, which meant they could not start life over in another country, and they would be under FBI surveillance for the rest of their lives.

Ruined by accusations and investigations, many people in similar predicaments quietly dropped from sight, sometimes changing their names so that they could reconstruct their lives and get jobs. The Keeneys, on the other hand, would not censor themselves to conform to the social and political temperament of the Cold War, asserting their rights to think and say what they wanted and to associate with whom they wanted. The Keeneys openly socialized with known party members (some also suspected of espionage) and supported leftist causes that had been labeled as Communist fronts, even after they themselves came under attack. Although Americans eventually recoiled from the harsh treatment of suspected Communists or sympathizers (those called "fellow travelers"), few former targets of "red baiting" were anxious to talk or write about their ordeals. Mary Jane Keeney, by contrast, was anxious to leave behind her version of the suffering she and her husband had endured. In "The Political Persecution of Philip and Mary Jane Keeney" she crafted a description of the couple as besieged citizens who loved their country and took their freedoms very much to heart.

Mary Jane did not write "The Political Persecution" as a mere exercise. She hoped to be remembered by posterity in just the way that she had depicted herself, as a brave outspoken victim. Shortly before her death in 1969, she bundled her raggedly typed manifesto together with assorted documents that included old letters, yellowed newspaper clippings, and autobiographical sketches and charged her attorney with giving them to the Bancroft Library at the University of California in

Berkeley. There, under the file name "Personal Papers of Philip and Mary Jane Keeney" the sheaf of materials lay untouched for twenty years. Being childless and having few relatives, the Keeneys faded into obscurity as their friends died. Only chance prevented the Keeneys from being forgotten.

That chance event occurred in 1987, when Rosalee McReynolds happened to read about an incident that occurred at Montana State University (now called the University of Montana) in the late 1930s. Philip Keeney, the university librarian, had objected when the state's board of education ordered the removal of a controversial novel from library shelves throughout Montana. The incident turned into a dispute that attracted national attention. Philip eventually won his case in the court of public opinion and in Montana's State Supreme Court, but he paid for the victory with his job and his health. In 1937, one of the darkest years of the Great Depression, an ailing Philip Keeney was turned out into the world with his wife Mary Jane.

The Keeneys' plight captured McReynolds' imagination, and she wanted to know what became of them. At first, it was easy. Articles about the censorship dispute in Montana appeared in the library and mainstream presses of the period. It was a cakewalk to discover that the Keeneys had spent the war years in Washington, D.C., and had worked for government agencies where they were accused of sharing the classified data to which they had access with the Soviet Union. Transcripts of Congressional hearings were easy to find, neatly indexed in the *Monthly Catalog of United States Government Publications* and shelved in depository libraries. The *New York Times* also offered up a raft of articles detailing the Keeneys' political and legal problems. Nothing, however, answered the most basic question: were Philip and Mary Jane Keeney really spies or were they victims of Cold War hysteria?

The question continued to gnaw at McReynolds, and she began the arduous process of trying to find the answer. The mission began to take on a double purpose: to answer this gnawing question and to test her abilities to find information. She exhausted standard reference works, print ones in the beginning, digital ones as the years passed. She spent hours combing through unpromising sources, reveling when she discovered any scrap of information that could propel her search forward. Ultimately, she contacted individuals who had known the Keeneys and sought out archives where relevant materials might be found. Virtually all of them treated her obsession with the utmost respect and rendered assistance.

At the Bancroft Library in Berkeley McReynolds discovered that, despite the file name, the "Personal Papers of Philip and Mary Jane Keeney" were very impersonal. The records were devoid of anything that would give the Keeneys a human face: no affectionate letters, no candid photographs, and no revealing diaries. Two years later, in New York, McReynolds would read Mary Jane's last will and testament in which she directed her heirs to destroy any and all personal files. She wanted to leave nothing that would contradict the one-dimensional portrait in her "Political Persecution of Philip and Mary Jane Keeney."

Ironically, a warmer, more interesting image of the Keeneys emerged from their FBI files, which McReynolds requested through the Freedom of Information Act (FOIA) in 1987. Over the next five years, fragments of the couple's 3,000-page file trickled in. The material was heavily censored, but through the uncensored portions she was able to begin to piece together the government's evidence against the Keeneys and to get a sense of their daily lives. After about 1,500 pages, however, the mailings just dried up. Subsequent appeals to the FBI for more materials met with marginal success; sincere but harried clerks asked her to be patient. Written inquiries generated form letters from the Bureau assuring her that the request was being handled. Besides, many of the unreleased pages duplicated material already sent, they said. Eventually, about ten years after her initial inquiry, McReynolds accepted the fact that nothing more would be coming from the FBI. And she discovered that, despite its bulk, the Keeneys' FBI file did not decisively answer the question about whether they had been rightly or wrongly suspected of espionage.

What the files vividly revealed, however, was the extent to which the government transgressed the couple's privacy, often without regard to legal niceties. The FBI tapped their phone, opened their personal mail, and broke into their apartment to photograph Mary Jane's diaries—all apparently without warrant. An open file on the couple remained in effect until the Keeneys died in the 1960s. It was a scenario repeated again and again with many other Americans who were suspected of disloyalty, and the toll on civil liberties arguably exceeded the damage to national security resulting from any information they might have supplied. McReynolds sheepishly admitted to a certain gratitude for the U.S. government's surveillance tactics. Besides providing greater insight into the Keeneys, the FBI's files are an intriguing study in fact gathering and analysis, one that can make a historian uncomfortable.

Further understanding of government intelligence methods was provided at a July 11, 1995, ceremony honoring veteran officers of the CIA and the NSA. Following a series of speeches lauding the agents' work, the NSA unveiled the curiously named "Venona," a secret operation that had decrypted cables exchanged between Soviet intelligence organizations and their operatives in the United States. The cables spanned the period between the late 1930s and the end of World War II but were not translated by American cryptologists until at least the late 1940s and the early 1950s. Although the project officially ended in 1980, the NSA concealed it for another fifteen years, long after the cables ceased to have any impact on American security. Eventually, Senator Daniel Patrick Moynihan of New York persuaded the NSA to release the cables, which the agency posted on the World Wide Web in the late 1990s.

A generation had passed between the Keeneys' deaths and the declassification of their FBI files and the Venona cables. When put alongside the more recent information, Mary Jane's version of events unravels, and the story that emerges in its place is more complicated than the one she left behind. In contrast to "ordinary citizens" caught up in Cold War anti-Communism, these newer documents suggest two people who engaged in a series of mishaps and adventures that led them into the inner circles of foreign intelligence agents. So, did that mean that the Keeneys were spies?

After fifteen years of asking, McReynolds was still grappling with that issue when the ovarian cancer with which she had been diagnosed in 1997 overtook her. She died, with her work well under way but unfinished, in August 2002. Prior to her death, she asked members of the small library history community if someone would undertake to finish her work. McReynolds knew that I had written about censorship and loyalty investigations and focused on the time period her work covered; I undertook the task, aware of the solemn responsibility entailed, but unaware of the difficulties I would face that have taken six more years to overcome.

Like the agents working for the FBI, historians gather their data one document, one interview, one book, one revelation at a time. The data gathered accumulates gradually and comes together in bits and pieces, with an iterative process of integration of information and seeking of missing pieces. Each new fragment may cause new questions to be asked of earlier material. The researcher knows when she has finished the process when the picture makes sense and any new material is repetitive of the old and brings no new insights to bear, does not shift the focus, or change the picture. Like the FBI agents, the researcher then draws the best conclusion available from the data, draws a picture and shares a story.

In this instance, however, I acquired all of Rosalee McReynolds' accumulated research at once, and at times felt I was buried in a load of gravel, fighting my way through the documents to make the information and the subsequent story my own. Initially I thought I would be just an editor, but I found that only chapters 1 through 5—the Keeneys' lives before spying—were complete, and others that had been started had to be reconceptualized in the light of new knowledge. I suppose the agents who received Elizabeth Bentley's 1945 story of government espionage experienced the same kind of information overload and the need to make sense of it. J. Edgar Hoover was able to make an argument for more agents based on the need to pursue those whom Bentley had named; I had to use the snatches of time a busy department chair can find. It has taken me much too long. New materials have been, and continue to be, uncovered and published; I had to digest thousands of pages of FBI files and try to match them with Venona decryptions to make sense of partial information. I ultimately had to develop my own set of ambiguous feelings about the Keeneys. I had to jump to my own conclusions, conclusions that had to be modified even after the book arrived on the editor's desk.

The analogy with the FBI is disquieting; the differences make the difference. The FBI agents kept their sources secret, their methods secret, and did not allow for those on whom their gaze was fixed to provide counterinformation or counterinterpretations. Historians do their best to leave a bright trail so that those who wish to challenge their facts or interpretations can do so.

Of course, spies do not make discovery of their work easy. The historian researching and writing about spies—even minor league ones like the Keeneys—can feel some sympathy with the difficulties the FBI faced in investigating and bringing to justice the Americans who illegally provided information to the Soviet Union. Even those who were clumsy with their spy craft were clever and stubborn enough to leave little evidence. The FBI did not have the advantage of present-day scholars' discoveries in the KGB archives to fill out their picture.

The pieces as they fit together follow: Chapters 1 and 2 deal with the Keeneys' lives before they meet. Chapter 3, "The Librarians," deals with their careers in Michigan, uneventful except for their marriage, and in Montana, eventful indeed. Chapter 4 tells of their penurious lives in California between Philip Keeney's Montana ouster and their move to Washington, D.C. It was during this time that the Keeneys' relationship with the Communist Party appears to have begun in earnest. Chapter 5, "The Progressive Librarians' Council," looks at the Keeneys' leadership of a short-lived leftist organization, now regarded as a Communist Front group, which tangled with the library establishment, isolating the Keeneys from the library community, and hastening them on the road to radicalism. Chapter 6, "The Spies at Home," and chapter 7, "The Spies Abroad," look at the Keeneys' careers as federal government employees and their activities as spies for either Soviet military intelligence, the

GRU, or the secret police, the KGB. Chapter 8, "Caught in the Web," shows how the confluence of events worked to expose the Keeneys, players on the periphery of interlocking scenes. Chapter 9, "The Un-Americans," details their ordeal of hearings and trials, and their life after leaving federal service. Chapter 10 makes an attempt to assess to a small degree the Keeneys' impact on their associates, their relationship to the library world, and what significance, if any, their story holds.

Librarians today espouse a strong belief in free access to information as essential to an educated citizenry. But they did not and do not condone spying, providing secret information to which they have access to a foreign government, compromising national security—and compromising the foundations on which the right to access to information stands. Philip and Mary Jane Keeney violated their obligation to protect classified information to the point of disloyalty to their country—but the U.S. government responded in a manner that risked its democratic foundations. In the twenty-first century, as the United States becomes increasingly defined by its reliance on information, and we once again face the use of invasive tactics of surveillance and what many see as violations of democratic principles in response to a threat external and internal, the story of Philip and Mary Jane Keeney may serve as a cautionary tale about the difficulty of balancing national security with our democratic values.

CHAPTER 1

Philip

Aware that he was being watched, but seemingly indifferent to the consequences, Philip Olin Keeney left his Greenwich Village apartment on the night of December 10, 1948, and headed to a pier on New York's East River. Several days earlier he had booked passage aboard the *Batory*, a Polish ship that would take him away from his home in America to a new life in Eastern Europe. His ultimate destination was Czechoslovakia, where friends and a job were waiting for him.[1] No less important, there was a government harmonious with his political views. In the United States, he had been jobless for more than a year, blacklisted after being fired from his War Department position helping to establish libraries in postwar Japan because of his leftist sympathies. He had been labeled a Communist and a security risk. His chances of working again were essentially nil.

As Keeney walked toward the ship, two U.S. Customs agents came forward to meet him. He knew they were there to prevent him from boarding, and he knew exactly why. He had no passport. It had been confiscated from him when he was fired, and the State Department refused to issue him another one. Furthermore, the government suspected him of engaging in espionage. He hardly looked like a stock character from a spy novel, however. At 58, he was very thin, stooped, bald, and carried himself with a slight limp.

Realizing that he could never bypass the agents through physical acrobatics or stealth, Keeney had another idea, something truly American. He brought his lawyer with him. But the Customs officers were unmoved by her insistence that prevailing law did not require Keeney to have a passport to leave the country and that his certificate of identity, along with Polish and Czech visas, were sufficient travel papers.

Correct or not, the legal argument was hopeless. Determined that Keeney would not leave, the agents simply turned to the *Batory*'s representative and threatened to impound the ship if any Americans boarded without passports. With departure time quickly approaching and with no desire to spark an international incident, the ship's representative capitulated. Keeney's luggage, which had been loaded on the ship earlier in the day, was removed and given back to him. And then the *Batory* sailed away. Their job completed, the agents made no move to arrest Keeney, leaving him on the pier to watch the ship escape from sight. As he stood there, an aging man at war with his own country, he must have felt that his last chance for a new life had literally gone out to sea.[2]

Growing up in Rockville, Connecticut, Philip Keeney would have been incredulous if someone had told him that one day he would be accused of betraying his country by spying for a nation that did not even exist until he was a grown man. What examples of American spies did he have to refer to during his childhood? Nathan Hale was a martyr and a hero of the American Revolution. Benedict Arnold might have been the historical figure that everyone loved to hate, but at least his motives and loyalties were clear enough. The same could be said for the spies who gave their allegiances to the Union and the Confederacy during the Civil War. Their motives seemed clear. From the time of its creation in 1917 until the end of World War II, however, the United States' relationship with the Soviet Union varied from cautious to hostile to sympathetic.[3] Hence, ambiguity tinged the criminality of giving information to the Soviets, at least for Philip and many others, who seemed to believe they were simply providing more information to an ally than the overly cautious government was providing.[4]

Philip grew up oblivious to the concept of national information security, chiefly because he was born at a time when the United States was a country that seemed to have little understanding of the currency of information. He was raised in a comparatively open society where—at least ideally—information meant education, education meant knowledge, and knowledge meant wisdom. The concept of knowledge as something that could be stolen would likely have been limited to the arenas of patent and copyright, even for well-educated people. As Philip came of age in the early twentieth century, the FBI was the fledgling Bureau of Investigation and the CIA did not exist.[5] America lagged behind its European counterparts, including Russia, in creating domestic and foreign intelligence services. Furthermore, other governments had relatively little interest in U.S. government secrets. Even the Soviets did not begin to systematically spy on the United States until the late 1920s, and these early efforts had something of a buffoonish quality about them. One of the first Russian[6] agents in the United States later told the House Committee on Un-American Activities that his fellow spies simply gathered publicly available information and sent it home: "I feel sad . . . You can buy these books in any bookstand and they were silly in buying them."[7]

Within a decade of these fledgling efforts, however, the Soviet espionage network in the United States was considerably broader and had infiltrated federal government offices in Washington, D.C. Historian Earl Latham has suggested that the New Deal provided an unexpected opportunity for the Russians, not because the New Deal was communistic (as its critics charged), but because it created an abundance of jobs at a time when many liberal and leftist intellectuals were out of work as a result of the Depression. "The hospitality that the new Deal showed towards unmoneyed intelligence attracted a certain kind of new recruit— the bright young person with a social conscience, drawn into the public service not just because there was a job to be had, but because there was a job to be done."[8]

Several "repentant" ex-Communists, the most notorious of whom were Whittaker Chambers and Elizabeth Bentley, came forward after World War II to publicly disclose the Soviet infiltration of the American federal agencies during the New Deal. These deserters from the revolution became the darlings of the far Right and the demons of the Left. Even self-defined moderates were repelled by and suspicious of the Cold War pageant of former reds that testified before Congressional investigating committees. Chambers and Bentley were frequently characterized during their lifetimes as neurotics, alcoholics, and consummate liars. Chambers and Bentley had their flaws, but the passage of time and the release of previously classified information, like the Venona cables and FBI files, have largely vindicated them. Their stories may not hold up in every detail but appear to be substantially true.[9]

Whittaker Chambers claimed that he served as a contact between a Soviet agent named J. Peters and a group of federal employees attached to the Department of Agriculture. Harold Ware headed the group, and it retained his name after he died in an automobile accident and was replaced by Nathan Witt, another member, and even after its various members found employment in various other government agencies. Individuals who later admitted to being part of the Ware group gave different explanations for its existence. One member, Lee Pressman, said that it was just a Marxist study group. In 1948, Chambers stated that Alger Hiss, a high-ranking Roosevelt aide during the war, had been a part of the group, a charge Hiss denied. Eventually, Hiss was convicted of perjury and spent three years in prison.

Elizabeth Bentley described her attachment through her handler and lover Jacob Golos to the so-called Silvermaster group, headed by Nathan Gregory Silvermaster and his wife, Helen. Like Ware, "Greg" Silvermaster had worked for the Department of Agriculture but after the United States entered the war transferred to the Board of Economic Warfare and finally to the War Production Board. According to Bentley, employees in several different agencies funneled classified documents through Silvermaster. Once the documents reached the Silvermaster home, they were retyped. When they became too numerous for retyping William Ludwig Ullman, housemate of the Silvermasters, photographed them in a basement studio. Every two weeks, Bentley traveled between New York and Washington, D.C., to pick up the film from the Silvermasters and pass it along to her Russian contacts. When Bentley confessed to the FBI that she had been an agent for the Soviet government, the Keeneys would be implicated as members of the Silvermaster group.[10]

*   *   *

Nothing about Philip's early life suggested that he would be anything but a patriot, much less involved in trading his nation's secrets. He was the product of an ancestry and an upbringing reflecting traditional American values. His father was a shopkeeper, his mother a former teacher. On both sides of his family, he descended from pre-Revolutionary forebears. Mary Jane proudly pointed out that her husband's mother, Susanna, was a member of the James family of Philadelphia. His father Henry descended from the Olins and Keenes of New Hampshire and the Sumters of Connecticut. This pedigree was no guarantee of wealth, however. The Keeneys never got rich, and sometimes they faced economic strain. Over the course of Philip's childhood, his family moved four times within Rockville, Connecticut, each time to rented apartments in working class neighborhoods.[11]

Born on February 3, 1891, Philip was the Keeneys' only son. As he grew up alongside his four sisters (Helen, Muriel, Miriam, and Harriet) he applied himself to his studies at the local public schools and spent much of his spare time working at the family store. He apparently had no interest in taking over the business, aspiring instead to study chemistry at the Massachusetts Institute of Technology (MIT), but because money was tight he could not put together his tuition until he was 20 years old. He enrolled at MIT in 1911. His much anticipated education was cut short two years later, however, when he injured his leg in an accident and soon afterward suffered a bout with typhoid that forced him to leave school in 1913. Instead of returning to school when he got better, Keeney went to northern California to raise olives through the newly developed Orland Irrigation Project sponsored by the U.S. Bureau of Reclamation. His reasons for going are unclear, but in the early years of the century quite a few people recovering from serious illness sought the California climate and outdoor work to regain their health. Philip was adept enough to make a living—albeit a hardscrabble one—for a decade. After he gave up on the project, he was philosophical about the experience: "Though I did not make a fortune out of the venture. . . I learned several lessons valuable to an Easterner—how to get on with my varied neighbors, how to handle labor, and how to control myself under exceedingly adverse circumstances." He also was satisfied, despite a limp he carried as a vestige of his 1911 accident, that the venture had helped him to recover his health.[12]

Eventually, wanderlust hit the entire Keeney clan. By 1917, his parents and sisters had joined him in California, and it appears that they had given up on Connecticut for good. Their motives for leaving Rockville are just as obscure as Philip's. They might have been financially motivated or driven by a sense of adventure. There is no doubt, however, that California held hope and promise, while the East offered the Keeneys nothing new or exciting.

It is not clear that Philip's family helped him to manage the olive grove, but he was able to take off for six months during World War I to perform military service. Rejected for combat because of his leg injury and because he was underweight, Philip's contribution to the war effort consisted of working as a chemical analyst at the Hercules Powder Plant in Pinole, California. After the war he returned to cultivating olives, a task to which he would devote another five years of his life. In 1922, his father died and his mother and sisters were settled in Berkeley. Two years later Philip joined them as his life on the land came to an end.

Ten years after dropping out of MIT, Philip resumed his education. He enrolled at the University of California at Berkeley in 1923 and by 1925 had completed a bachelor's degree in history. At first, he considered a teaching career but was ambivalent because he had a slight speech impediment, a stammer. He then settled on a close alternative, librarianship, a propitious choice because merely by virtue of being a man he could expect to enjoy advantages in hiring and promotion over his female colleagues, although they dominated the field in numbers.

The U.S. census estimated that some 88 percent of American librarians were women in 1920, a leap of 68 percent from 1870. This phenomenon inspired concern among both male and female librarians of the

1920s, because many of them feared that the feminization of the profession would erode its salaries and prestige. C. C. Williamson's 1923 report *Training for Library Service*, commissioned by the Carnegie Corporation, reinforced those fears. In addition to criticizing the lack of standards for library education, Williamson asserted that the shortage of men as library faculty and students lowered the prestige of library schools *vis-á-vis* other professional schools. Not exactly poised to alter the social conventions that devalued women's work, librarians of the period logically concluded that the solution to the problem was to recruit more men. In short, there could not have been a better time for Philip to enter the field.[13]

In 1927, Keeney obtained a certificate in librarianship from Berkeley, but without a master's degree his job choices were limited, despite the benefit of his gender. His first job after completing certification was managing a graduate reading room at the University of Michigan library, hardly a prestigious position. His salary was $1800 a year, small even by the standards of the time. His pay increased considerably within a few months as he moved up to the post of assistant librarian in the order department for an annual salary of $2400. His advancement apparently was not contingent on his willingness to work long hours, because he had enough spare time to take courses toward a master's degree in library science—which may account for his more responsible position.

The studious life had bitten Keeney, and as he hovered on the brink of middle age his future seemed crystal clear. He would pursue the path of the scholar librarian. His life would be respectable, predictable, and subdued. It also would be lonely. Isolated in Michigan, far from his family, Keeney divided his time between the classroom and the library with few other diversions. But just as he was settling into this tidy and rather sad existence, his world was about to be invaded by a force he could not have imagined. He was about to meet Mary Jane Daniels.

CHAPTER 2

Mary Jane

Philip Olin Keeney and Mary Jane Daniels were born and raised a thousand miles apart, but against backgrounds so similar that they might have been brought up under the same roof. Like Philip, Mary Jane grew up in an atmosphere of small town Protestantism. Like Henry and Susanna Keeney, Frank and Margaret Daniels prided themselves on hard work, valued education for their children, and cherished their Anglo-Saxon bloodlines. Although Mary Jane was impressed by her husband's lineage, she was no less pleased with her own. An ancestor on her father's side had arrived aboard the Mayflower, and she was proud to say that her forebears included the names of men who had fought on both sides in the War for Independence.[1] This paternal side of the family apparently prospered, became staunch patriots, and settled into a solid middle-class lifestyle in Illinois.

Her mother's side of the family had not fared so well. Margaret Bailey's father had brought his wife and children to America from England in the 1870s after selling his freehold in Devon. Within two years, they returned to England, having lost their money in failed investments in the United States. Ten years later, Mary Jane's maternal grandparents immigrated back to America with their children and proceeded to squander a recently inherited fortune. Mary Jane did not disclose much more about their fate, except to say that by marrying Frank Daniels in 1888 her mother gained American citizenship.

Compared to the Keeneys, the Daniels family was financially and socially comfortable. Pillars of the community, they had no cause to strike out for better fortunes in the West. Mary Jane's father, Frank Daniels, was a graduate of Northwestern University's pharmacy school and managed a drugstore in Woodstock, Illinois, a town of 5,000 in the early twentieth century. He was highly respected, and when he died unexpectedly of a heart attack at the age of 52 his obituary was front-page news. All the local businesses closed so that the whole town could attend his funeral. During his lifetime, Frank Daniels had helped to found the town library, the fire department, and the hospital. He was the first president of the Woodstock Business Men's Association, which later became the Chamber of Commerce.[2]

Mary Jane had considerably less to say about her mother, a homemaker who took an active and pious role in the Presbyterian Church. Margaret Daniels's exacting daughter wrote her off as timid and conservative, a woman with nothing more than a "sentimental sympathy for the underdog." Clearly it was Frank Daniels to whom Mary Jane looked for guidance and inspiration. He, in turn, doted on her. Frank Daniels was quite remarkable in that he encouraged Mary Jane to compete on equal ground with her brother Luman to get a good education and attend college. For Frank Daniels, it seemed that his children could never know too much and never tell the world too much. This confidence in his children apparently was well deserved. In 1915, Mary Jane graduated as the valedictorian of her high school class and went to the University of Chicago on a scholarship. There she joined Luman, who had graduated first in his high school class three years earlier.

By her own account, Mary Jane always was a precocious child. She had impressed her family at a tender age with her extensive vocabulary and with entertaining short stories that she wrote from the age of 5. Before she entered grammar school, her father had gotten her a library card, and she was reading her way through the Woodstock Public Library. At age 10 she was reading Dickens and Thackeray. "I never read 'girls books' such as the Little Colonel series and Elsie Dinsmore which my playmates loved and wept over."[3]

Despite the encouragement she received from her father, the adult Mary Jane faulted him and her mother for failing to invest their children with a social conscience. By this she meant an appreciation of Socialism and Communism. It is hardly surprising that her parents overlooked this part of Mary Jane's education, given their conservative lifestyle and Republican politics. Nevertheless, Mary Jane conceded that her father might have inadvertently nudged her to the left by telling her about an extended "visit" that the people of Woodstock received from union leader Eugene Debs after the Pullman Strike, one of the largest labor actions of the nineteenth century.

In 1895, three years before Mary Jane was born, Debs spent six months as a prisoner in the McHenry County jail in Woodstock as punishment for his pivotal role in coordinating a work stoppage by employees at the Pullman Palace Car Company. Located in a Chicago suburb named for the company's owner, Pullman manufactured sleeping cars in an era when trains provided the only viable means of overland travel. George Pullman ruled his business and the town like a feudal lord, making arbitrary decisions that affected nearly every aspect of his employees' lives. During the depression years of the 1890s, like other employers trying to stay in business, he slashed wages. At the same time, however, as the only landlord in Pullman he charged his employees higher rents than those in nearby Chicago. He even assessed residents for using the local library. Want and desperation were epidemic, and after failed attempts to persuade Pullman to improve conditions, the workers at his plant walked off the job.[4] Although Debs had not called for the walkout, he threw his support and that of his organization, the American Railway Union (ARU), behind the striking workers by refusing to switch any Pullman cars from one railroad track to another, thus preventing them from traveling between destinations.

The influence of big business over the legal system was demonstrated on July 2, 1894, when a federal court in Chicago issued an injunction against the ARU for supporting the strike against Pullman. The judges claimed that interference with the interstate railway system amounted to obstructing a federal "highway" and ordered an end to the boycott. Confronted with sacrificing the strike or breaking the law, the ARU board boldly defied the injunction, but it was a hopeless situation. In the end, the strike was scuttled when the ARU leaders were charged with contempt of court for violating the injunction and, more seriously, with conspiracy to obstruct a mail train. As punishment, Debs and his colleagues were sentenced to six months in Woodstock's McHenry County jail.

This was no place for hardened criminals and proved to be a comparatively blissful place for the ARU "convicts" to spend their sentences. Because Sheriff George Eckert sympathized with his prisoners, he reduced security in the jail to the point that they came and went practically at will. The charismatic Debs frequently engaged in local baseball games, dined with the sheriff, and conducted the business of the ARU from his cell. Recognizing his good fortune immediately after he arrived in Woodstock, Debs wrote to his parents on January 8, 1895: "Am in the very best of health and spirits. We are in the best jail in the state, out in the country where we eat with the sheriff's family, have clean comfortable beds, lots of room & everything we care for."[5]

Despite his disapproval of Debs's political and social views, Frank Daniels was one of many townspeople who took a shine to him. In Mary Jane's words, her father "came to know him as a singularly lovable character." Hearing her father talk kindly about Debs led Mary Jane to conclude that the apparently conservative town of Woodstock "was rather tolerant towards Socialists as people."[6]

The tale about Debs may have kindled Mary Jane's interest in leftist politics, but her telling of it was longer on effect than on accuracy. Debs did not openly embrace Socialism until 1897, two years after his stay in the Woodstock jail, and the American Socialist Party was not established until 1901. Mary Jane's distorted description of Debs's stay in Woodstock gave it a mythical quality that helps explain why she converted to the Left. In its distorted form, the message she took from her father's reminiscence of Debs was that Socialism was somehow acceptable to the most revered person in her young life. The importance of her father's approval—even from the grave—was vital.

Mary Jane's radical transformation began in earnest after she was in college. When she first arrived at the University of Chicago in 1915, she studied the classics and the social sciences, and for the first time she found herself intellectually challenged by her teachers and fellow students. In addition, she had a full social life through participation in amateur theatricals and various informal clubs. As the feature editor of *Green Cap*, a student newspaper, she made the acquaintance of many faculty members, including Charles Gilkey, a young theology professor. In Gilkey and his wife Geraldine, Mary Jane found friends and mentors. Newly married and not much older than she, the Gilkeys apparently served as big brother and sister and as surrogate parents. They were reform minded and may have encouraged Mary Jane's political awareness. Geraldine Gilkey was active in the Young Women's Christian Association (YWCA), which in the years prior to World War I worked to improve living conditions for the underprivileged.[7]

In addition to his teaching role at the University of Chicago, Charles Gilkey was a minister concerned with social issues. At some point he became an officer of the Chicago chapter of the League for Industrial Democracy, founded by Jack London and Upton Sinclair in 1906 as the Intercollegiate Socialist Society (ISS). As the ISS, the organization's objective was to educate students about Socialism. After it evolved into the League for Industrial Democracy (LID) in 1921 its focus changed to labor issues, and its publication the *Intercollegiate Socialist* became *Labor Age*. As an officer of the LID, Gilkey helped to sponsor committees that came to the aid of strikers and the unemployed. Despite its new emphasis on labor, appealing to young people remained a goal of the

LID, and the student wing of the organization transformed into the Students for a Democratic Society in 1960.[8]

Between her native intelligence and her social successes, everything about Mary Jane's early days at college suggested a bright future. Within a short time, however, things began to go awry, just as they had for Philip Keeney when he was in college. In 1916, a scarlet fever epidemic swept through her dormitory, and stricken with the illness, she was forced to leave school. The following year she was devastated by her father's sudden death from a heart attack. Together, these events kept Mary Jane at home for two years. When she resumed her education in the fall of 1918, she had trouble finding her direction. She had lost her joy about the intellectual stimulation of college and now characterized the experience as "an education which gave me a mass of curiously unassorted information and a training in techniques and procedures, but not an education which had any connection with reality."[9] Soon after returning to school she sought out a more applied program, nurse-training at a hospital, but within months she returned to the University of Chicago and enrolled as a premedical student. Her brother Luman was then a graduate student in physiology, and he encouraged her to help him with a series of experiments he was conducting. "I used to attend classes and laboratory from seven to twelve," Mary Jane related, "operate on dogs all afternoon, and study at night. Finding this regimen rather tough, I later varied my work and took some graduate courses in sociology."[10]

It appears that Mary Jane's psychological state became as erratic as her academic career. She wandered around Chicago by herself, believing that this was a learning experience superior to anything she could get in the classroom. She became a regular in the periodical rooms of local libraries, where through liberal weeklies and newspapers she found the world of political thought that would influence her for the rest of her life. "I had for the first time an intimate and critical view of men and affairs."[11] Her experiences also built on her childhood affection for reading and encouraged what would become a lifelong devotion to libraries and independent learning.

If Mary Jane's wanderings through Chicago amounted to a search for meaning, she apparently found what she was looking for on November 11, 1918. On Armistice Day, she walked amid a thick of revelers celebrating the end of the war, but "I found no emotional release in mingling with the crowd."[12] Although she professed to be a nonbeliever, something instinctive from her Presbyterian youth led her to a church where she joined hands with strangers reciting the Lord's Prayer and singing the Doxology. "I had my one deep religious experience . . . Suddenly, I had an intuition of the oneness of mankind and the living force of a collective spirit."[13]

Mary Jane's account of this event and her early life appeared in an autobiographical article titled "The Making of a Radical," which was published in the September 1939 issue of a short-lived leftist publication, *Black and White*. Loyal Communists were expected to provide autobiographies that emphasized their political evolution, and this may have been the purpose of the *Black and White* article. On the other hand, despite her obvious political leanings, Mary Jane denied ever being a card-carrying Communist or a member of any political party.[14]

Even if she had wanted to, Mary Jane could not have joined an American Communist Party in 1918 because it did not yet exist. It is possible that her imagination was first captured by the left wing of the Socialist Party, which was on the brink of breaking out into a separate Communist entity at the end of World War I. This speculation is supported by Mary Jane's expressed disappointment that "the significance of the November Revolution was lost in the wave of rejoicing which swept America with the Armistice."[15] She was referring to the fall of the Hapsburg Empire in Germany and its replacement with a Socialist government, an event for Mary Jane as significant as the Armistice.

For anyone newly enamored of the Left, there was no better place to be than postwar Chicago. In the summer of 1919, delegates arrived in the city with the goal of establishing an organization of American Communists. Their fractious and divisive meetings ended by producing two opposing parties, the Communist Party, led by Russian émigrés, and the Communist Labor Party under the leadership of John Reed, the American whose eyewitness account of the Russian Revolution was recorded in *Ten Days That Shook the World*. Within these groups there were additional factions along lines of ethnicity and language—not surprisingly, because the majority of members in both groups were foreign born. Of the 24,000 reported members of the Communist Party in 1919, less than one-tenth were native English speakers. The smaller Communist Labor Party with 10,000 members had about 1,900 native English speakers.[16] The parties united in May 1921 as the Communist Party of America.

Although she lived in Chicago, there is no way of knowing if Mary Jane was present at the formative meetings of the American Communist movement. If so, she would have been conspicuous not only as a speaker of English but as a woman. At most, women made up 15 to 20 percent of party membership in the 1920s, and they usually were linked to male members, either as wives or lovers. In theory, Communists advocated sexual equality, but in practice women assumed subservient roles.[17] The place of Blacks in the movement also was uneven, with none at the founding conventions in 1919, and none represented on the Party's central committee until 1929. In the decade between, only a few hundred Blacks became members of the party.[18]

It is difficult to gauge Mary Jane's political activities during this time because later in her life she went to extreme lengths to hide her whereabouts for the period between 1920 and 1928. She concocted the tale of an exotic and mysterious illness that supposedly confined her to her mother's home: "In 1920, my formal education was permanently interrupted by illness, diagnosed finally as hyperthyroidism induced by the secondary infection of scarlet fever."[19] During this period of invalidism, she described herself as a "voyageur au ma chambre," claiming to have spent her long convalescence educating herself through independent reading, concentrating on poetry and the literature of the Renaissance. In addition, she said that she taught herself French, Spanish, and Italian, discovered contemporary novels, became conversant in the history of books and manuscripts, and kept up with current affairs through subscriptions to the *Manchester Guardian* and the *New York Times*. She may have accomplished all of these things, but not in a sickbed in Woodstock, Illinois.

Chicago in 1919 was not just the site of the formative American Communist Party. It also was home to a young political radical and poet named Legare George. Although she deleted George from any personal narratives of her life, Mary Jane acknowledged in a 1945 passport application that she had been married to him.[20] It would be more accurate to say that she acknowledged leaving him, because information she supplied on the application indicated that she had divorced George in Los Angeles in 1928, but she provided no clues as to when they were married or where they spent their years together. In all likelihood, the two probably met in Chicago around 1919 or 1920.

A conscientious objector, George spent the last weeks of World War I as a medic in France. Soon afterward, he made his way to Chicago where he came to the attention of Harriet Monroe, whose *Poetry* magazine was publishing the leading and promising poets of the day. By age 25, George had published poems in *Poetry* and in *Dial*, another prestigious literary magazine. In the 1930s, the Modern Library anthologized his work alongside that of Stephen Spender, Allan Tate, and Wallace Stevens. It may be that George never achieved their notoriety because he was not very prolific and because he changed his name to the less distinctive William Stephens in the 1930s. In addition, many of his poems were not published until twenty years after his death in 1958.[21]

The brief biography that accompanies *Standard Forgings*, his posthumous book of poetry, does little to shed light on the shadowy Legare

George. It makes absolutely no reference to Mary Jane. In the same way that Mary Jane attempted to erase the memory of Legare George, she was expunged from the story of his life. This may have been the work of his third wife, Margaret Thomsen Raymond, who had the poems published in 1978 under his later name, William Stephens. Neither Raymond nor Mary Jane, nor his second wife, the mother of his three children, is mentioned by name in George's biographical sketch. His children also do not figure in his brief biography, and neither does the fact that he was once poetry editor at *Esquire* magazine.[22]

What does appear in his biography is the story of a troubled youth who at the age of 15 ran away from his home in California. After a year of living on his own, George's family hauled him back and sent him to the California Junior Republic. Brainchild of self-proclaimed reformer William Reuben George (no relation to Legare's family), the Junior Republic has been characterized as a home for wayward youths and, indeed, Legare George suffered from a compulsion to steal. Still, it is not completely accurate to describe the Junior Republic as a reform school. More precisely, it was an idealistic experiment in salvaging delinquent youth through inculcation in democratic and capitalist principles. The Republic included a town hall, small businesses run by the residents, and a jail to which the lazy and undisciplined were remanded.[23]

The Junior Republic's goals were not always achieved; in fact, some turn-of-the-century observers believed that its system was akin to a Communist utopia and that it may even have cultivated rebelliousness. Historian Jack Holl suggests that "A number of young activists found the Junior Republic an ideal outlet for their liberal, and even radical, impulses. Although founded on the rock of political and economic orthodoxy, the Republic not only liberated its young citizens from the corrupting influences of the city and factory, but more importantly for the radicals, it implicitly repudiated the role of the family, the church, and the school in rearing and educating youth."[24]

This helps to explain how Legare George developed his leftist political impulses. The Junior Republic, it seems, also encouraged his literary talents. According to the biographical sketch in *Standard Forgings*, "the wife of the director became personally interested in his talents, got a job for him in the school library, and urged him to send his poetry to such men as Randolph Bourne and Edwin Arlington Robinson, who in turn encouraged him to continue writing poetry."[25] The encouragement paid off when he was discovered by Harriet Monroe.

Legare George's poems also provide the best clues to life with Mary Jane. Over his lifetime, he wrote almost exclusively about two things, the trials of the working class and tortured love. During the late 1920s, love must have been weighing heavily on his mind. From 1925 to 1928, he wrote poetry describing a woman who was distant and unresponsive to his affections—"She closed the windows and the door / To shut him from the place"[26]—and given the deeply personal nature of his poetry, it is safe to assume that George was capturing the demise of his marriage to Mary Jane. But even the poetry does not provide the exact cause of their breakup. Perhaps she found his politics unsatisfactory or perhaps the depth of his despair had taken a toll on her. A letter Mary Jane wrote to Harriet Monroe in December 1926 does establish that Legare was inclined to be gloomy. It also establishes that the couple was in Chicago at the time. Mary Jane writes to thank Miss Monroe for a recent issue of *Poetry* and "for being kind and encouraging to Legare. He needs badly just the spurring on that publishing in *Poetry*, and the friendliness of you, Mrs. Mitchell and George Drilan have given him. I, who may be pardoned for believing that he has an authentic gift, hearten him in despondent moments as best I can, but I can never offer so tangible inspiration as recognition."[27]

Less than two years after Mary Jane sent this letter her marriage to Legare George ended in California. After the divorce was final (a date coinciding with the miraculous recovery from her "illness"), Mary Jane went directly from Los Angeles to Michigan where, according to her autobiography, she got her first job. The disconsolate George spent the next few years drifting through the Midwest, "learning the ways of hobo jungles and town jails."[28] It is unclear if he was learning those ways directly or as an observer. He continued to write and publish poetry, much of it about the difficulties faced by factory workers and the heartlessness of industrial moguls. He also eventually resumed his reporting career, working as a labor correspondent for the *Chicago Daily News*, as well as for the *People's Press*, a Congress of Industrial Organizations (CIO) newspaper.

Comprised largely of seasoned Communists and expatriates from the American Federation of Labor (AFL), the CIO was formed in 1935 as an alliance of predominantly unskilled workers, in contrast to the AFL, which primarily represented craft workers.[29] The leading force of the CIO was John L. Lewis, president of the United Mine Workers of America. Although no friend of Communists, Lewis was willing to cooperate with them to shape his own labor organization.

In turn, the Communist Party (CP), which was able to supply several skilled organizers for the nascent CIO, was disposed to working with Lewis as part of Moscow's newly mandated "Popular Front." This was a strategy for achieving revolution by collaborating with non-Communist individuals and organizations. The relationship between

Communists and non-Communists in the CIO was often tense, however. Anti-Communist elements within the organization, abetted by growing anti-Communist sentiments in American society at large, undermined the might of CP members in the CIO, and this might explain why George's involvement with the CIO had ceased by 1940. Thereafter, perhaps as a concession to his new employers at *Esquire*, he apparently refrained from political activities. Ironically, Legare, who must have abetted Mary Jane's budding radicalism in the 1920s, would actually conduct himself ever more conventionally even as she became more of a steeled Communist.

Between the time of their divorce and the beginning of World War II, Legare George and Mary Jane Daniels followed different paths, but in their own ways crusaded for similar causes including economic justice, workers rights, and—no less important—literature. Mary Jane never developed her former husband's facility with language, but she defended words and thoughts by defining herself as crusader against censorship. She was not above making an exception, however. She never allowed the principle of free access to information to be applied to the details of her own carefully guarded life.

CHAPTER 3

The Librarians

Although proud to call herself a radical, Mary Jane was closemouthed about her affiliation with the American Communist Party. She persistently denied being a member of the party, and if she had joined, it is understandable why she would not admit it. Even during the relatively tolerant 1930s, when leftist sympathies were fashionable among the American intelligentsia and some elements of the wealthy, many of those in the party hid their membership. The mainstream population was, after all, suspicious of radicals. From another perspective it is irrelevant whether she carried a party card or not. Most important, her heart was in the revolution, at least her uniquely garbled version of it. Throughout her life, Mary Jane's radicalism was fraught with contradictions. She criticized her mother for sentimentalizing the poor but paid little more than lip service herself to the plight of the disenfranchised. Rather than living among the workers, she read progressive novels that celebrated them. She also enjoyed listening to Mozart, visiting art museums, and serving meals on her heirloom china, hardly the pastimes of the laboring classes. "I did not believe," said Mary Jane, "that my place was on the street corner."[1] And what a sight she would have made, attired in her white gloves and a hat, hawking the *Daily Worker* on the sidewalk.

She saw herself as part of the revolution's intelligentsia, even though she never extolled a coherent political philosophy, but this is as much a reflection on the state of the American Left during her lifetime as it is on her. Mary Jane came of age in the Progressive Era when liberal activists sought to erase injustices through reforms, strikes, and preaching from the pulpit. Socialists advocated more fundamental changes in the American economic system but lacked revolutionary will. Despite the presence of strong personalities like Robert LaFollette, Eugene Debs, and Norman Thomas, both groups failed to develop a powerful central authority that could unite their many ideological factions.

As the American Communist movement emerged after World War I, it too was fraught with internal conflict, but it did not want for discipline, which came from the Communist International (Comintern), formed in 1919. Ostensibly, the Comintern was a federation of Communist parties throughout the world, but its power base rested squarely with the Soviet Communist Party. Faithful party members had to comply with orders from Moscow, a requirement that initially gave the American Party a sense of stability.[2] It was at the Comintern's direction in 1921 that the rival Communist Labor Party and the Communist Party united into a single organization, the Workers Party, which by 1929 would evolve into the Communist Party of the United States of America (CPUSA). Unification was, in fact, a condition that American Communists were forced to observe to gain membership in the Comintern.[3]

Discipline did not translate into consistency or predictability. Moscow frequently demanded abrupt, sometimes irrational, changes in American party leadership and rank-and-file behavior that put members at personal risk. For example, in the wake of government raids on the headquarters and meeting halls of several leftist groups in 1919 and 1920, several American Communists chose to meet in secret or "underground." This perfectly logical action shielded party members, many of whom were deportable immigrants, from the attention of hostile authorities. As another condition of Comintern membership, however, Moscow decided in 1922 that American Communists would have greater legitimacy if they operated openly or "legally." Some defied Moscow by remaining concealed but were inevitably marshaled out of the party. Other members, unable to endure the Comintern's iron-fisted discipline, simply left the party in disillusionment.

Moscow would vacillate on other issues as the years went by. In the early 1920s, the Comintern forced American Communists to follow a strict regime with regard to several key issues, including the party's ethnic composition. Immigrants, divided into groups according to language, dominated the party in numbers and authority in its early years. Not surprisingly, the Comintern determined that Russian speakers would have the greatest internal authority over the party. But in the 1930s the Comintern reversed itself and deemed it necessary to attract more English speakers, and recruiting efforts among native-born Americans increased to the degree that foreigners were discouraged from joining the party at all.

In the all-important area of organizing workers, the Comintern flip-flopped between directing American Communists to form their own unions or to work within established unions. In the early 1920s, convinced that international revolution was imminent, Comintern leaders directed American Communists to create unions that would compete with more conservative labor groups, particularly the American Federation of Labor (AFL). By the mid-1920s it became apparent that the world was not on the brink of revolution and that Communist unions were not attracting sufficient numbers of members. Consequently, American Communists were directed to take a greater role in the AFL, essentially to bore from within. The latter approach was relatively short lived, as well. As soon as Stalin had consolidated his power in Russia by 1929, world Communism entered its so-called Third Period. Fiercely isolationist in tone, Third Period policy again mandated Communist-led unions to rival conventional trade unions. Six years later, Moscow renounced its Third Period approach and declared the era of the Popular Front, which justified collusion between American Communists and the non-Communist founders of the Congress of Industrial Organizations (CIO).

This stand on labor unions paralleled wavering views in Moscow on when its followers should participate in, or isolate themselves from, conventional institutions and politics. In the early 1920s, after American Communists were directed to operate in the open, or "legally," the party was renamed the Workers Party, making it seem more within the American social mainstream. With the commencement of the Third Period, the Workers Party was renamed the Communist Party of the United States of America (CPUSA) to solidify its identity. With the ushering in of the Popular Front in 1935, it again became acceptable to work with non-Communist groups, including mainstream political groups. At that point, defeating Fascism at any cost—even consorting with the bourgeoisie—justified the reversal of the Third Period militancy.

The Popular Front had a positive side effect for the CPUSA. The party's membership peaked at 100,000 in 1939, but it was a triumph that would be short lived when the Soviet Union committed a contradiction that many American party members could not stomach. On August 23, 1939, Hitler and Stalin signed a nonaggression pact that facilitated the German invasion of Poland and the Soviet seizure of the Baltic States. Stunned American party members resigned in disgust. Those who remained within the fold defended the Soviet Union's actions as being necessary for its survival, and as long as Stalin was united with Hitler,

American Communists campaigned against the United States' joining the Allies in the war effort. But this position against intervention changed as soon as Hitler reneged on the pact by invading Russia on June 22, 1941.[4]

The Soviet Union's virtual control over American Communists during these years seems indisputable, yet the question of this control formed the heart of a bitter argument between conservatives and leftists throughout the twentieth century. American Communists avowed that theirs was a homegrown organization, independent of any foreign government. Skeptics asserted just the opposite, insisting that American Communists answered directly to Moscow. In the post–Cold War era, this may not seem worth debating, but it was extremely significant at a time when Communist Party membership was equated with the will to overthrow the American government, a crime that could lead to prison time, to deportation, or (theoretically) to capital punishment. Over time, the number of people believing that American Communists were subservient to the Soviets expanded to include former party members, liberals, and the "renegade" intellectuals that Mary Jane vilified in "The Political Persecution of Philip and Mary Jane Keeney." The opportunity to resolve this dispute did not arise until the Soviet Union was dismantled.

In the wake of the 1989 coup that brought down the Communist regime, the Yeltsin government opened up old Soviet security files to American researchers. Between 1993 and 1996, American historian Allen Weinstein and Russian journalist Alexander Vassiliev were given access to the operations files of the KGB and its predecessor agencies. Harvey Klehr, an Emory University professor of political science, along with John Earl Haynes, twentieth-century political historian at the Library of Congress, were allowed to plumb Soviet files on the American Communist Party and the Comintern. Working independently of one another, the research teams concluded that the documents they examined proved that the Communist Party of the Soviet Union had virtually complete control over the CPUSA from the time the latter was established in 1919.[5] Haynes and Klehr conceded that the rank-and-file might have naively believed that they belonged to an American-based organization, but that the party leadership was knowingly submissive to Moscow. This obedience included the willingness to recruit Americans who would commit espionage for the Soviet Union.

The conclusions of the researchers who had used the Russian archives were met with praise and apprehension. Critics pointed out that the researchers' living and travel expenses were paid by conservative organizations that supported the hypothesis that American Communists were subservient to Moscow. Because Haynes, Klehr, and Weinstein were established proponents of that theory, it was hardly surprising that they were accused of subjectively using documents to affirm their own beliefs. When the Russian government abruptly cut off access to the archives in 1996, no one else would be able to verify or discard these conclusions at the source.[6] Despite lingering doubts, however, the findings based on materials unearthed from the Russian archives in the 1990s generally have been accepted, especially since the release of the decrypted Venona cables in 1995.[7]

As a person comfortable with contradiction and as a self-proclaimed radical, Mary Jane would have been unlikely to have objected to the Soviet leaders' dictatorial style or to their ever-shifting directives to American Communists. She demonstrated time and time again that she could accommodate political and economic incongruities if it suited her. There is no better example of this than the direction she took after parting company with Legare George. Even though she had become a confirmed anticapitalist at this point (largely because of the execution of Sacco and Vanzetti), she made the decision to accept an effete job with a rich capitalist employer.

Immediately after her divorce became final, the 30-year-old Mary Jane traveled from California to Michigan to catalog the rare book collection of Albert May Todd. Known as the Peppermint King of Kalamazoo, Todd was a chemist and entrepreneur who became wealthy in the late nineteenth century through his cultivation of aromatic herbs. Although he was rich, Todd was no conservative. In fact, like Mary Jane, he combined antithetical qualities. He acquired and perpetuated a vast fortune that enabled him to become a social activist. In addition to being one of the first members of the American Civil Liberties Union (ACLU), he spent his adult life promoting municipal ownership of railroads and public utilities. He founded the Public Ownership League of America, which survived from 1916 to 1922, as well as his own Todd Foundation "for the enlargement of mankind."[8] His brief political career began with an unsuccessful run for governor of Michigan in 1894. Three years later he was elected to the U.S. Congress as a fusion candidate of Michigan's Democratic, Union Silver, People's, and National parties. After he failed to gain reelection in 1899, he took an interest in assorted causes, including the American Proportional Representation League and the National Child Labor Committee. He also traveled to Europe, the Middle East, and Asia to study the social and economic systems in those regions.[9]

In the wake of antiradical sentiment following World War I, Todd came to the attention of disapproving public watchdogs. In 1920, the state of New York conducted one of the first government-sponsored investigations of domestic and foreign radical organizations. Todd was cited as a financial contributor to the *Intercollegiate Socialist*, the publication of the Intercollegiate Socialist Society, which later became the League for Industrial Democracy (LID). In time, Todd became the Michigan representative to the organization. Because Mary Jane's friend Charles Gilkey from her University of Chicago days also belonged to the LID, this may explain how she became acquainted with Todd.[10]

As Todd's librarian, Mary Jane had an ideal situation: a politically liberal employer and the opportunity to spend her days amid early manuscripts, antiquarian books, and modern fine press editions. By her own admission, the only qualification she had for cataloging the collection was an interest in bibliography that she had developed during her supposed illness. She estimated the number of items in Todd's library at 25,000 and claimed to have completed her task within fifteen months. That achievement defies the imagination, even if the collection contained only 10,000 items, as stated in Todd's *New York Times* obituary. In any event, Mary Jane stated that her final catalog never reached the light of day because Todd's family was unwilling to pay for its printing after his death in 1931.[11]

The reluctance of his relatives to carry the project through does not seem to have soured Mary Jane's relationship with them, at least not all of them. Todd's nephew, Laurence Todd, remained her lifelong friend, and like his Uncle Albert, Laurence was drawn to the Left. He was a Socialist from 1904 until 1919, when Michigan's members were expelled from the larger Socialist Party for being too radical. In 1919, the Michigan contingent teamed up with one of the newly created Communist factions, only then to be accused of being too conservative. At that point the Michigan Socialists formed the Proletarian Party. Laurence Todd's part in these events is vague, but he retained his keen interest in postrevolutionary Russia. From 1923 to 1952, he was managing director of the Washington office of Tass, the Russian news agency.[12]

With her job in Kalamazoo ending in the spring of 1929, Mary Jane moved to nearby Ann Arbor where she had been hired to catalog a collection of early scientific books for the University of Michigan. Because she worked in the library it was likely that Mary Jane would have met Philip Keeney. That their acquaintance would lead to marriage seems less likely, for in appearance and nature the two were complete opposites. The diminutive Mary Jane was dynamic, ambitious, and had big ideas. The phlegmatic Philip was tall, struggled with the limp from his youthful accident, and never suffered from an overload of dynamism or dreams. A sympathetic former colleague described him as "not a prepossessing looking individual . . . he didn't look very sturdy and was not a very energetic person."[13]

The most reasonable explanation for Mary Jane's attraction to Philip is that she was searching for someone very different from her first husband. A fuzzy photograph of Legare George that appears in his posthumous book of poetry is still crisp enough to see that he was handsome. A cigarette dangles from his hand as he gazes, steady and relaxed, at the camera. It also is hard to imagine muses more at odds than those who spoke to Legare and Philip. While Mary Jane's former husband wrote sensitive poetry, the latter wrote practical articles with titles like "Flexibility of Library Organization" and "Democratic Aids to Staff Responsibility."[14]

When they first met, Mary Jane considered Philip flawed, not in his body, but in his political and social awareness. She sniffed at his "petit bourgeois background" and called him a humanist of the Irving Babbitt school, "a thinker rather than a man of action."[15] She appreciated his love for the arts and education but was disturbed by his cynicism about life in general. He believed that the world was destined to go from bad to worse and equally certain that he could do nothing about it. As a man who didn't even exercise his right to vote, Philip was ripe for rehabilitation and Mary Jane was clearly the woman for the job.[16]

Raising Philip's political consciousness became the centerpiece of the couple's courtship, and because they were librarians it is not surprising that books played a large part: "We began with Gibbon," said Mary Jane, "and progressed to Marx."[17] Luckily for her, Philip was very pliable, and within a short time he accepted her highly ambitious worldview. As Mary Jane put it: "Science, technology, engineering—these had a place within our grasp of the possibility of peace and abundance for all. It was an obligation laid on all who caught the implication to help convert the possibility into reality. In mutually accepting this duty, my husband's and my identification became complete; henceforth, we were one."[18]

They were married in August 1929 in Kalamazoo, presumably without the presence of Mary Jane's mother, who still lived in Illinois, or her brother, who was practicing at the Mayo Clinic in Minnesota. Nor is there any reason to believe that Philip's mother or sisters came from California for the wedding. The couple's wedding license does not even list witnesses. If anyone attended the ceremony, it was probably members of the Todd family.

The Keeneys' financial situation was considerably shakier than their grounding in Marxism. The stock market crashed two months after they married, and Mary Jane lost her position in the library because of a university policy against retaining married women in jobs that could be given to men with families. Their finances were threatened not just by the Depression, but by Philip's failure to ingratiate himself with people who could further his career. Although men were in demand in the library profession, an old-boy network determined which positions would go to whom. There is no doubt that Keeney's frail physique worked to his disadvantage since the library world wanted not just more men, but vigorous ones. His marriage to Mary Jane did not help much, either. As Jesse Shera, a well-known librarian who met Philip years later put it, "Mary Jane definitely wore the pants in the family."[19] Her assertiveness would not have appealed to leading male librarians of the day, whose biographies indicate that most of them had quietly supportive wives and children.[20]

Philip's future rested in the hands of such patriarchs. William Warner Bishop, director of the University of Michigan Library at the time Philip worked there, was one of the most prominent librarians in the United States. Proximity to power did not necessarily benefit Philip, partly because of his retiring nature, and partly because Bishop was notoriously mercurial. In his position, Bishop could make or break Philip's future career, and it seems that he exerted his power by using—or refusing to use—the good-old-boy network.[21] He neither recommended Keeney for other jobs nor promoted him up the ranks at Michigan. Consequently, Keeney stayed put in his lackluster job in the library's Acquisitions Department.

By the time Philip and Mary Jane marked their first anniversary, they had little reason to celebrate. Nearly forty years old, Philip had finished his master's degree in library science but had virtually no job prospects. Making the most of his situation, he had entered the doctoral program in history at Michigan. Thirty-three-year-old Mary Jane also took courses, with no particular plans to finish a degree. The two of them were aging students without professional reputations and had few chances of finding good academic jobs as universities throughout the United States cut positions in response to the poor economy.

In the spring of 1931, however, the Keeneys' luck abruptly changed when Gertrude Buckhous, head librarian at Montana State University in Missoula, died.[22] No one in the university's administration knew how to go about replacing Miss Buckhous, who after twenty-eight years in her job had become a fixture. A befuddled President Charles Clapp sought help from Sidney Mitchell, head of the library school at the University of California in Berkeley, and stipulated that he wanted a man to fill the head librarian's position. Unfortunately for Clapp, Mitchell could recommend any number of capable women but cautioned that male librarians were a sought-after species who could choose the best jobs. Few would be enticed to distant Montana to head a library whose collection was at best medium sized. Mitchell could offer only one reasonably qualified man who might be willing to take the job, his former student Philip Keeney.[23]

Philip was more than willing; he was desperate. Once alerted by Mitchell to the opening, he wasted no time contacting Clapp and obtaining letters of reference.[24] Within days after Clapp summoned him to Montana for an interview in September of 1931, Philip was appointed the head librarian at Montana State University. All of this was unbeknownst to William Warner Bishop, who was away on an extended European book-buying trip and from whom Philip did not solicit a reference. On the contrary, Philip went to some pains to conceal his plans from Bishop, presumably because the latter might have obstructed his efforts to get the job in Montana. Bishop would not discover until his return from Europe that Philip was no longer his employee, a slap at the "great man" of the library world.

If Philip had observed the gentleman's code of the profession, his career might never have advanced, and the job in Montana was definitely a step up. In his new position, he held a full professorship and realized a 60-percent increase in salary over his job at the University of Michigan. As he began his new duties, Philip could not have imagined that within a few years he would be embroiled in a censorship dispute in Montana that would become a national cause celebre and that would to help define the legal limits of academic freedom and tenure.

Shortly after the Keeneys arrived in Missoula there were signs of trouble, but they had nothing to do with censorship. The all-female staff at the library was less than pleased with Clapp's choice of a head librarian. One woman in particular had reason to be bitter because she had wanted the job for herself. A staff member who was interviewed decades later speculated that the women also bristled at Philip's political views, which they found too radical.[25] That may have been true, but they also had legitimate objections to some aspects of his management. He brought his dog to work, spent a good part of his morning reading the *New York Times*, and was given to leaving on vacation without notice. He also failed to keep good track of expenses and book orders.[26]

Despite his shortcomings, Philip made a sincere effort to appease his staff. He gave them more flexible schedules and encouraged them to attend professional conferences. He even managed to give them raises during the Depression, but they had longer memories of a time when he kept money for himself that was arguably theirs. As head librarian, Keeney was supposed to teach a basic course in library science. Uncomfortable as an instructor, largely because of his stammer, he delegated his responsibilities to the staff. When the university's payment for the course arrived, he gave a few dollars to each of his assistants but held onto the rest to pay his train fare to a conference. Keeney's performance aside from this appears to have been at least competent, depending on who assessed it.[27]

Mary Jane may not have initially noticed Philip's problems at work because she was dealing with issues of her own. She loathed Missoula, finding it a hopeless backwater, even though it served as the cultural and commercial hub of the surrounding region. It wasn't the cowboys, miners, and farmers who put her off nearly so much as the local gentry. These people, having little sympathy with her politics, she dismissed as xenophobes jealous of her intellect and sophisticated lifestyle.[28] She later reported to a Civil Service investigator that she even believed they were suspicious of her delight in serving unusual foods: "I had been giving my guests borscht for several years before I learned that I was actually offending people by so doing. . . . [T]hey read into this act on my part, an act which had the innocent basis that I happened to have Spode dishes of a matching color, an over-fondness for Russia."[29]

Although repelled by Missoula's bourgeoisie, the Keeneys apparently never sought the company of the town's proletariat. Instead, they drifted into activities befitting a faculty couple, such as planning literary programs, editing a poetry column for the *Montana Woman*, and attending parties given by people they supposedly disdained. The only pastimes that truly appealed to them were the "salons" they hosted or attended at the homes of their few friends, where the entertainment consisted of discussions and literary readings. They also enjoyed inviting students to their home because this provided an opportunity to expand the young guests' cultural and intellectual horizons.[30]

Although they managed to find a social niche, the Keeneys had a way of offending people. One night at a book reading in another faculty member's home, Mary Jane appalled those present by reciting profanity-laced passages from Robert Cantwell's *Land of Plenty*, a contemporary progressive novel. On another occasion, tongues wagged when Philip appeared intoxicated at a local cafe. In yet another incident, the Keeneys lent their apartment to a visiting professor to host a party for a writers' conference, and what began as a simple reception ended with some of the guests going downtown and having a public brawl. President Clapp was especially disturbed by the fact that drinking was involved because Prohibition was still the law in Montana when these events occurred.[31]

The Keeneys' life in Missoula was not all parties and drinking bouts. During their early years in Montana, they engaged in a few projects to benefit the community. Philip set up a program to loan books from the university library to Montana's farmers in remote areas.[32] Mary Jane, using her medical training from Chicago, helped to treat sick children. The couple even managed to import Rockwell Kent and Norman Thomas, royalty of the Left, to speak at the Missoula campus. These undertakings hardly satisfied the Keeneys' lust for revolution, but their isolation in Montana prevented them from participating in more serious leftist activities. This must have been particularly disappointing because Communism was enjoying an unprecedented popularity in large American cities, and the Keeneys could only observe from a distance.

For the Keeneys to take part in the movement, Philip obviously had to get another job in a major urban area. Not content to move to a less prestigious position, Philip unsuccessfully applied for other library directorships. Mary Jane attributed his inability to get another job to Montana's remote location, much too far from professional conferences and organizations where he might make a name for himself. Understandably, the Keeneys may also have suspected that the profession's old-boy network stood in Philip's way. Leaving the University of Michigan without Bishop's blessing certainly could not have helped Philip in the long run.

Unbeknownst to the Keeneys, the biggest threat to Philip's career was really the president of Montana State University. In fall 1934, reacting to Philip's tardy return from summer vacation, Clapp's patience reached the breaking point. The president created a list of complaints in preparation for a disciplinary meeting with Philip, possibly to lay the groundwork to dismiss him. Among the notes that Clapp had jotted were "Upsetting to library staff . . . Disorganized leave for Pacific N.W. Assoc . . . . Lack of interest in library and institution . . . dog complex . . . Do Not Bring Dog to Office . . . Lack of stamina . . . Personal peculiarities—rather marked. The most potentially humiliating comment about Philip was "Wanted *man* & not *woman*."[33]

By the time that the meeting actually occurred, Clapp apparently had lost his nerve and merely scolded Keeney only for being away too long. Some people at the university later speculated that Clapp would have lowered the boom eventually, but before the two men could meet again Clapp was diagnosed with a terminal illness. He died in May 1935, and what followed at the university was absolute chaos. After his death, Clapp's skill for holding dissent at bay soon became abundantly clear. Campus factions that had been simmering for years quickly rose to the surface. Young professors voiced resentment against their older colleagues, a resentment that was reciprocated. Poorly paid teachers vented frustrations over perceived salary inequities. Most important for Philip, the socially and politically conservative majority lined up against the liberal minority.

Philip certainly fell into the latter camp, but despite the perception that he was a wild-eyed extremist he usually took a conventional approach to his job. Indeed, the only vaguely radical acts he committed as librarian were subscribing to the Socialist magazine *New Masses* and instituting a program called the Open Shelf, nothing more than a prominently displayed bookcase in the library that contained literature and nonfiction. Avant-garde novels and books about Socialism were represented, but they rested alongside standard histories, biographies, and science books.[34] Despite reservations that some people had about Philip, the Open Shelf excited little comment until it became interwoven with the search for President Clapp's successor.

Among the contenders for the position was John Morris, a former history instructor who had lost his job at the university the year before Clapp died. Morris, who had taken to farming to support his many children, convinced himself that he could snap up the president's job by campaigning to uphold high moral standards at the school. To make the scheme work, he had to win over the Montana State Board of Education because its members were responsible for hiring the new president. Once the determined Morris insinuated his way into the board's September 1935 meeting and was given the floor, he launched into a tirade about the low character of campus life at the university. To make his point, he began reading from Vardis Fisher's *Passions Spin the Plot*, a book that had come from the Open Shelf. The book was clearly chosen for its shock value because it dealt frankly with a young man's reaction to the discovery of his fiancée's sexual activities.

Morris failed to convince the board that he could lead the university, and his listeners cringed as he read graphic passages from the book. One board member, a chivalrous man fearful that the women in the room would be embarrassed, abruptly interrupted the reading with a proposal to ban *Passions Spin the Plot* "and all books of similar character" from the university libraries of Montana.[35] The resolution quickly passed, and Morris was asked to leave. Provoked by an awkward situation, the board failed to consider the implications of the resolution. They certainly did not see themselves as censors of books.[36]

Upon hearing of the resolution, Philip treated it at face value, notified the board that he had removed *Passions Spin the Plot* from his library, and asked for advice in identifying other books that should be removed from the shelves.[37] This was hardly the response that would be expected from the anticensorship crusader that Philip later proclaimed himself to be. It is impossible to know what he was thinking at the time. Supposedly, details of Morris's performance were not circulated outside of the board, so Keeney probably did not know what prompted the resolution;

and it does not appear that he asked for an explanation. Was his appeal for guidance a sign of blind obedience or was he testing the waters in preparation for more decisive action?

If he expected a timely response from the board, he would be disappointed. Consumed with the effort to find a new president for the Missoula campus, the board failed to answer Philip for three months. Philip might have perceived this as a snub or as a sign that the board was conspiring to wage a censorship campaign against the state's universities, a campaign he must defeat. Whatever his reasoning, by the end of October, still waiting for a reply to his letter, he and Mary Jane began organizing an anticensorship protest against the board. Although her name is absent from any documentation, the protest showed all the hallmarks of Mary Jane's thought and energy.

To protect Philip's job, the Keeneys had to act covertly. Criticism of university administrators was not viewed as the stuff of academic freedom during the 1930s, even in public institutions where safeguards for such expression were largely undefined until the 1960s.[38] If Philip had complained openly, he could have been treated as nothing more than a troublemaker and summarily dismissed. The Keeneys therefore gave control of their anticensorship effort to Stephenson Smith, a University of Oregon professor who had become friends with the Keeneys when he taught at Montana State University in the early 1930s. With the Keeneys' consent, he circulated an anticensorship petition among academics in the Northwest calling upon the Montana board to reconsider the ban on *Passions Spin the Plot*. Instead of simply asking that the censorship motion be reversed, the petition suggested that problem literature in Montana be transferred to "the vault or lock shelf" from which it would be issued only to mature students by a faculty member or by the librarian. It addressed the Montana board with at least a hint of sarcasm: "We recognize that your Board is the authorized spokesman for the moral convictions and tastes of the people of Montana, and we do not for one moment mean to call in question your final jurisdiction in these matters."[39]

To hone the element of surprise, Smith did not circulate the petition in Montana, so the board had no idea that trouble was brewing. Although Smith's methods were somewhat devious, they protected Philip, at least for a while. In very little time, it became obvious that the advantages of Smith's involvement were offset by his cockiness and by his refusal to let go of the censorship issue even when it was dying on its own. In early December 1935, the executive secretary of the board wrote to Philip and told him that the resolution against *Passions Spin the Plot* was not what it appeared to be. Briefly describing what had led to the resolution, the secretary assured him that the matter was closed and would remain so "unless there is some effort from the outside to open it up."[40] The simplest thing for Philip to do at this point was to stay mum and quietly return *Passions Spin the Plot* to the shelf. But it was too late to halt the Stephenson Smith zephyr, and even if the Keeneys had tried to stop him, Smith probably would have plowed ahead with the anticensorship crusade on his own. Whether they liked it or not, the Keeneys were involved in the campaign and there was no turning back.

As the crusade accelerated, it continued to be linked to the board's frustrating search for Montana State University's new president. After failed attempts to find suitable candidates from other universities, the board capitulated to demands of local businessmen for their choice of president: a young assistant professor of zoology whose doctorate was less than a year old when he came to teach at Montana State University in 1934. G. Finlay Simmons had been formally presented as a candidate, but his lack of academic experience made him an inconceivable one in the minds of the other faculty. This hardly fazed the town's merchants and bankers because they wanted a president who would be a highly visible booster and promote the town's economic interests. A sociable man with a record of lively speech making at Rotary Club meetings, Simmons was their man. His résumé read like an adventure story that included stints as a police reporter, a Red Cross ambulance driver during World War I, and the director of a Darwinesque voyage to collect specimens for the Cleveland Museum of Natural History.[41]

When they heard that the board had picked Simmons to be the next president, the faculty was horrified. Among the most outraged was Philip Keeney, who took it upon himself to circulate another petition—this time openly—calling upon the board to rethink its choice of president. There would be no reconsideration, however, because Montana's governor suddenly died a few days after Simmons's confirmation, removing the spotlight from the troubles in Missoula. Besides this, Simmons enjoyed the support of the new governor. With backing from the state's chief official, who also served as a member of the board of education, there was no chance that Simmons would be asked to step down.

The demoralized faculty suspended their effort to recall Simmons, but not before he had a chance to size up his enemies, boding ill for Philip. The very sight of the librarian, Simmons once said, made him "unhappy."[42] To make matters worse, the socially conservative Simmons had been present when Mary Jane had read from Cantwell's *Land of Plenty*, and he regarded her as a woman of exceptionally poor taste.[43]

As Simmons was assuming office in January 1936, Stephenson Smith called in the anticensorship petition, which contained the signatures of sixty faculty members from Washington and Oregon. Initially destined for Montana's board of education, Smith decided to send it to Finlay Simmons instead. Smith's original purpose, to assist Philip in defeating censorship, would get lost in a battle of nerves with Simmons, but Smith could not resist playing the gadfly. Along with the petition he sent a letter urging Simmons to challenge the very people who had just put him in office: "It is my hope," wrote Smith, "that you will act on this matter and see that the proper modification of the Board's order is made."[44]

Recognizing that Smith was testing him to see if he would choose the principle of academic freedom over loyalty to his supporters, Simmons framed his reply carefully and defended the board against charges that they were censors. Deflecting responsibility from himself (after all, he was not yet president when the resolution passed), Simmons suggested that the petitioners simply communicate directly with the board.[45] The calm tone of Simmons's response to the petition masked his rage, which escalated when, immediately after taking office, he was presented with yet another anticensorship petition. This second petition, signed by 400 students and faculty members from the Missoula campus, convinced Simmons that he must assert his authority. In doing so, he proved to have something in common with the hapless John Morris because he decided to achieve his mission by lifting the university's moral character. Simmons, it turned out, was a consummate prude.

The first object of his disapproval was a student production of *Ah, Wilderness,* which raised his ire because it included a character who was a prostitute. The very idea that a young female student would be cast in this role was unthinkable for Simmons, and he pressured the head of the drama department, who agreed to substitute a different play. Another Simmons target was H. G. Merriam, the editor of the university's literary magazine *Frontier and Midland,* which Simmons felt was too liberal. Simmons also suspected Merriam of involvement in the anticensorship petitions because he was chairman of the English Department, where Stephenson Smith had been visiting professor.[46] By focusing on Merriam, Simmons failed to grasp Philip's part in the scheme for several weeks.

The truth began to unfold in March 1936 after an article appeared in a popular West Coast publication, *Pacific Weekly.* The author, writing under the pseudonym James Steele, criticized the board's censorship action and their selection of Simmons as president. Readers were urged to protest the ban of *Passions Spin the Plot* by complaining directly to Simmons, again suggesting that he was responsible for it.[47] Simmons protested to the *Pacific Weekly*, but the editor refused to divulge the identity of James Steele. The editor was, however, willing to reveal that information for the article came from the librarian at Montana State University. The revelation spelled disaster for the Keeneys. If Philip's star began to fall at this point, it flamed out the following month when all the newspapers in Montana received a letter, alleged to be from the Alumni Progressive League of Montana, which called for an immediate end to censorship on the Missoula campus. Upon investigating, Simmons determined that the Progressive Alumni League, like Steele, was fictitious, and he was certain that Philip was responsible for the letter.[48]

Simmons wanted to fire Philip immediately, but cooler heads convinced the president that this would just lead to more campus turmoil.[49] Simmons then ostensibly held out an olive branch to the librarian by telling him that he was anxious to work out their problems. At the same time, Simmons made it plain that the 1936–1937 academic year would be crucial in determining Philip's future at the university.[50] Recognizing that his job was in jeopardy, Philip kept a low profile, continuing to search for a new job and protecting the one he still had by kowtowing to Simmons. For Philip that meant surviving in an atmosphere of mounting censorship, and if he were honest with himself he would have to admit that he was partly responsible. The resolution against *Passions Spin the Plot*, which the board passed in the heat of John Morris's embarrassing performance, was essentially a nonevent that, largely thanks to Philip and Mary Jane, had snowballed into something big. In turn, when the inexperienced Simmons found himself under siege he overreacted in his determination to show that he was in charge. As a consequence, freedom of expression at the university really was suppressed, and once he began to feel his oats, Simmons took his campaign statewide.

In April 1936, he convinced the Board of Education to pass a resolution establishing review committees at all of Montana's public universities. The role of these committees was to maintain high standards in the selection of library materials and in the production of student plays. Varnished with language that gave faculty control over the selection process, this resolution actually compromised their authority with a clause demanding "cooperation from all concerned in the type of plays performed and in the character of material used in student and faculty publications, in order that a proper high level of good taste and public decorum may obtain."[51]

Another key provision of the resolution was that "any writings found unsuitable for immature student reading shall not be admitted to the general or open shelves of the library."[52] Philip inevitably came under scrutiny; he meekly gave a list of Open Shelf books to the local review committee. Deferring to a warning from Simmons against stressing "isms" in the library, Philip purged a dozen of the books without any prompting. Now the self-appointed champion of intellectual freedom had become a censor himself.[53] When he wasn't removing parts of the library's collection from public view, Philip applied himself to his duties. Not once during the 1936–1937 academic year did Simmons complain, and it seemed that he was content merely to savor his victory over the head of the library.

Philip's falling-out with Simmons happened to coincide with a nationwide drive by the American Federation of Teachers (AFT) to organize faculty members at universities. One of the professors who had signed Stephenson Smith's petition suggested to the AFT that Philip might be asked to put together a local at Montana State University. Obviously this individual was unaware of Philip's predicament since organizing a union would have amounted to career suicide for him. When the AFT contacted Philip in January 1937 he regretfully explained that he couldn't possibly engage in such activities. But he also made it clear that he was ready to consider the idea for the future: "I am enormously interested," he declared, "and do not think that I will lay [sic] down if there is the slightest chance to get a chapter here."[54]

Philip's change of heart came quickly. Within two months, he had mustered his courage and was scouring the Missoula campus for faculty members to start an AFT chapter. He would later say that he was emboldened by other faculty members who had approached him with an interest in unionizing.[55] In reality, he had gotten wind of a rumor that Simmons planned to fire him at the end of the academic year. At that point, forming a union actually appeared to be Philip's salvation. Under the Wagner Act, ratified by the U.S. Congress only days before he heard of his imminent dismissal, Philip could not be legally fired for organizing a union. During the first week of April 1937 he collected in excess of two dozen names, enough to form a local, and was frantically begging the AFT to send a representative to Missoula. Before anyone could arrive, however, Philip received a letter from Simmons informing him that his services as librarian were no longer desired; his contract for the upcoming academic year would not be renewed.[56] Philip insisted, not very convincingly, that his efforts to form an AFT local had caused his dismissal. Knowing the law and prepared for this ploy, Simmons replied that he let Philip go solely because of his incompetence as a librarian and his disruptive behavior.[57]

In an effort to short-circuit any sympathetic publicity for the deposed librarian, Simmons immediately contacted editors of Montana's labor newspapers and warned them to beware of Philip's exploitation of the union issue, about which Simmons said he had known nothing until "long after the decision to replace Mr. Keeney was reached."[58] But if Montana's labor sector was concerned that Philip's effort to form a union grew out of his own self-interest it hardly showed. When his dismissal became public, the state's unions responded with an outpouring of support. News of Philip's plight traveled quickly and far, accompanied by the buzz that Simmons was conspiring with industry moguls to break up the new AFT chapter. Solidarity around Philip quickly spiraled into a movement. By the summer of 1937, scores of written protests from unions throughout the United States flooded Simmons and the board. Amid this support Philip gained the courage to fight for his job. His resolve grew even stronger when the ACLU and the American Association of University Professors (AAUP) took an interest in the case.

In addition to these organizations, a number of librarians spoke up on Philip's behalf, but the American Library Association (ALA), the group most representative of his professional interests, distanced itself from the case. By doing so, the ALA lost its opportunity to speak out against the suppression of books, a matter of natural concern to the association. The case also was extremely timely for librarians who by the late 1930s were consciously rejecting their old role as social arbiters of public reading tastes. Instead, they were embracing a mission of providing a comprehensive and balanced body of literature to library users. The Keeney case provided the ALA with a forum to proclaim the profession's changing identity.[59]

Philip's expectations that the association would stand behind him were reinforced by a letter that ALA executive director Carl Milam sent him in response to the publicity drifting out of Montana. Milam compared Philip's dismissal with that three decades earlier of Pulitzer Prize–winning historian Vernon Parrington from the University of Oklahoma "to their everlasting disgrace." Milam further expressed hope that "ALA might find some way to make the administration at Montana squirm."[60] Just three weeks after Milam wrote his letter, however, it became clear that these promises were empty. Paul North Rice, chairman of the ALA committee authorized to review cases of wrongfully dismissed librarians, informed Philip that the association had no budget to send an investigator to Montana. Not the least bit apologetic, Rice cast doubt on Philip's integrity as a librarian. "I have no sympathy with any censorship of books in a college library which stress a different point of view than that of the administration," wrote Rice to Philip, "but neither have I sympathy, and I assume that with this you will concur, with using a college library for propganda [sic]."[61]

Although there is no evidence that Philip was using the library to spread propaganda, Rice was undoubtedly swayed by an unsolicited letter that Simmons had sent to the ALA in which he argued his side of the case and assailed Philip's character. Simmons insisted that he had not fired the librarian, merely declined to renew his annual contract.[62] Without asking Philip to respond, ALA president-elect Milton Ferguson published an editorial in *Library Journal* suggesting that Simmons, not Keeney, was the wronged party. In the editorial, Ferguson casually stated that Philip was a Socialist and repeated a claim made by Simmons that the fired librarian threatened to "spread his case and our difficulties in every radical sheet across the country." Ferguson further questioned the right of any librarian to ignore the opinions and wishes of higher authority and wondered "how far will academic freedom and right of free speech permit a faculty member to project his personal convictions into college affairs and the administration of the library."[63]

Although *Library Journal* was not an ALA publication, it worked hand-in-glove with the association and often served as its unofficial mouthpiece.[64] Ferguson's statement belied ALA's impartiality, and, to add insult to injury, Philip read the editorial for the first time when his issue of *Library Journal* arrived in the mail. Stunned, he fired off a rebuttal to Ferguson denying that he was a Socialist "in the sense that I am a member of that party. I am a member of no party." He conceded that he belonged to the ACLU and to the American League against War and Fascism, "both of which have been described by President Simmons as communistic organizations."[65]

Despite the shabby manner in which he had been treated, Philip asked for only one concession: to present his side of the story in a future issue of *Library Journal*. This was hardly a request that Ferguson could reject in good conscience, and he assured Philip, "I will be pleased to urge the editor to print any brief statement you may send her."[66] It is doubtful that Ferguson kept his promise because *Library Journal*'s editor, Bertine Weston, turned Philip down when he asked her to print his response. Paul North Rice also chided Philip for objecting to the editorial, describing the protest as intemperate and regrettable.[67]

It is difficult to account for the ALA's reluctance to get involved with the Keeney case. The official explanation, that the organization had no money for investigations, is hard to believe. In 1937, the ALA's budget was some eight times greater than that of the AAUP, which regularly investigated firings in academic institutions. Unlike the AAUP, however, much of the ALA's treasury was built from sources other than its members' dues.[68] As they were beholden to any number of individuals and foundations outside of librarianship, the ALA's officers could not automatically act on behalf of colleagues who faced dire consequences for living by their professional creed. To do so risked offending donors whose positions on censorship were unpredictable. Another factor in the ALA's behavior was its oligarchic structure. The association's permanent staff, including Milam, was accountable only to a small circle of insiders, virtually all of whom were themselves administrators. Officers of the association were drawn from a pool of librarians like Philip's old boss William Warner Bishop, who was ALA president in 1918. It is tempting to speculate that Philip's offense against Bishop in bolting from Michigan to Montana without "permission" and Bishop's generally low opinion of Philip partly accounted for the ALA's chilly behavior, but there is no solid evidence of this.

The attitude of the ALA elite might suggest that Philip Keeney was too much of a maverick to succeed in a uniformly conservative profession, but there were strong pockets of liberalism among librarians of the 1930s. Sociologist Nathan Glazer, who gathered data about Depression-era Communists concluded that members of "certain intellectual occupations (teaching, social work, librarianship)" often drifted toward Communism.[69] To buttress his theory, Glazer pointed to Alice Bryan's classic study of librarians in which she reported in 1948, even as conservatism was on the rise, that 17 percent of librarians preferred Socialist, Communist, or Progressive candidates for President, "suggesting a rather leftist group."[70] It was probably even more leftist during the 1930s when American Communism enjoyed its greatest popularity during the period of the Popular Front.

What these statistics really attest to is the gulf that existed between the profession's elite and its more liberal rank and file. Long before the Keeney case, ALA members were discontented with the association's lack of democracy and accountability. By the late 1930s, the association supposedly was making a greater effort to respond to its members' demands. Among these demands was greater assistance for librarians who had been fired from their jobs under questionable circumstances. Philip was neither the first nor the last librarian to appeal to the association for help, but as late as 1940 the Association had allocated only $100 to investigate unjust dismissals. The following year it budgeted nothing at all.[71] The slow progress made by the ALA suggests that the staff and officers were considerably less enthusiastic than its members about making changes.

The hesitancy of the ALA to respond to members' requests for help is evident in this 1942 letter from a colleague to Carl Milam: "My inclination is to ignore tenure cases until we know what we are supposed to do and are granted funds with which to proceed. Laborious collecting of facts and filing them away accomplishes nothing but a waste of . . . time."[72] Two years later, the association was still laboring over its standard for the principles of tenure.

The ALA's failure to take action in the Keeney case also had something to do with the association hierarchy's disapproval of organized labor, and Philip came to believe that the ALA was punishing him for trying to establish the AFT chapter. This was not an unreasonable assumption given that Milton Ferguson publicly condemned the notion of library unions during his 1938 inaugural address as ALA president.

In addition to Ferguson, Rice, and Milam, Philip managed to alienate the influential Charles Brown, the ALA's 1940 president-elect, even though the two men hardly knew each other. Jesse Shera, then a library school student who petitioned the ALA to investigate the Montana case, attested to this animosity between Philip and Brown. As an old man, Shera recalled that Brown gave him some fatherly advice to steer clear of Philip, declaring that the latter was "no good." Ignoring Brown's warning and regarding himself as something of a firebrand, the young Shera continued his campaign on Philip's behalf and wrote him supportive letters before actually meeting him in the early 1940s. "The whole business was a mess," said Shera, "and there was right and wrong on both sides, and the ALA handled it all about as badly as it could."[73]

Luckily for Philip, he had ample encouragement to fight on even without the ALA. Each of his biggest organizational supporters—the Montana Federation of Labor, the AFT, the ACLU, and the AAUP—had a stake in the case. Labor leaders believed that it would have far-reaching implications for unions and agreed to pay Philip's legal expenses, a major financial commitment for Montana's labor sector, which had suffered severely during the Depression years.[74] Keeney's second major supporter, the ACLU, was convinced that the First Amendment was under attack, and the AAUP hoped to use the case to further the cause of academic tenure. The AAUP sent an investigative team to Montana State University that concluded that Philip's dismissal was completely without cause. This was followed by the AAUP's censure of the university, a major embarrassment in the academic world.[75]

Philip had the potential to be a labor hero and a champion of free speech. Initially, his best legal argument appeared to be that his right to organize a union had been violated.[76] A judge in Montana's First District Court concurred and immediately ordered the board of education to reinstate Philip in September 1937. Within days, Simmons and the board contested the ruling, and it became obvious that Philip's lawyers could not sustain the argument that he had been fired because of union activities. Finlay Simmons testified convincingly that he was ignorant of

Philip's plans to form an AFT local when he decided not to renew his contract. Not revealed in court, but further undermining Philip's position, was a letter Simmons received from Charles Hope, regional director of the National Labor Relations Board (NLRB) that monitored violations of the Wagner Act. Hope expressed serious doubts that Philip's case would hold up before the NLRB.[77]

As labor's prospects faded, Philip's hopes shifted not to the First Amendment, but to the relatively mundane matter of the contracts he had signed between 1931 and 1935. A clause on the contracts automatically awarded tenure to full professors after three years in their jobs. Philip, who was a full professor, had been at Montana State University for five years when Simmons fired him. In addition, Philip had not been given the opportunity to appeal his dismissal through the university's standard grievance procedure.

Simmons claimed that Philip was not entitled to tenure or to a grievance hearing, bolstering this assertion by producing the memo President Clapp had prepared for the showdown meeting planned for Philip in 1935. Discovered by the late president's secretary as she was cleaning out his desk, the memo promised to be the smoking gun in the case. Besides criticizing Philip's inferior performance as librarian, Clapp had included the notation "not entirely satisfied, reason [for] *annual contract.*"[78] This was proof positive, said Simmons, that automatic tenure did not apply to Keeney. Simmons insisted that he simply was opting not to renew Keeney's annual contract, an option that Clapp appeared ready to exercise two years earlier.

The judge decided that the case had to be reconsidered on the merits of these contracts, but it would not be a speedy process. The suit would drag through the courts for nearly two years and end up in the Montana State Supreme Court. In the meantime, Philip's reinstatement based on his right to organize a union was nullified. He was barred from his office and his paychecks ceased. At age 46, he was unemployed and a pariah among the elite of his profession. In 1937, one of the darkest years of the Great Depression, Philip and Mary Jane Keeney faced a period of great hardship. They were not, however, going to fold their tents and just disappear. While they waited for the Montana court's decision, they reinvented themselves as crusaders for free speech. Any suggestion that they were even partly responsible for the events in Montana evaporated, at least in their own minds. Now their faith in revolution became one with their belief in free speech and free access to information. They constructed motives that matched their romantic notions of the misunderstood revolutionaries they wished to be.

CHAPTER 4

Struggle

For the middle-aged, there is probably nothing more humiliating than returning home to live with parents. Perhaps the only thing worse is sharing quarters with in-laws. In the autumn of 1937, out of work in the midst of the Depression, that is exactly where Philip and Mary Jane found themselves. They moved to Berkeley and set up housekeeping with Philip's mother. Unable to find a job, Philip began writing a book on the significance of libraries in world history. Mary Jane kept bread on the table by taking a job with explorer and writer Victor W. Von Hagen. Although her position was that of an editorial assistant, she may have fallen into her tendency to exaggerate when she claimed to have completely rewritten his book *Ecuador the Unknown*.[1] The job enabled her and Philip to move into their own apartment, but it was a penurious time during which they depleted their savings and sold many possessions.

It is a matter of some curiosity that Mary Jane's first husband moved to Berkeley during the time that Mary Jane and Philip were there. By then, Legare George had remarried and had a family, but it is unclear how he spent his time in Berkeley or if he was in contact with Mary Jane. If she even knew her ex-husband was in Berkeley, he was probably the least of Mary Jane's concerns. She and Philip were physically, psychologically, and financially exhausted as they anticipated the outcome of Philip's lawsuit. On March 16, 1938, Mary Jane wrote in her diary: "My beloved cracked under the intolerable strain of the combined world and personal situation and I cracked with him." But no matter how dire things got, the couple never wavered in their determination: "We decided again we would see the fight through to its bitter end and take death rather than a job in which we'd have no freedom."[2]

A few years later, Mary Jane wrote an informal autobiography in which she stated that she and Philip also considered the fight to be their civic obligation as good Americans. "Our knowledge of historical cause and effect, our belief in the principles on which the United States was founded, and our love for this wide and beautiful land which is so full of promise. . . . This duty caused us many hardships but because of them we grew to love our country more—the general experience, I believe, of anyone who contributes something to his country."[3]

For all their hardships, the couple had reason to be encouraged. They had a cadre of loyal supporters, some of them quite prominent. Jerry O'Connor, a Montana representative to the U.S. Congress, refused to release funds for building projects at the Montana State University until the Keeney case was resolved. Wayne Morse, Dean of the University of Oregon Law School and future senator, wrote to the U.S. Commissioner of Education to recommend Philip for a position in the Bureau of Education.[4] Hugh DeLacy, the AFT representative who came to Missoula to aid Philip in organizing the teachers union, was elected as a Seattle City Councilman in 1937[5] and in his new position continued to advocate for Philip. He admitted, however, that he wasn't entirely sure of Philip's good judgment and told him so: "You are too outspoken," DeLacy wrote Philip, "much too outspoken . . . you were never cut out for a politician . . . your wife has more possibilities."[6]

In addition to individual supporters, the Keeneys continued to enjoy the combined clout of the AAUP, the ACLU, and several labor organizations. Even the ALA, succumbing to pressure from its members, finally issued a perfunctory statement calling for a thorough investigation of Philip's case.[7]

During the two years that the case lingered through the courts, Philip made efforts to find a new job, but he knew that, despite the ALA's halfhearted statement on his behalf, he was blacklisted among the movers and shakers of the organization. Nevertheless, the power of Philip's support among the rank and file of the profession was not to be dismissed, and soon he found that he had an important friend in David Ralph Wahl, head of binding at the Library of Congress. Wahl made a concerted effort to help Philip obtain a job in the federal government.[8] There was almost certainly more to Wahl's assistance than another librarian's sympathetic response with Keeney's plight.

According to FBI files, the CPUSA, perhaps at the personal direction of Earl Browder, exploited Wahl's position at the Library of Congress.

In the FBI's view, Wahl was used during the Russo-German pact for the express purpose of gathering information regarding troop movements. The details, such as whose troops, are not elaborated upon in the file.[9] To the uninitiated, the Library of Congress might seem like an unlikely place for spies to be roaming about, but its collection is a gold mine of information, and the data that the party sought might have been in government documents at Wahl's fingertips.

All signs indicate that the Keeneys were solid Communists by the late 1930s, but that was not a litmus test of their willingness to steal classified information. Spying Communists, though numerous enough, were the exception, not the rule; however, it is unlikely that Wahl would have recruited Philip to Washington just on the off chance that the latter would be willing to pass along secret documents to the Soviets. Although they were 3,000 miles apart, Wahl and Philip may have conferred face-to-face at some point, most probably at the formative meetings of the Progressive Librarians' Council (PLC) that took place within conferences of the ALA. Philip continued to attend the association's conferences, even when he was unemployed.

If the two didn't meet at a PLC meeting, they might have been brought together through like-minded mutual friends, possibly ones that the Keeneys made in Berkeley after Philip was dismissed from his job in Montana. In Berkeley, Philip and Mary Jane found sympathetic company by participating in activities that took them farther into the circle of the American Left. Mary Jane's diary reflected that in January 1938 she and Philip attended a meeting sponsored by the Medical Bureau to Aid Spanish Democracy held at the Printing Pressmen's Union in Oakland, California. Mary Jane addressed the meeting and rallied the group to take up a collection for the Spanish Loyalists. Afterward the Keeneys went out with two new acquaintances, to whom Mary Jane referred as "comrades."[10]

Later that year, the Keeneys attended a meeting at the Oakland municipal auditorium, where Earl Browder, head of the CPUSA, was the featured speaker. Mary Jane described this meeting as the "most thoughtful political gathering I ever witnessed." She described Browder as having little magnetism but another speaker, an African American business agent of the Marine Cooks and Stewards Union, as possessing a great deal of personality. Although she was initially unimpressed with Browder, Mary Jane took the opportunity to meet him when he spoke at a Communist Party picnic on May 28, 1939.[11] It is entirely possible that it was Browder who facilitated the relationship between the Keeneys and Wahl, because the head of the CPUSA personally encouraged Communists to apply for government jobs in Washington.[12]

In California the Keeneys also met at least two people who later would be implicated in compromising the Manhattan Project: Joseph W. Weinberg, a physicist at the Radiation Laboratory at the University of California at Berkeley, and Haakon Chevalier, a professor of French at the university.[13] In the early 1940s, while working on the Manhattan Project, Weinberg passed along documents regarding the project to an American Communist Party official, who in turn gave them to a Soviet intelligence officer.[14] Chevalier's name would surface in August 1943 when Robert Oppenheimer, head of the Manhattan Project, informed project security officers that Chevalier had approached him the year before soliciting classified data. He refused Chevalier's request, saying that he would consider it a betrayal of his country. Oppenheimer's patriotism would do little for him down the road, however, as he lost his government security clearance in 1954.[15] Ostensibly, he was punished for waiting too long to report Chevalier's overture, but in the era of McCarthyism Oppenheimer's real offense was having once been a member of the Communist Party.[16]

Neither the connection with Wahl nor the friends that the Keeneys made in Berkeley resulted soon enough in what the couple needed most: gainful employment. Only a desperate need for work can explain what Philip did in June 1939 when he finally won his case in the Montana Supreme Court. The verdict vindicated him with back pay and reinstatement in his old job at Montana State University, and as Mary Jane pointed out, she and Philip could have just taken the money and gone on their merry way. Instead, they decided to go back to Missoula because, said Mary Jane, "We believed that we owed an obligation to those people and organizations who had helped us carry on the fight, to enforce the victory won with their help."[17]

With Finlay Simmons still at the helm of the university, it is hard to imagine that the Keeneys' supporters would have insisted that the couple return to Missoula. Anyone in his right mind would have known that Philip and Mary Jane would be put in a torturous situation, and so they were. After arriving back at the university in July 1939, the Keeneys were treated with complete contempt by Simmons and other administrators. They locked Philip out of his office and did everything conceivable to keep him from collecting his salary. In defiance of the state supreme court ruling that restored Philip's privileges as librarian, Simmons ordered him to refrain from speaking with the library staff, from handling library mail, and from administering any of the work of the library.[18] Simmons also began compiling a file of petty complaints going back to 1931 that could be used to justify firing Keeney yet again.

None of this could have surprised the Keeneys, but they had not anticipated the devastating toll that the experience would take on Philip's

Philip Olin Keeney as his picture appeared in the 1937 issue of the now defunct *Montana Labor News.*

health. Within two months he became ill with a gastric disorder, and by October he required hospitalization and recovery at home that lasted into early December. Still, he did not get better and was forced to go to the Mayo Clinic in Minneapolis for specialized treatment.[19] Without being specific, Mary Jane hinted that emotional stress was part of Philip's illness. "One of the conditions of restored health will be freedom from strain and anxiety, a condition we cannot hope to enjoy at the State University under the present regime."[20] This time, Philip's return to Missoula was completely out of the question because his job there was literally killing him.

Despite the cloud looming over them, the Keeneys quickly found that as one door closed another was opening. Archibald MacLeish, newly appointed Librarian of Congress, personally offered Philip a job in Washington, D.C. It is hard to say who was happiest about this, the Keeneys or the Montana State University administration. Upon hearing that Philip had a new job, Finlay Simmons wrote to H. H. Swain, executive secretary of the Board of Education: "I have just had a night letter from [Keeney] saying that . . . he is resigning as Librarian and Professor of Library at this institution in order to accept a 'permanent post' at the Library of Congress . . . I have heard rumors for some time that the new liberal Librarian of Congress, Archibald McLeish [sic], has been making a place for Mr. Keeney, since Keeney had the endorsement of John L. Lewis and had defended McLeish as an outstanding liberal at some meeting of the American Library Association."[21] An equally delighted Swain replied, "I am now profoundly grateful to Pres. Roosevelt for appointing Archibald McLeish. I wonder if the 'post' helps to hold up the main floor."[22]

In the end, it was Philip who got the last laugh. When he sent the telegram to Simmons announcing his resignation, he reversed the charges.[23]

CHAPTER 5

The Progressive Librarians' Council

As it turned out, the ALA helped Philip Keeney get his job at the Library of Congress. The favor was hardly intentional and resulted not from a rapprochement, but from blunders by the ALA that played into Philip's hands.

With time weighing heavily on them in Berkeley, the Keeneys could dream up creative ways of irritating their enemies, and the ALA was high on the list of targets. By July 1938 Philip realized that the ALA's leaders would not come to his aid in the Montana case and decided that it was because they were philosophically opposed to his attempts to unionize professionals at the university.[1] The Keeneys' plan of retribution against the ALA was simple, but highly effective. They began their own organization, the Progressive Librarians' Council (PLC). With membership dues of fifty cents and virtually no budget, the PLC could never rival the 60-year-old ALA with its 17,000 members. But that was not the purpose of the PLC. Instead, it was meant to be a gnat torturing an elephant, and it tortured very well. Under the Keeneys' leadership the PLC's members turned up at awkward moments, garnered publicity, and embarrassed the ALA.

The PLC took shape in San Francisco at the ALA conference of June 1939, right on the heels of Philip's victory in Montana and following informal meetings of like-minded people at the two previous annual conferences.[2] His friends, including David Wahl, feted him at a small but highly visible banquet where he was elected chairman of the new organization. ALA officers turned a blind eye to the whole affair, but they would not be able to ignore the PLC for long. Launching the council during the ALA's conference was certain to confuse some people into thinking that the ALA had sanctioned the PLC, although nothing could have been farther from the truth.

Shortly after the PLC was founded, Philip wrote a placating letter to newly elected ALA President Ralph Munn in which Philip insisted that the PLC "was not formed at a rump convention or as a subversive faction. . . . My being chairman is quite likely to be misinterpreted as my leading an organized personal following of dissidents in order to create trouble for the ALA."[3] These gestures could not have been intended to fool Munn, just annoy him. Philip only superficially disguised his role and the purpose of the council, and it was widely known among the ALA hierarchy that the PLC was Philip and Mary Jane's brainchild, pure and simple. In Philip's absence at the group's 1940 meeting, Mary Jane served as moderator, and the couple frequently contributed to the *PLC Bulletin*. To diminish the Keeneys' blatant control of the PLC, individual chapters were established across the United States, and the *PLC Bulletin* was printed in Chicago under the direction of the group's secretary, Bertha Schuman, an employee of that city's public library system.[4]

One of the PLC's first public acts was to applaud President Franklin Delano Roosevelt's appointment of writer Archibald MacLeish to the post of Librarian of Congress. The appointment, confirmed by the U.S. Senate in June 1939, had been vigorously opposed by the ALA with the argument that an experienced librarian, not a man of letters, should replace the outgoing Librarian of Congress, Herbert Putnam. The ALA pulled out all the stops in fighting the MacLeish appointment, with Milton Ferguson, president of the ALA when MacLeish's nomination was announced, leading the charge. The ALA sent President Roosevelt an open letter signed by 1,400 librarians in which the nomination was declared a calamity.[5] The Senate Library Committee, which had to confirm the appointment, was bombarded with correspondence from outraged librarians. Even apart from the "calamity" letter, Ferguson was particularly barbed in his remarks. He publicly opined that MacLeish was not qualified to manage a respectable public library. Ferguson further ridiculed Roosevelt's choice of MacLeish for being as illogical as appointing a secretary of agriculture because he likes cut flowers or making the skipper of a racing yacht the chief of naval operations.[6]

One of the more impudent actions against MacLeish took the form of a letter written by former ALA president Harrison Craver to Roosevelt's uncle, Frederick Delano. Craver, urged on by the anti-MacLeish faction, knew that Roosevelt often took advice from Delano and hoped that the latter might persuade his nephew to reconsider the nomination. What

Craver may not have known was that MacLeish had served as secretary to Delano in 1926 on a mission to survey the opium trade in what was then Persia. MacLeish and Delano may not have been fast friends, but Delano had enough confidence in his secretary that he signed his reports after barely reading them. Delano did not reply to Craver's letter.[7]

The ALA's *Sturm und Drang* was carried out largely for the benefit of Carl Milam, the ALA's longtime executive secretary who had misled Philip to believe that the ALA would come to his aid in Montana. Milam coveted the post of Librarian of Congress for himself, and though his campaign was understated his ambition was no secret, so the PLC's congratulatory remarks about MacLeish were an affront to Milam. It was bad enough that the president of the United States had snubbed him; now he was being humiliated by a pipsqueak upstart organization.

In reality, Roosevelt never intended to appoint a professional librarian as head of the de facto national library. In May 1939, he had written to his friend Justice Felix Frankfurter to ask for help in making the appointment. "I have had a bad time picking a Librarian to succeed Putnam. What would you think of Archie MacLeish? He is not a professional Librarian nor is he a special student of incunabula or ancient manuscripts. Nevertheless, he has lots of qualifications that said specialists have not."[8]

In reply, Frankfurter confirmed Roosevelt's instincts: "According to the best American and European tradition, the librarians that have left the most enduring marks have not been technical librarians. . . . [T]he danger of the technical librarian is that he over-emphasizes the collection and classification of books—the merely mechanical side of the library—and fails to see the library as the gateway to the development of culture."[9]

If librarians of the day had been privy to these letters, they surely would have been wounded by the dichotomy that Roosevelt and Frankfurter saw between "technical" librarians and visionaries. There is no clue that the president and the justice believed any professional librarian could also be someone "who knows books, loves books, and makes books," qualities Frankfurter believed essential for Librarian of Congress.[10] To a great extent, however, librarians had themselves to blame for the apparent distinction since they had labored since the Melvil Dewey era to be businesslike, scientific, and efficient.

The ALA was not alone in objecting to the MacLeish nomination. J. Parnell Thomas, Republican congressman from New Jersey and member of the House Special Committee to Investigate Un-American Activities (Dies Committee, later called HUAC), contended that MacLeish was overly sympathetic with Communist causes and with members of the American Communist Party. Much was made of MacLeish's affiliation with the left-leaning League of American Writers and of his support for the Republican government of Spain during that country's civil war. In the late 1930s, MacLeish had joined the American Friends of Spanish Democracy and had collaborated with John Dos Passos and Ernest Hemingway in producing *The Spanish Earth*, a documentary that depicted the toll the conflict had taken on the Spanish people.

Ironically, in the early 1930s the Communists had lambasted Mac-Leish for being a capitalist. He would have been better described as an independent thinker who had benefited from the capitalist system but who would cooperate with Communists in fighting for a moral cause. During the period of the Popular Front, the feeling, of course, was mutual. MacLeish's cooperation with the CPUSA did not really endear him to the Communists, but in 1939 the party was willing to join forces with anyone who could potentially further its revolutionary goals. Anti-Communists would make hay of this "fellow traveling" during the Cold War, but anti-Communism had not yet reached the proportions needed to squelch MacLeish's nomination as Librarian of Congress. On June 29, 1939, the Senate confirmed his appointment with 63 votes in favor, 8 against, and 25 not voting.[11] Senators voting against MacLeish expressed virtually no concerns about his lack of professional library qualifications, just his political leanings.

The confirmation was a humiliation for the ALA, especially because the Senate displayed no interest in his library skills. For Philip, MacLeish's confirmation provided an opportunity to gloat and a chance to reenter the world of libraries. In the guise of the PLC, he and Mary Jane continued to court and flatter MacLeish, and MacLeish responded favorably. Amicable relations between the couple and the new Librarian of Congress were also furthered by personal coincidences. MacLeish and Mary Jane shared a mutual friend in Charles Gilkey, Mary Jane's mentor from the University of Chicago. Gilkey was the MacLeish family pastor and had officiated at the funeral of MacLeish's beloved brother Kenneth in 1918. MacLeish's father, Andrew, was a trustee of the University of Chicago from 1890 to 1924 and had previously served as a trustee of the Baptist Union Theological College (later the university's divinity school) and of Rush Medical College.[12] Rush was the school from which Mary Jane's brother, Luman, graduated in 1920.

Besides these personal ties, Mary Jane and MacLeish shared the link of geography. Close in age, the two had grown up in the Chicago area around the turn of the century; Mary Jane in Woodstock, MacLeish in Glencoe. Socially, their paths never would have crossed, even though their fathers were both merchants. It was just that Frank Daniels managed a small town drugstore whereas Andrew MacLeish managed and owned the Carson Pirie Scott department store in Chicago. Nevertheless, Archibald MacLeish was always mindful that his father, who never finished high school, was just a shopkeeper who had made good.[13]

Despite reservations he may have harbored about Philip's abilities, MacLeish cleared the way for him to get a job at the Library of Congress.[14] MacLeish's concerns were described by Philip in his own personnel file: "I came to the Library of Congress in January, 1940 and worked for a few months in the Reference Dept. I took this post as a professional assistant with the understanding that I would be given a responsible position as soon as the then new librarian, Archibald McLeish [sic] was satisfied with my library training and experience."[15] At $2,000 a year, less than he had made at the University of Michigan a decade earlier, Philip's job as a reference librarian was hardly lucrative, but it wasn't long before his fortunes at the library improved. In May 1940, MacLeish made him acting head of the Accessions Division at a salary of $4,600.

Mutual friends and a mutual disdain for the ALA brought the Keeneys together with MacLeish, but it was shared political beliefs that cinched their alliance. This was especially true of their sympathies with the Republican government of Spain. Using the PLC as a bully pulpit to support the Spanish Loyalists, the Keeneys apparently felt obliged to draw a connection between the war and libraries. "A country hitherto without library service saw the establishment under the [Republican] Ministry of Education of hundreds of popular libraries. The militia marched off to the front with a book under one arm, a gun in the other. Leaders in the popular library movement were two graduates of the University of Madrid, Sra. Teresa Andres, and Dr. Juan Vincens."[16]

Putting aside the rather ludicrous image of beleaguered soldiers toting *Don Quixote* along with their guns, the PLC is to be admired for putting its pitiful resources and its corporate mouth in the same place. The group "adopted" Andres and Vincens, who found exile in France during the course of the Civil War. Falangists had assassinated the father and eldest brother of Teresa Andres. Another brother had been killed in battle, and a third was imprisoned in Spain. As war spread in Europe, the safety of these librarians in France became increasingly tenuous and the PLC took on the task of raising funds to pay their way to a safe haven in Mexico.

Within a year, the organization had raised over $600, half-again more than was needed to get the Spanish librarians from France to Mexico. Before the money became available, Vincens succeeded in getting there by other means. Andres, along with her husband, Emilio Nadal, and infant son, disappeared until the end of the war. Unable to locate her, the PLC sent most of the funds they had collected to Vincens in Mexico with the understanding that he would funnel them to endangered librarians trying to flee Europe. Andres never escaped, but the PLC money that she eventually received saved her family from starvation. In late 1945, Mary Jane traveled to France and managed to track them down. Sadly, Andres's health had been so impaired by the war that she died the following year.

Other issues taken on by the PLC included tenure and salaries, censorship, and the ALA's progress in transforming into a more democratic organization. Whenever there were opportunities to criticize the ALA, the PLC took full advantage of them.[17] It really wasn't a fair contest because the ALA, like a big lumbering bear, was such an easy target. The PLC did its best to depict the larger ALA as heartless and socially irresponsible. Alas, the portrait was not always exaggerated.

One of the biggest gaffes by the ALA concerned its ambiguous position on accommodations available to African American librarians in cities where the ALA held its conferences. After the 1936 conference in Richmond (where Black librarians were denied rooms in conference hotels, forced to use different entrances than Whites, and seated in segregated areas during sessions), the ALA took seemingly convincing steps to eliminate such discrimination at future meetings. It adopted a policy that "in all rooms and halls under the control of the ALA for conference use, all members should be admitted in full equality."[18]

Under pressure from White Southern librarians, however, the ALA soon began to waffle. Although conferences were held in the South only every five years, these librarians insisted that holding all meetings in the North, West, and Midwest would impose an unreasonable travel burden on them. In deference to the Southern members, a special committee of the ALA was appointed in 1940 to reconsider the 1936 resolution. Many librarians were disturbed by the ALA's about-face, and the PLC vigorously protested the ALA's tepid stance on racism. The PLC sent copies of a letter to the library press and to ALA president Ralph Munn: "[T]he issue is not one of . . . travelling expenses every fifth year to conferences; it is the much larger issue of persecution of a minority. We who raise our voices against anti-Semitic persecution abroad cannot defensibly tolerate racial discrimination at home, especially when it is our proud professional boast that the libraries wherein we work recognize no distinctions of race, color or class. . . . The world of books knows no color line."[19]

In May 1940, the ALA reaffirmed its 1936 resolution, but without taking a stand against racism as an institution. Indeed, the ALA's leaders were well aware that Cincinnati, where the June 1940 conference was to be held, was no mecca of integrated facilities. Prior to the meeting, the *ALA Bulletin* published a notice encouraging its Black members to find rooms at a hotel that was a mere four miles from the conference head-quarters "with several car lines passing without transfers."[20]

Besides criticizing the ALA's position on race, the PLC condemned the ALA for rejecting the PLC's appeals for contributions toward the cost of passage for the Spanish librarians Teresa Andres and Juan Vincens.[21] What the PLC failed to acknowledge was that in the mid-1930s the ALA had embarked on its own program to assist refugee librarians. Eventually, a placement service was set up during the ALA's 1941 conference, but it was noted at the time that the employment of European librarians was impeded by the refusal of many American libraries to hire Jews and Catholics.[22]

Then there were the two matters so close to the Keeneys' hearts: censorship and job protections for librarians. After the Keeney case in Montana was resolved, the ALA acknowledged an obligation to stand behind librarians who had been unfairly fired, but this support generally took the form of sympathetic letters or statements on behalf of those who had been turned out of their jobs. Unlike the AAUP, the ALA was reluctant to make on-site visits to institutions where disputes occurred, and persistently failed to put the organization's monetary resources behind investigations.[23]

The ALA took an equally cautious approach to intellectual freedom with its Library's Bill of Rights, issued in 1939. On one hand, it favored free access to literature and information by advocating that libraries provide materials that represented "all sides of questions on which differences of opinion exist." On the other hand, it recognized the obligation of individual librarians to use public funds to purchase books and other reading matter that reflected the values and interests of their communities. In short, any book not in keeping with "community values" could be justifiably excluded from a library under the terms of the Library's Bill of Rights.[24]

The PLC was far more explicit in its condemnation of censorship and lobbed numerous volleys at the ALA for refusing to address specific cases where public access to literature had been violated. In 1941, the PLC included among its objectives "to uphold the civil rights of library users by acting against censorship of books." One of the most admired and vilified books of the day was John Steinbeck's *The Grapes of Wrath*, and it became the PLC symbol of the censorship problem in American libraries. The council repudiated libraries in New York State, Missouri, New Jersey, and Ohio for banning *The Grapes of Wrath* from their shelves.[25]

The PLC claimed the moral high ground when criticizing the ALA, but the ALA remained aloof from its little rival for as long as possible. Patience on the part of the ALA's leaders must have been severely tried,

however, when they discovered that the PLC had once again piggy-
backed its meeting on the ALA's 1940 conference in Cincinnati. It was
there that the battle of nerves between the two groups came to a peak.
America's impending role in the war was the issue that would lead to an
enormous blowup between the two groups.

Officially, the ALA was neutral on America's entry into the war, but
Executive Secretary Carl Milam was known to personally advocate intervention. The ALA also informed government officials that it was prepared to support the military in the way it knew best, with information.
As in World War I, the ALA affirmed that its greatest contribution to
preserving democracy was in providing books to soldiers at the front
and assuring that foreign publications would continue to arrive in America despite blockades.[26]

The PLC took a contrasting stand on the war. It opposed American
intervention and passed a resolution to that effect at the 1940 meeting in
Cincinnati. Had the PLC limited this announcement to the conference
goers, the ALA leaders would have been unfazed. Instead, the smaller
organization trumped the ALA by wiring to President Roosevelt:

> Alarmed by the rapid drift of this country toward involvement in the Euro-
> pean war, we, librarians assembled at the sixty-second annual conference
> of the American Library Association in Cincinnati May 26 to June 1, re-
> spectfully urge you to keep this country at peace. We believe that if Ameri-
> cans are to save western civilization our first duty towards mankind is to
> remain at peace, to preserve and improve our standard of living and to
> maintain the civil liberties with which libraries are so greatly concerned.[27]

Dubbed "the Peace Letter," this message to Roosevelt sent the ALA
into a tailspin. Upon learning of the telegram, the ALA's officers were
infuriated. Their deepest fear was that Roosevelt would misconstrue the
position of the PLC as that of the ALA, or worse, think that the PLC was
the ALA—although the PLC had signed the telegram. Countering with
its own communication to Roosevelt, the ALA condemned the PLC as a
minority group with no authority to speak for librarians on the war or
on any other subject. As Dennis Thomison, historian of the ALA, has
pointed out, the ALA was no less presumptuous in speaking for America's librarians by asserting that most of them would reject the position
expressed in the PLC telegram. In fact, no one had ever polled the nation's librarians to ascertain their sentiments on the war.[28]

For some members of the PLC, the Peace Letter represented sincere
pacifist sentiments. For Philip and Mary Jane, however, it reflected an

allegiance to the Communist Party's opposition to the United States' joining the Allies' fight against Germany while the Hitler–Stalin Non-Aggression Pact was in effect. Signed in 1939, the pact guaranteed that the Germans and Russians would not attack each other. The American Communist Party opposed Hitler, but support of Stalin took precedence above all else. Many could not live with the contradiction, however, so an exodus of disillusioned members from the American party followed. About half of the PLC's members dropped out of the organization after the Peace Letter was issued, but they were replaced by an equal number of new members.[29] Despite their own anti-Fascist sentiments the Keeneys remained sympathetic to the Soviet Union after the pact. In her unpublished autobiography, Mary Jane brushed aside the implications of the pact, calling it "a thunderbolt which we did not understand at the time." She elaborated no further on how she and Philip ever found the alliance palatable, but she never questioned it.[30]

Opposing views on American intervention in the war not only caused a blowup between the ALA and the PLC; it also threatened MacLeish's good will toward the Keeneys. Mistakenly assuming that MacLeish shared their view against American intervention, the Keeneys invited him to be the PLC's guest of honor at their 1940 Cincinnati meeting with the belief that he would speak on the benefits of isolationism. Instead, he called for united support of Great Britain and denounced the Soviet Union. A PLC member who attended the meeting recalled three decades later that the Keeneys could hardly be civil to MacLeish after that.[31]

Unwilling to accept MacLeish's failure to speak against American intervention, the PLC brazenly attempted to link his name with the Peace Letter by implying that it carried his endorsement. A. B. Korman of the PLC sent the Peace Letter to the ALA and asked that it be distributed during the ALA's 1940 conference. Korman was merely the messenger; the scheme never would have gone forward without the Keeneys' approval. The ALA turned down the request to distribute the letter but made a compensating offer to publish the text in the *ALA Bulletin*. Before that happened, Carl Milam smelled the proverbial rat and sent the Peace Letter to MacLeish, ostensibly to give him a chance to correct any errors. MacLeish immediately repudiated the letter. Instead of stating a position on American intervention, MacLeish simply referred the editor of the *ALA Bulletin* to "The Irresponsibles," a paper that he had delivered in April 1940 to the American Philosophical Society and that was printed in the *Nation* magazine the following month.

A reading of "The Irresponsibles" does not provide an easy answer to the question of MacLeish's views on the war. The thrust of the paper is a lament over the social indifference of scholars, writers, and artists to the assault on Western civilization going on around them: "[T]here are no voices which accept responsibility for speaking. Even the unimaginable indecencies of propaganda, even the corruption of the word itself in Germany and Russia and Spain and elsewhere, even the open triumph of the lie produced no answer such as Voltaire in his generation would have given." He called for a fight against tyranny, not with guns, but with thoughts and words. The bleak prospect of war facing the world, suggested MacLeish, was largely due to the failure of artists to speak out in time. "The Irresponsibles" demonstrated that MacLeish could not be easily buttonholed as a hawk or a dove.[32]

No strangers to headstrong and self-defeating behavior, the Keeneys' actions in Cincinnati were reckless even by their own standards. It would be an understatement to say that they erred in attempting to link MacLeish to the Peace Letter without consulting him. If the Keeneys were indifferent to the ethical niceties of their relationship with MacLeish, they might at least have given some thought to the fact that he was now Philip's boss. As a member of the federal employees union at the Library of Congress, Philip may have felt immune to the possibility that MacLeish might even fire him, but there was one thing that he really didn't consider: a rapprochement between MacLeish and the ALA. After Milam alerted MacLeish to the PLC scheme, the chilly relationship between the two men began to thaw. They hardly became chums but managed to collaborate on issues affecting libraries, particularly in regard to the war and to a massive reorganization of the Library of Congress. Milam and MacLeish even exchanged a few personal visits and started to address each other by their first names in correspondence.[33]

By contrast, Philip and Mary Jane faced unpleasant consequences from their ill-advised attempt to use MacLeish's name in their antiwar effort. Watching Milam and MacLeish mend fences must have been hard enough, but although Philip would not lose his job, the Keeneys' bond with MacLeish had been permanently damaged by their attempt to use his name in their cause. The August 1940 *PLC Bulletin* carried what could be considered a grudging apology to the Librarian of Congress: "[T]hough it [the PLC] does not share Mr. MacLeish's opinion concerning the war, it is proud to have conducted a forum of opposing points of view, and sensible, too, of the honor he did us by appearing at our breakfast."[34]

All cordiality between the Keeneys and MacLeish essentially ended in the summer of 1941, when Philip learned that he would not be the permanent head of the library's Accessions Division even though he had been acting head for over a year. Instead, MacLeish demoted him back to the position of reference librarian with a major salary cut. After supervising thirty-five people, Philip oversaw a staff of three. It should not be assumed that MacLeish's move was a reprisal only for the use of his name in conjunction with the Peace Letter. MacLeish was not a man who nursed grudges.[35] Instead, when he became Librarian of Congress, he decided to be a good "technical" librarian and immediately began streamlining the library's organizational structure, which had become byzantine during Herbert Putnam's tenure.

To accomplish his ends, MacLeish was prepared to reassign anyone whose work did not measure up to his standards. One casualty was Wilfred C. Gilbert, director of the Legislative Reference Service (LRS) at the library and a former classmate of MacLeish's at Harvard Law School. With a stream of complaints from congressmen about inadequacies of the LRS, MacLeish appointed Luther Evans director and made Gilbert deputy director. If MacLeish would downgrade a man with the old school tie, he was prepared to demote anyone, although it probably did not give him too many pangs of guilt to send Philip down the organizational chart.

Philip's demotion did not go unremarked within the Library of Congress. The library's chapter of the United Public Workers of America (in which Philip actively participated) noted the change in its August 1941 newsletter. Philip was praised for wiping out backlogs in the Accessions Division and for raising staff morale. Without naming MacLeish as the responsible culprit, the newsletter was critical of the fact that Philip was left to flounder only as the acting head of Accessions "while his successor was made permanent. The difference in titles constitutes discrimination whether or not it was intended."[36] This venting may have given Philip a degree of satisfaction, but the union never filed a formal complaint on his behalf.

From the middle of 1940 until the summer of 1941—the period between the debacle of the Cincinnati conference and Philip's demotion at the Library of Congress—the Keeneys continued to be the major presence in the PLC. Philip remained as chairman of the council, the quarterly *Bulletin* increased in volume, and the artist Rockwell Kent appeared as the group's guest of honor at its June 1941 meeting in Boston. Kent was enough of a public figure that his address was aired on NBC radio, and in him the PLC found a more unequivocal ally than MacLeish had been the year before. Kent, without subtlety or nuance, roused his audience to join the "world front" against Fascism.[37] What this meant in terms of American intervention in the war was complicated by the earth-shaking event that occurred the very day on which Kent addressed the PLC. On June 22, 1941, Hitler reneged on his pact with Stalin and invaded the Soviet Union.

Members of the PLC were caught off guard by the invasion, and in its aftermath the *PLC Bulletin* no longer carried a recurring statement against American participation in the European conflict. The PLC did not, however, immediately adopt a pro-intervention stance. That would not come until after the bombing at Pearl Harbor. At that point, the librarians of the PLC pledged to the president of the United States "their willing and loyal services as citizens in whatever capacity they may be needed."[38] Like the Peace Letter, a copy of this resolution was sent to President Roosevelt. It was as if the PLC's position against American intervention in the war had never existed.

By the time the PLC announced its support for America's declaration of war, the Keeneys' role in the council was quickly subsiding. Philip had given up his position as chairman, and he and Mary Jane had assumed their places as emeriti of the organization. The reasons for this were several. First, the new job Philip had recently begun proved to be more of a responsibility than he had first imagined. He was now the reference librarian for the research and analysis unit of the Office of Strategic Services (OSS). The predecessor of the CIA, the OSS served as America's "spy" organization during World War II. Suddenly, Philip Keeney was expected to provide materials from the Library of Congress to researchers who would write classified reports used in military strategy. With Philip's attention distracted from the PLC, the council began to decline. Second, as an organization appealing to younger people, it lost a sizable number of members to the armed forces. Besides this, the ALA suspended its annual conferences for the duration of the war, eliminating the convenient venue for PLC meetings. The group continued to produce a newsletter until June of 1944 and held a meeting as late as 1946, but the disengagement of the Keeneys spelled the end of the organization. They had started the PLC and had gotten from it what they needed—attention, revenge, and employment. By 1942, they were ready to move on. They had other work to do in the name of world revolution, and that would include giving classified information to the Soviet Union.

CHAPTER 6

The Spies at Home

Exactly what Philip and Mary Jane Keeney's work on behalf of the Soviet Union amounted to is hard to decipher. Spies, after all, do not usually advertise their activities. Although the Keeneys were hardly as circumspect as we might today expect, their lack of caution was in part simply a sign of simpler times. Not only did U.S. concern about Soviet espionage at first take a back seat to concerns about Axis spying during World War II, when the USSR was regarded as our ally, but the Soviet spy apparatus in the United States was in a state of transition or outright chaos during much of the Keeneys' government (and espionage) careers. The CIA was just coming into existence, and counterintelligence was in its infancy. Nevertheless, the preponderance of evidence, though failing to delineate their degree of success in supplying information to the Soviets, or the nature or importance of the information they supplied, points to considerable effort on their part to contribute something of value to the Soviet cause in which they believed.

Hope of greater clarity generated by the 1995 unveiling of the results of the Venona project—a long-term effort by the National Security Agency (NSA) and its forerunner the Army Signal Intelligence Service to decrypt cables dating chiefly from 1941 to 1945 containing information about Soviet espionage—was diminished when it became apparent that, at least with regard to the Keeneys, the content of the cables was sparse and, in some cases, virtually incomprehensible. In their 1999 book *Venona: Decoding Soviet Espionage in America*, John Earl Haynes and Harvey Klehr indexed the cables, matching cover names and newly released information with knowledge from other sources, but even this could not make all of the messages coherent or meaningful. This decoded communication regarding the Keeneys demonstrates the problem: "KAVALERIST has explained that KEENEY [KINI] and his wife were signed on apparently by the NEIGHBORS [SOSEDI] for work in 1940." So reads a cable sent on August 29, 1944—more than four years after the Keeneys' arrival in Washington, D.C.—by a Soviet intelligence agent based in New York to General Pavel Fitin in Moscow. Fitin, head of KGB foreign intelligence, was the recipient of most of the cables cracked by the Venona project.[1]

Despite its brevity and enigmatic quality, this message can be loosely interpreted, especially because the Keeneys are mentioned by name (in the majority of cables, cover or code names are used). "Kavalerist," or Cavalryman, was the cover name for Sergey Kurnakov,[2] a Russian national residing in the United States who recruited Americans to work for the KGB, the Soviet secret police. When he approached the Keeneys in 1944, he found that they had been recruited in 1940 by "neighbors," or a different branch of intelligence, probably the Soviet military intelligence, GRU.

Although the identity of the early contact is unclear, Venona cables dated May 17 and 22, 1942, appear to describe Philip's recruitment by "Sound," Jacob N. Golos, in 1942, shortly after Philip moved from his Library of Congress acquisitions position to "Izba" or the Office of the Coordinator of Information, later the Office of Strategic Services or OSS. Because Kurnakov reported that the Keeneys were recruited in 1940, it appears that the Keeneys were identified as potential recruits at least twice and possibly three times, with the earliest time being a GRU contact preceding the Golos and Kurnakov contacts. Possibly Keeney's earlier contact was his PLC friend, David R. Wahl, in 1940 head of Binding at the Library of Congress. Wahl is the previously unidentified active KGB agent "Pink," uncovered through a 2007 translation of handwritten notes taken on KGB archival material.[3] Wahl and his wife Edith, like Philip and Mary Jane Keeney, were social friends with Nathan Gregory Silvermaster (code named "Pel" and "Robert") and his wife Helen and their housemate William Ludwig Ullman. The Silvermasters and Ullman were principal actors in the "Silvermaster group," who provided valuable materials to the KGB through Golos.

Golos and Kurnakov were espionage "talent spotters" and managers for Soviet intelligence. There were differences, however. Golos was a member of the CPUSA who had long recruited and managed spies for the KGB. Born Jacob Raisen, he had escaped from a Siberian prison and had become naturalized as an American citizen by 1915. He told Elizabeth Bentley that he had been in the Soviet Union sometime during the 1920s and had become involved with the secret police, but he was in the

Reissue(T104)

From: NEW YORK

To: MOSCOW

No: 1234

                                      29 August 1944

To VIKTOR[i].

        Your no. 3464[a]. GONETs[ii] is working as deputy chief
of the PROVINCIAL[PROVINTsIAL'NYJ][iii] department of the "Columbia Broadcasting System." He was used by us earlier for the
most part on liaison with ARTUR[iv], as a meeting point[YaVKA]
[b] for couriers. At the same time we used him on the processing[OFORMLENIE] of PROVINCIAL

                [17 groups unrecoverable]

as a FELLOWCOUNTRYMAN[ZEMLYaK][v]. We are using him here on
the processing of the CBS and of the diplomatic representation
of the COUNTRY[STRANA][vi] in the PROVINCES[iii].

        KAVALERIST[vii] has explained that KEENEY[KINI][viii]
and his wife were signed on apparently by the NEIGHBORS[SOSEDI]
[ix] for work in 1940.

No. 688   MAJ[x]
    29 August

Notes: [a]   Not available.
       [b]   i.e. presumably, his business establishment was used
             as a meeting point for couriers.
Comments:
       [i]   VIKTOR: Lt. Gen. P.M. FITIN.
       [ii] GONETs: i.e. EXPRESS MESSENGER, Ricardo SETARO.
       [iii] PROVINTsIAL'NYJ, PROVINTsII: PROVINCIAL and PROVINCES
             are Latin-American and Latin America respectively.
       [iv] ARTUR: Unidentified cover-name.
       [v]   ZEMLYaK: Member of the Communist Party.
       [vi] STRANA: The U.S.A.
       [vii] KAVALERIST: i.e. CAVALRYMAN, Sergej KURNAKOV.
       [viii] KEENEY: Phillip Olin KEENEY and his wife Mary Jane
             KEENEY.
       [ix] SOSEDI: Members of another Soviet Intelligence or-
             ganization.
       [x]   MAJ: i.e. MAY, Stepan Zakharovich APRESYaN.

                                      2 May 1972

Venona Cable #1234, showing Kurnakov's approach to Keeney in 1944. Note that
the cable was deciphered in 1972.

United States in time to help found the Communist Party and was a full-time party functionary by 1923. His roles were two: to run World Tourists, a legitimate business under contract with the official Soviet travel agency to arrange trips to and from the USSR; and to recruit and manage underground spying activities. World Tourists helped fund Soviet enterprises in the United States and gave cover for Golos's clandestine operations.

Golos was more independent than Moscow or the New York KGB chief liked, and attempts were made to recall him to Moscow. He stayed in the United States and thereby saved himself from the Stalinist purges, which disrupted the developing espionage capacity of the KGB by depriving it of many of its experienced operatives. At the time of Golos's death in 1943, the KGB was trying to isolate him and take over his agents. The KGB believed—rightly—that he had been constantly under surveillance since a 1940 plea bargain on charges that World Tourists was an unregistered agent of a foreign government, and was thereby making the entire apparatus vulnerable to discovery. Following Golos's plea bargain, he opened a second business, United States Service and Shipping, with his lover Elizabeth Bentley as its day-to-day manager. Bentley also assumed his spymaster role when he died and became known after her defection to the FBI as the "Blond Spy Queen."[4]

Sergey Kurnakov had left his native country after the Russian Civil War in 1921 and spent most of the following years as a writer for *Russkii Golos*, a Russian language journal with a Bolshevik slant published in New York. He also produced articles for the *Daily Worker* and *New Masses*. His early life, recounted in an autobiography written in 1935, made Kurnakov an unlikely Communist spy. A member of an aristocratic family, he fought for the Czar in World War I and was horrified by the collapse of the empire. After Alexander Kerensky took power, Kurnakov was reduced to despair at the sight of St. Petersburg in chaos and incredulous as he watched drunken soldiers shoot their officers.[5] He became an enemy of the Bolsheviks with the onset of the Russian Civil War in which he fought for the White Army. It is unclear when he changed his loyalties or why.

Pavel Sudoplatov, who had leading roles in the secret police, stated in a 1994 memoir that his agency depended heavily upon Kurnakov to recruit Americans who were willing and able to provide classified information to the Soviets.[6] For a time during World War II, Sudoplatov worked to combine the operations of the GRU with the KGB, which had the same kind of sometimes frosty and competitive relationship as the FBI and the CIA. The Keeneys' relationship with Kurnakov, therefore, may also reflect the changing internal configurations of Soviet intelligence, with the GRU at least temporarily subsumed by the KGB.

In addition to the competition between the two Soviet spy agencies, the Soviet espionage apparatus during this period was working to professionalize its operations, to improve its tradecraft. Jacob Golos, protective of his American sources and suspicious of the Russian newcomers he considered culturally insensitive and inept, represented the old school, criticized by Moscow for its sloppiness, while Kurnakov appeared to be a practitioner of the new postpurge regime.[7] Thus the Keeneys, like others of their Communist friends, such as the Silvermasters, were caught in the middle of a drama the impact of which would only become apparent years later.

Given the confusion within the Soviet espionage apparatus—a confusion that deepened after Elizabeth Bentley's November 1945 interviews with the FBI—as well as the secretive and confusing nature of spying and the lack of access to documents from the Soviet era KGB archives, it is not surprising that the Keeneys' story would be murky at best.[8] We do, however, have references to Keeney in the Venona cables and in some Soviet archival material just coming to light, as well as an accretion of other evidence that together builds an evidentiary mosaic of spying—albeit a circumstantial one with fragments missing, especially pertaining to their early years in Washington. From 1940 through Golos's contact in 1942 to Kurnakov's initial contact, we know little. At the outset, though, it appears that the Keeneys, if not providing information directly to Golos, may have been providing information to Wahl, who may have been their first recruiter. It is also possible that they gave information to Silvermaster, who regularly turned over large numbers of documents to Golos and later Bentley, who became Golos's courier and replacement. Because Silvermaster was the intermediary, and the Venona cables report only on what the KGB received from Silvermaster, it is impossible to know definitively what the Keeneys turned over to their spymasters, if anything. At least one 1944 Venona cable, however, reports that Silvermaster provided forty-three rolls of film, among which was "a review by the Ministry of Economic Warfare on the economic situation in Germany," to which Mary Jane—who worked on issues pertaining to the German economy—and Philip—who was by that time head of document security at the Board of Economic Warfare (BEW)—would have had easy access; but so would others, such as BEW's Frank Coe, named by Bentley.[9]

If the Keeneys did provide material to the Silvermasters, however, they did it unbeknownst to Elizabeth Bentley, who in 1945 said that she did not know them, and that up until the time in 1944 when she discontinued her visits to the Silvermasters, the Silvermasters had not "used" the Keeneys. "Their jobs may not have been sufficiently important," the FBI file reports Bentley advising, or one of the Keeneys "may have been considered to be unstable."[10]

They apparently were stable enough for another attempt at recruitment. Philip and Mary Jane's first contact with Kurnakov was a surprise visit recorded by Mary Jane in her diary on November 5, 1943, less than three weeks before the death of Jacob Golos, and during a time that Golos was trying to protect his "probationers"—the word used for agents—from reporting directly to the KGB, rather than to Bentley and through her to him. That visit, the record of which called Kurnakov by name, was followed in July 1944 with a dinner at the home of their friend George Faxon[11] at which "Colonel Thomas"—the cover name they used for Kurnakov—was also present. "Discovered he came to see us," Mary Jane writes. When Col. Thomas takes them to dinner the following night, he "discovers he came on a wild goose chase," she comments, apparently alluding to the fact that they had already been recruited to espionage by the GRU, because that is what he reported in the 1944 cable. It may be that at this time Kurnakov was under instructions to take over the management of the Keeneys' activities from their previous contact as part of the effort to professionalize espionage activities.

Although they occasionally saw or spoke to "Colonel Thomas," however, their main intelligence contact during this time was an American, Joseph Milton Bernstein, whom the FBI believed to be engaged in GRU espionage. The Venona files identify Bernstein with the code name "Marquis."[12] It may well be that, having discovered that the Keeneys had been recruited by the GRU, Kurnakov made an effort to connect them with a GRU contact, Bernstein. Certainly in January 1945, when "Cerberus" (Keeney) asks "Robert" (Silvermaster) to get him back in touch with "the man through whom he was connected with the Fellow-countrymen [Communist Party]," Stepan Apresyan, the New York agent in charge, asks Pavel Fitin in Moscow to "allow us to inform the head 'Neighbor' [here the GRU] about Cerberus's request."[13] Apparently the Keeneys began and ended their Washington employment working for Soviet military intelligence, although they kept in touch with Kurnakov, Wahl, and Silvermaster, as well as Bernstein.

Ironically their contact, Joseph Bernstein, a translator and editor, had been a graduate student at Yale in the late 1930s, a time when the university was incubating a generation of future American intelligence agents. Among his friends at Yale was undergraduate James Jesus Angleton, who would become head of the CIA's counterintelligence division in 1954. There is nothing to indicate that the relationship between the two men was based on a mutual fascination with espionage, but rather on a shared fondness for Baudelaire, Rimbaud, and Verlaine.[14]

NY 65-15648

~~TOP SECRET~~

In order to intelligently portray the association between BERNSTEIN and the KEENEYs, the information
received from Confidential Informant ▓ mentioned previously,
from MARY JANE KEENEY's diaries and correspondence is being
set forth in chronological order.

November 11, 1943

"JOE BERNSTEIN down here from New York. Long
talk about Japan and then long talk about other matters which
seem quite complicated."

December 7, 1943

"JOE B. comes in at 8:30. Get to bed very late.
JOE encounters technical difficulties but gets off on 9:00 train."

December 27, 1943

"JOE down."

January 27, 1944

"Off at 9:00 for New York. See JOE B."

January 29, 1944

"To (ABE & ELIZABETH) FEINGOLDS in Brooklyn...
To JOE B's for dinner and we are joined in evening by SAM SIL
(SAM GILLEN)."

February 2, 1944

"JOE B. down."

March 7, 1944

"JOE down. We pass on our birthday gift to the
Jefferson School."

April 11, 1944

"JOE down. Has SUE's book and candy and is
pleased with my exploits."   ~~TOP SECRET~~

357

- 12 -

This page of the Keeneys' FBI file, 101-467-187, p. 357, shows excerpts from Mary
Jane's diary that reveal the pattern of meetings they had with Joe Bernstein.

And what information did Philip or Mary Jane Keeney have that a
foreign power could possibly want? As acting head of Acquisitions from
June 1940 to June 1941, Philip was in a position to know about virtually
everything that the Library of Congress added to its collection, including
war-related documents. His value to the Soviets grew considerably when

he was transferred to the office of the Coordinator of Information (COI) in July 1941. Within a year the office was enlarged and renamed the Office of Strategic Services (OSS), with a Research and Analysis unit in the Library of Congress. The Soviets were anxious to penetrate the OSS, which they code-named "Izba," and they were particularly interested in reports that were being written about their own country by the staff of Research and Analysis.

As chief librarian, first of the COI and then of Research and Analysis, Philip worked at the epicenter of sensitive information compiled by researchers who wrote reports on areas affected by the war.[15] The staff was made up of academics, largely from the Ivy League, with foreign language skills and specializations in every region of the world. Many of their reports were destined for the desks of military strategists and the inner circle of the White House. Like any reference librarian helping a student write a term paper, Philip had the opportunity to see which resources were used to write those reports. It is entirely likely that he got to see the researchers' final products, which would become part of the "Izba" collection, but his librarian status would have been unlikely to raise red flags for those concerned about security. For a time, Philip reported directly to William Langer, the chief of Research and Analysis, providing an opportunity to observe not only the work of rank-and-file researchers, but that of the highest-ranking members of national intelligence.

Politically, Keeney was in his element at OSS Research and Analysis, where many of the academics shared his political sentiments. A contemporary variation on the OSS initials was "Oh So Socialist," a reference to the openly liberal makeup of the staff. William "Wild Bill" Donovan, head of the OSS, knowingly hired Communists, even as intelligence officers in the field. Among these agents were veterans of the Abraham Lincoln Brigade, Americans who had fought for the Spanish Loyalists under the aegis of the Comintern. In Donovan's view, political philosophy was far less important than having skills necessary to do a job, but his hiring practices risked security leaks. John Earl Haynes and Harvey Klehr believe that at least twelve OSS staff members reported to the KGB or to the GRU during the war. Besides Keeney, three were located in Research and Analysis. Many of the other names listed by Haynes and Klehr—Maurice Halperin, Helen Tenney, and Donald Wheeler, for example—appear in the Keeneys' FBI file and were social acquaintances. In short, it was not very difficult for Philip to get information out of OSS to his Soviet handlers.[16]

Jesse Shera, an up-and-coming librarian who had ardently supported Keeney during the Montana case, worked at the Library of Congress during part of this time and saw nothing that suggested espionage. "I not only got to know Keeney well, but worked with him closely, or at least as closely as anyone could work with a man who did absolutely nothing," Shera said later. What Shera saw was a bitter whining man. "I never really knew whether Keeney was a bad librarian from the start, or whether, by the time I got to know him, he was a 'broken spirit' because of the affair at Missoula."[17] This negative appraisal was a personal and professional defeat for Philip because he forfeited the faith that Shera had put in him at a critical time. In his old age, Shera remained convinced that there had been a miscarriage of justice at Montana State University but concluded that as a librarian Philip was "everything Charlie Brown [former ALA President] said, and worse."[18]

This characterization of Philip's library skills may be debatable, but Shera was dead wrong about one thing. Philip was not spending his days doing absolutely nothing, but much of his work was deliberately inconspicuous. Philip's superiors at the library apparently were oblivious of, or indifferent to, his unauthorized activities. At least nothing he did hurt his career or compromised his access to classified information. In 1943, he got a nice salary increase when he transferred easily to the position of chief of document security, Enemy Branch, Economic Intelligence Division, at the Foreign Economic Administration (FEA). According to the personnel file document that recommended his appointment, his responsibilities included having "custody and control of all secret and confidential documents pertaining to the work of all branches of the Board of Economic Warfare" as well as "reading, analyzing, abstracting, and correlating" intelligence material. Later, as he was applying for another transfer, Keeney characterized the work as the analysis, collation, and processing of "all classified material from sources foreign and domestic . . . including the rapid distribution of this material so that it could be readily used for the reports and other assignments originating in the various offices and divisions of the FEA." Once again Philip was in charge of access to information that the Soviets were likely to find valuable. His performance ratings at the FEA were excellent.[19]

By the time Philip had transferred to the FEA, Mary Jane was working as an assistant economic editor in the Office of Economic Warfare (OEW), a division of the Board of Economic Warfare. Hired in October 1942, she was promoted quickly to more responsible positions where she had even greater access to classified materials. In September 1943, she was made a full editor and transferred to the OEW's Blockade and Supply Unit. In the last year of the war, the Board of Economic Warfare was absorbed by the FEA and in October 1944 Mary Jane was promoted to the position of foreign affairs economist.[20]

While working in these divisions, Mary Jane edited many reports on
the economies of Axis countries. She personally authored reports on the
light metals industry in Germany, U.S. business holdings in Germany
and Austria, and the German machine industry. One of her employers
praised her work, saying Mary Jane was "more familiar than anyone
else on the staff with the entire body of analytical work" that had been
done by the Enemy Branch of the FEA.[21] Information that may well have
come from Mary Jane is reported in the Venona files as coming from
Silvermaster. The line between economic and military intelligence is
blurry, especially during wartime, and Mary Jane's reports included production statistics and specific locations of factories that might become
objects of attack. This was information that the United States might
have shared with its allies, including the Soviet Union, but not at Mary
Jane's discretion. It may be said of the Keeneys, and of anyone considered a spy, that to some degree their transgression lay in claiming the
right to disseminate information that higher government authorities did
not consider to be theirs to give away.

This rule of thumb was not necessarily obvious. Government agencies routinely shared information with newspaper and magazine writers in an atmosphere of relative openness before the United States
became involved in the war, and even then they were more concerned
about the information getting to Japan or Germany than to the Soviets. Discretion over which documents would be released often rested
with the individuals who produced them. William Langer, head of the
OSS Research and Analysis unit (and Philip Keeney's boss for a time)
used classified documents from his office in writing his books *Our
Vichy Gamble* and *The Undeclared War*. OSS Director William Donovan had the habit of divulging secret information during the casual
patter of cocktail parties. Significant information about the most sensitive of topics—the atom bomb—was exchanged completely outside the
government arena. As late as 1940, physicists were publishing their
research on the subject in respected venues like *Physical Review* and
Naturwissenschaften.[22]

Their agency heads may have been oblivious to the Keeneys' activities,
but an increasingly wary Congress demanded investigations of government employees likely to give away sensitive information. Suspects included those on the radical Right and radical Left, individuals who could
fit some loose definition of disloyalty. Pressure for these investigations
came from the Special House Committee on Un-American Activities,
established in 1938 and better known as the Dies Committee after its
chairman, Representative Martin Dies of Texas. Although a Democrat,

Dies was no admirer of the Roosevelt administration, which he considered to be dangerously liberal.

The Dies Committee was aided in its efforts to investigate federal employees with the passage of the Hatch Act in 1939. The act made it illegal for federal employees to be members of organizations that advocated the overthrow of "our constitutional form of government in the United States." Feeling pressure from Congress, Roosevelt imposed a Hatch Act loyalty oath on federal employees, in essence forcing them to swear that they would not join any organizations that were deemed Communist fronts, a term that Dies applied to any organization of which he disapproved. For good measure, right-wing groups such as the German-American Bund were proscribed, but, unquestionably, the Dies Committee was fixated on leftists, especially after the Nazi–Soviet pact.

Following close on the heels of the Hatch Act were the 1940 Voorhis and Smith acts. The Voorhis Act required the registration with the U.S. government of any organization representing foreign governments, and of any paramilitary and other organizations that advocated overthrowing the government by force. The Smith Act extended these provisions and added a proscription against teaching or advocating overthrow of the government. These acts were intended, among other things, to force American Communists to sever their ties with the Soviet Union. Beginning in 1948, the Smith Act would be the basis of the prosecution of the leadership of the CPUSA.[23]

Ironically, anti-Communist legislation in the United States gained momentum at a time when Communists were at their most "American." In the 1936 election, the CPUSA had lent its tacit support to Roosevelt, a bold departure from the party's earlier rebuff of mainstream politics, even though this support only took the form of opposing Alf Landon in the effort to direct votes to the Democrats.[24] Four years later, however, the party's support for Roosevelt was more direct, and Earl Browder made other changes to his party to make it more palatable to the White House. In 1944, the Communist Party of the United States of America was renamed the Communist Political Association (CPA), and it was transformed into a nonpartisan left-wing pressure group that could work through the two-party system. Under Browder's leadership, American Communism became so conventionally liberal that the Popular Front in the United States became known as the Democratic Front.

Although Browder's actions were out of step with the international Communist movement, there were hints that he could balance his courtship of the Democratic Party with Moscow's regime. At the time he was courting Roosevelt, relations between the United States and the Soviet Union were better than they ever had been. The two countries were now officially united in the war against Fascism. As a concession to the Allies, Stalin went so far as to dissolve the Communist International, facilitating, he declared, "The organization of all freedom-loving nations against the common enemy—Hitlerism."[25] Although the move was little more than window dressing, Browder chose to interpret it as a sign that Moscow wanted the party members under his guidance to be more integrated into American democratic life.

President Roosevelt, pressured by Congress, directed the Civil Service Commission to investigate federal employees against whom allegations of disloyalty had been made. It is not clear who implicated the Keeneys (their FBI file refers only to "a source of information"), but their political activities made it inevitable that they would be subjects of an inquiry. Besides their role in the Progressive Librarians' Council, Philip and Mary Jane had aligned themselves with a number of liberal and leftist organizations in Washington, D.C. Philip was in the United Public Workers of America, the CIO union at the Library of Congress, and was a member of the American Peoples' Mobilization. At the beginning of the war, this organization had called itself the American Peace Mobilization and was strongly opposed to U.S. intervention in the war. After Germany invaded Russia on June 22, 1941, the organization changed its name and its position. Many in Congress were inclined to believe that the American Peace/Peoples' Mobilization was Communist inspired because its stance on the war paralleled that of the American Communist Party. In fact, just about every organization or individual that changed position on the war on June 22, 1941, was suspected, not surprisingly, of Communist leanings.

The Civil Service scrutinized Mary Jane largely because of her volunteer work for Russian War Relief and the Washington Bookshop. The Washington Bookshop was the special object of Martin Dies's wrath. Formed as a cooperative in 1938, the bookshop offered books and phonograph records to its members at a substantial discount, but it was more than a business venture. It was a social club, an art gallery, and a lecture hall. Many of the members were federal employees who had moved to Washington, D.C., for wartime jobs and found themselves starved for companionship and a cultural life. In return for their annual dues of one dollar, members could attend lectures and concerts for free. One former member reminisced in the 1990s about the pleasure she derived from playing the violin in the Bookshop's string quartet. She recalled that the other violinist in the quartet was the Keeneys' good friend David Wahl, whom she remembered fondly.[26]

Dies seized upon reports that the bookshop sold the *Daily Worker* and works by Marx and Engels. He chose to ignore ample evidence that in most respects the bookshop's stock resembled that of other Washington area bookstores like Brentano's and Ballantyne's. Major publishing houses and book distributors attested that shipments to the Washington Bookshop were similar to those sent to these other bookstores. Publisher Alfred A. Knopf himself wrote a memo to the shop's trustees saying "It would be impossible for us to distinguish between your purchasing and that of any other bookshop of your size."[27]

Neither this nor the inevitable comparisons to German book burning dissuaded Dies from his pursuit of the bookshop. Guest speakers that the bookshop sponsored disturbed him as much as the store's inventory and membership rolls. Most notably, Eleanor Roosevelt addressed the members, an event that must have incensed Dies, an outspoken opponent of President Roosevelt and the New Deal. Besides Mrs. Roosevelt, speakers included Joseph E. Davies, ambassador to the Soviet Union between 1937 and 1938; a host of novelists; and two Black Howard University professors, Doxey Wilkerson and Sterling Brown. In the opinion of Selma Williams, herself the subject of a federal loyalty-security investigation, it was this absence of a color bar at the bookshop that most rankled Dies. Washington, D.C., was still very much a southern city in the early 1940s, and the bookshop was unique in that it admitted members irrespective of race or religion.[28]

Bookshop members were openly proud of their nondiscriminatory policies. As Angus McDonald, one of the founders, wrote at the height of the investigations: "We tried to be liberal. We said we favored anything that was democratic. In the constitution that we drew up we tried to follow the good old United States Constitution. We said we wouldn't keep anybody out because of race, color, or previous condition of servitude. In other words, if a man was a member of the National Association of Manufacturers or had even been in Congress, we said that if he came down and wanted to turn over a new leaf that we would forget about his past."[29] McDonald's humorous tone is remarkable considering that the investigations had become deadly serious.[30]

Like many federal workers, Philip and Mary Jane were subject to extensive background checks prior to being interviewed by the Civil Service. Investigators went so far as to question the Keeneys' friends in Berkeley, and FBI agents visited the campus of Montana State University to confer with G. Finlay Simmons. Simmons was only too willing to tell the agents that Philip was a notorious radical and agitator, but he stopped short of calling him a Communist. Kathleen Campbell, a librarian at the university, related her observations of Philip's early efforts to organize the "radical" PLC at the 1938 conference of the ALA. She told agents about a speech he had delivered from the convention floor, a speech that caused pandemonium because of "the Communist principles advocated by him." His remarks, said Campbell, were like waving a red flag. She, too, would not go so far as to say that Philip was a card-carrying Communist, but she did express her conviction that he was at least a Communist sympathizer.[31] So anxious were Simmons and Campbell to condemn Philip that Bureau agents quickly concluded that Philip's dismissal from the university grew out of personal friction, not Communist activities.[32] In fact, they found no reason to conclude that he was a Communist, much less a threat to the American way of life, a noticeable contrast to later FBI reports that interpreted Philip's actions and remarks as suggestive of disloyalty to his country.

The FBI interviews at the Library of Congress provided yet another opportunity for co-workers who disliked or distrusted Philip to vent their criticisms and to speculate on his political activities. One library employee, James Boyland, stated that he had joined the PLC to learn more about the technicalities of library work and was unhappy to find that the leaders of the organization had pronounced radical tendencies. In Boyland's opinion, the organization had been formed to spread "radical documents" and to oppose American intervention in the war. Once the Germans attacked Russia, he said, the position of the PLC abruptly changed to advocating intervention, the litmus test in the opinion of many for Communist sympathies.[33] Boyland added, presumably for the benefit of the investigators, that Keeney had asserted that the country would be a lot better off without the FBI, and that the day would come when the country would be rid of it.[34]

Another interviewee, Charles Gould, a self-described leftist sympathetic to the Keeneys, may have done them more harm than good by pointing out that Philip was interested in labor movements, Spanish Loyalists, civil liberties, and "the international situation." He described Philip as "friendly with the more liberal minorities in the union" at the Library of Congress and added that Philip had "many friends among liberals in all the government agencies."[35]

Although the Civil Service was responsible for investigating federal employees under the Hatch Act, it was the FBI that interviewed Philip in March 1942. As if he were reading Philip his Miranda rights, the agent began the session by stating that the Bureau had been empowered by Congress to investigate federal employees "who are alleged members of subversive organizations or who advocate the overthrow of the Federal Government." He then went through a rote process of asking Philip about the title of his job, the date of his employment, and the standard questions: "Are you now or have you ever been a member of any organization which you have reason to believe is controlled by the Communist Party? Do you now or have you ever advocated the overthrow of the present form of Government we enjoy in the United States?"[36]

Philip answered "no" to these questions but waffled in response to a question about his involvement in the American Peoples' Mobilization. He conceded that he had attended mass rallies of various kinds while in Washington, but he was not aware that any of them had been for that particular organization. That was essentially it. The interview could not have lasted more than ten minutes. Philip asked why he had been summoned; the agent said that he could not tell him. Philip replied "Yes, certainly. I understand," but his contempt for the experience came out when the FBI telephoned him to ask if he would like to sign the typed transcript of the interview. He answered tersely that he would not and hung up the receiver.[37]

As Philip's superior, Archibald MacLeish received a copy of the report, and it was he who had the authority to decide if Philip would stay in the federal service. Three months after the interview, MacLeish sent the FBI a letter indicating that he saw nothing in the reports to indicate that his employee had engaged in subversive activity or that he was anything other than a loyal American. Consequently, said MacLeish, he would not take any disciplinary action against him. It is a testimony to MacLeish that he would not take an easy opportunity to fire Philip, even though the two men were no longer friendly. Whatever he thought of Philip, MacLeish apparently thought less of the loyalty investigations.[38]

The FBI's investigation of Mary Jane led to an interview on September 10, 1943, with two members of the Civil Service Commission. No official transcript of this session exists in the Keeneys' FBI file, but Mary Jane's recorded impressions of the experience found their way from her diary to the file: "My Civil Service interview lasts for three hours, two men [names blacked out], the former a nasty man, and a stenographer. They shoot and boat at once with Communist allegations from Montana. Am philosophical and discursive and manage to make everyone laugh at the end but it is a detestable business all told."[39]

Mary Jane portrays herself as the one in charge of the event, answering questions in minute detail and going on after the interviewers had asked her to stop talking. Given what they asked (assuming Mary Jane didn't embroider the story), it is not surprising that she felt compelled to vigorously defend herself and drop the names of powerful friends like Senator James E. Murray and Congressman Mike Mansfield of Montana.

First Question: Mrs. Keeney, the Commission has information that during the time you lived in Montana, you were widely considered to be a member of the Communist party; that the activities in which you engaged were of a Communist nature; that you were constantly very critical of the United States; and that you frequently compared that government unfavorably with the government of Russia. Do you care to comment on this?

MJK (half rising and slapping gloves against handbag for emphasis): I certainly do want to comment on these idle and malicious tales.

And so she did, lambasting what she called the frustrated and malicious people of Missoula. She stated her belief that they resented her because she was more cosmopolitan than they, jealous of her refinement, her unique cooking style, and her familiarity with the fine arts: "[T]hey thought I was 'stuck up' and resented—because they envied—my knowledge of the field. I was told I had frequently been accused of being too much interested in foreign 'isms' which in this case were nothing more than impressionism and 'pointillism' (Spells it)."[40]

Undaunted by Mary Jane's first answer, which ran to an hour, the interviewers continued to ask her questions. They wanted to know who her friends were; she reminded them that she was a friend of Mansfield and Murray, as well as Wayne Morse, then at the War Labor Board but quickly ascending to Oregon's congressional delegation. They asked about an article by the Keeneys' friend David Wahl in the *PLC Bulletin* that was critical of Martin Dies. She defended the article and added her own unflattering remarks about Dies, pointing out that he had been photographed with "notorious Bundists" and that the vice president of the United States had been quoted as saying that Dies was doing Hitler's work in America.

Despite her interviewers' growing weariness, there was no way that they would allow Mary Jane to leave without being questioned about her memberships in Spanish Aid and the Washington Bookshop. Again, she made no apologies for her support of the Spanish Loyalists, or for her love of books and records, or for her delight in finding a bargain: "We found that the savings to members were substantial if one bought many books and records in a year. In general, we have found the Washington Bookshop a well-run commercial venture." When the questioning came to an end, Mary Jane refused to give the Civil Service interviewer a pat answer when he asked if she believed that he had conducted a fair and impartial hearing:

I'm afraid that I have tried your patience this afternoon because I have not answered the questions with a simple "yes" or "no.". . . It is a cherished principle of law that anyone accused of anything may have the opportunity to face his accusers. . . . To comment to my utmost satisfaction, and to the Commission's, I must necessarily have the right to face these accusers, for then I would know what was the basis for the malice shown. Therefore, in the absence of this cherished principle of law, I cannot say that this hearing has been fair or impartial.[41]

For all their indignation, the Keeneys must have gone into these interviews with some degree of fear. At the time they were questioned, or shortly thereafter, Philip and Mary Jane were actively working with their Soviet contacts and had no way of gauging what the government knew about them. But the lack of consequences that followed both interviews must have convinced the Keeneys that they were in the clear. Mary Jane's diaries indicate that she and Philip socialized constantly with the Wahls and the Silvermasters. No later than November 11, 1943, she began to record meetings with Bernstein which continued on a regular basis for more than a year until Bernstein came under suspicion, at which time he took a hiatus until March 1945.[42]

Fraternizing with Silvermaster was a risky business, whether the Keeneys knew it or not, because the FBI had paid considerable attention to him since the late 1930s. He had aroused suspicion because he was Russian born and because he had once worked at the Department of Agriculture, labeled by Communist hunters as the "reddest" agency in the U.S. government. Silvermaster had come to the United States as a child. As an adult, he lived in California for a number of years before moving to Washington, D.C., in the 1930s. He was, coincidentally, a doctoral student at Berkeley in the mid-1920s when Keeney was working on his certificate there in library science. There is no evidence, however, that the two men knew each other during this period. Silvermaster's move to Washington predated the Keeneys' by a number of years.[43] The FBI speculated that Golos may have introduced the Keeneys to Silvermaster, whose providers included, among others, Harry Dexter White, a high-ranking Treasury official; and Lauchlin Currie, deputy administrator of the FEA. Although Bentley did not list the Keeneys among Silvermaster's sources, they saw themselves as part of the Silvermaster social group if not their espionage circle.[44]

The Keeneys' role in supplying classified documents to their various contacts escaped the notice of the FBI throughout the war. When the war ended, the Soviet appetite for those documents did not diminish, but the spy ring was in danger of losing its access to information. With the shutdown of wartime operations, many government positions began to be eliminated. The Keeneys' jobs were among those to be phased out, throwing a wrench into the couple's espionage endeavors and confronting them once again with the prospect of unemployment.

In 1945, that prospect was considerably less daunting than it had been in 1937 because Philip and Mary Jane had made powerful friends who could help them find jobs. From the time they arrived in Washington, the Keeneys (especially the sociable Mary Jane) had cultivated relationships with liberals and leftists, many of whom were high in the government, in the CPUSA, or in the public spotlight. As one of the couple's acquaintances put it, "I think they like bigshots better than little shots."[45]

One sympathetic acquaintance even offered to use her influence with Franklin and Eleanor Roosevelt to get Philip the ultimate library position, Librarian of Congress, which Archibald MacLeish had vacated in 1944 to become assistant secretary of state in charge of public and cultural relations. This accommodating lady was Josephine Truslow Adams, who claimed John and Abigail Adams as her forebears and Pulitzer Prize–winning historian James Truslow Adams as her cousin. "Josie" to her friends, Adams had taught art at Swarthmore from 1934 until 1941, when the college decided not to renew her contract. She avowed that she had been dismissed because of her political affiliations, and she was probably correct.[46] Adams was a sponsor of the 5th National Conference for Protection of the Foreign Born and of the American Rescue Ship Mission for Spanish Refugees. She was also a member of the Harry Bridges Defense Committee and the Conference on Constitutional Liberties in America.[47] Most important, Adams was visibly sympathetic to the American Communist Party. When party leader Earl Browder was jailed for passport fraud in 1941, Adams became deeply involved in the campaign to have him released from prison.[48]

As a result of publicity that accompanied her firing from Swarthmore and her efforts on Browder's behalf, Adams came to the attention of Esther Lape, a close friend of Eleanor Roosevelt. Lape admired Adams's artwork and in 1941 commissioned a painting for Eleanor. Apparently Mrs. Roosevelt expressed appreciation, and Adams did another painting for her. Adams persuaded Browder that she had developed an "intimate relationship" with both Roosevelts and that this newfound relationship presented a golden opportunity for the American Left to communicate with the White House. Adams accepted kudos for President Roosevelt's pardoning the Communist leader in 1942, only fourteen months into his four-year sentence. Beyond that, Adams agreed to act as an unofficial ambassador for Browder, sharing his views with the president and reporting back on Roosevelt's reactions. Adams also reported to Soviet agent

Sergey Kurnakov, clearly suggesting that her observations of the White House were going to Moscow, probably via both men.

Through her subterfuge, Adams became a heroine among American Communists and was invited to resume her teaching career at the Jefferson School of Social Science. Founded in 1943 with funding from wealthy supporters, the Jefferson School served as the Communist Party's educational wing in New York City. Similar party schools with names celebrating American forefathers already had been established in other cities. In Chicago there was the Abraham Lincoln School; in New Rochelle, the Thomas Paine School; in Boston, the Samuel Adams School.

The Keeneys met Adams in August 1944, when they enrolled as students in a two-week summer course she was teaching for the Jefferson School, held at a Lake Arrowhead, New York, retreat owned by the Furriers Union.[49] They soon became fast friends. The three had much to unite them, especially the mutual experience of being banished from their university jobs. And then there was Kurnakov, the Soviet contact that they shared, and Earl Browder, their party hero. For the Keeneys, Adams's willingness to put in a good word for Philip with President Roosevelt must have exceeded their wildest dreams. The idea that Philip could be Librarian of Congress would have been the unlikely, but triumphant, conclusion of his checkered career. What a black eye this would have been for the bigwigs at the ALA, who were unaware that Philip was a shadow candidate. As far as the ALA was concerned, the only people in the running for the job were Keyes D. Metcalf, librarian of Harvard University; Ralph Ulveling, librarian of the Detroit Public Library; and Luther Evans, chief assistant librarian and acting Librarian of Congress after MacLeish's departure.[50]

According to the Keeneys' FBI file, Adams met with Mary Jane in February 1945 and assured her that Philip's interest in the job would be relayed to the president. When Roosevelt died in April 1945, the scheme to get Philip appointed ran into a major roadblock, but Adams was undaunted. Not long after Roosevelt's death she wrote to Mary Jane regarding her continued efforts on Philip's behalf: "I made connections with Eleanor Saturday evening. The interview was touching and from our point of view *good*. She seemed to think a way should be found for me to continue. So that I am trying to get through the tangled wires straight to Truman with the idea that this and other things were F.D.R.'s wish."[51]

As the Keeneys' FBI file glibly observes, Luther Evans was appointed Librarian of Congress in spite of Adams's efforts on Philip's part, but there is nothing to suggest that the Keeneys were surprised or disappointed.[52]

Perhaps most important, there is no hint that the Keeneys wondered if Adams had lobbied aggressively enough for Philip or if she really had the entrée to the White House she claimed to have. At least one FBI agent questioned Adams's credibility early in her relationship with the Roosevelts. Of course, the FBI had its own reasons for finding fault with Adams: her constant communications with the Roosevelts included criticism of the Bureau and demands that J. Edgar Hoover investigate organizations with supposed Nazi ties.

After Roosevelt's death, Adams made an effort to be on friendlier terms with the FBI. She even volunteered to work as an informant and as a liaison between the Bureau and America's Communists. The Bureau turned down the offer based largely on the perception that Adams was unreliable and mentally unstable. In 1951, Adams showed an FBI agent her scrapbook of letters from the Roosevelts, and he concluded that her claims of intimacy with the first family were vastly exaggerated. "No indication is shown in these documents," he reported, "that Adams acted as liaison between Earl Browder and President Roosevelt."[53] What the agent saw were form letters and courtesy notes from the White House, along with discursive memos that were supposedly sent by Eleanor Roosevelt but which bore more resemblance to Adams's penmanship and writing style.

Most of the letters were, in fact, forgeries; conversations that Adams said she had with the president at Hyde Park or at the White House frequently occurred on dates when he was not in either location. Yet Adams was so convincing in portraying the president's physical and spoken mannerisms that few doubted the closeness of her relationship with him and Mrs. Roosevelt. In particular, Earl Browder and the American Communist fellowship labored for years under the impression that Adams had represented their best interests. When confronted with overwhelming evidence in 1956 that Adams had deceived him, Browder still could not believe that she had fabricated her role as emissary between himself and Roosevelt. He could not fathom that Adams possessed the political sophistication to invent the information she brought him.[54]

After her charade became too obvious to be denied, Browder claimed that he really had not relied on Adams a great deal, but the memory of one of his contemporaries suggests otherwise. Gil Green, a party insider who knew Browder well, recalled the latter told him, "One of the reasons why I was able to keep such a steady course [during 1943 and the early part of 1944] was because I had this girl visiting me every week. I knew what was in Roosevelt's mind!"[55] The only certainty is that he knew what was in Adams's increasingly troubled mind. By the late 1950s, she had completely lost her grip on reality and was confined to a mental institution for the rest of her life.

In using Adams to get closer to the Roosevelts, Browder was complying with Moscow's wartime diplomacy toward the West, but cooperation with the Allies was a policy of necessity for the Soviet Union, the only hope for resisting Hitler's assault. With the end of the war, the USSR quickly scuttled this charade of cooperation and assumed its most hostile stance ever toward the non-Communist world, especially toward the United States. For nearly four decades afterward, the Russians and the Americans battled for domination in a world where virtually all nations seemed to fit neatly, though too simplistically, into two camps: Communist and anti-Communist. The Cold War rivalry between the United States and the Soviet Union did not result in armed conflict between the two nations directly, but their stockpiled weapons of mass destruction were a source of constant tension, and they engaged by proxies in various places in the world, such as Korea and the Congo. From the end of the 1940s until the demise of the Soviet Union in 1989, the two countries vied for the honor of owning the most atomic, then hydrogen bombs. Meanwhile, the rest of the world lived in fear that the superpowers would resolve their differences with a conflagration that no one could survive.

Earl Browder never got a chance to adjust to Moscow's radical change in policy toward the West in his capacity as leader of the CPUSA. In April 1945, Jacques Duclos, a leading French Communist, published an article denouncing Browder's conciliatory stance toward the American government and other Western powers. To observers familiar with how Moscow elevated and demoted party leaders throughout the world, the Duclos letter was a coded message that Browder's days in power were numbered.[56] Several months after the Duclos article was published, Josephine Adams reported to Philip and Mary Jane that Moscow had asked for a visit from Browder and that the State Department had agreed to let him go via England and Sweden, but not to France. She also said Browder was reluctant to go because he knew the reason for the invitation was to depose him as head of the American party.[57] Her communication with the Keeneys suggested that Adams was still in Browder's confidence, but this may have been a figment of her imagination.

Browder was expelled from the Party in February 1946, before he ever got to Moscow. James Ryan, Browder's biographer, describes a comparatively optimistic man, quite different from the one Adams represented to the Keeneys. In 1946, Browder, hoping to appeal his expulsion, was quite anxious to go to Russia. After managing to obtain a passport and visa to visit the Soviet Union, Browder embarked on the 5,000-mile journey at his own expense in May 1946. "Aware that Stalin's government had executed Lenin's contemporaries, the Old Bolsheviks," writes Ryan, "Browder displayed life-threatening courage and boundless self-confidence."[58] Browder would manage to return from Russia unharmed, but his aspirations for a personal audience with Stalin were dashed and he was reduced to a meeting with Molotov. The latter did nothing to encourage Browder's hopes for reinstatement and sent him back to America. He was never readmitted to the party.

Browder's ouster resulted in the exodus of his most loyal followers from the party, but membership actually enjoyed a slight rise between January 1946 and August 1948.[59] Although they had developed a cordial acquaintance with Browder, the Keeneys registered no regrets over his demise. They showed no signs of disappointment with Moscow's changing policy and continued to willingly supply whatever information they could to their Soviet contacts. By the time Browder was deposed by Moscow, the Keeneys had also managed to find new jobs with the potential of providing the Russians with a whole new variety of intelligence. They might not have realized that Josephine Adams could not deliver on the promises she made them, but they did not really need her. Philip and Mary Jane had lots of friends, and when it came to landing on their feet, the Keeneys were acrobats.

CHAPTER 7

The Spies Abroad

By acting quickly and appealing to influential friends, Mary Jane and Philip managed to extend their stay with the federal government and to get postings abroad. On November 1, 1945, Mary Jane departed from the United States for Paris after receiving an appointment to the Allied Commission Staff on Reparations (known as the Angell Commission after its leader, James W. Angell) based on the work she had done for the BEW. Three weeks later, Philip wrote to Mary Jane that Bowen Smith of the Department of State was putting together a special group to go to Japan for nine months at the request of Major General John H. Hildring.[1] Smith, a personal friend of the Keeneys, asked Philip to join the group as a researcher in the education section.[2]

Mary Jane was to be in Paris and Berlin to provide research and documentation support for the negotiators establishing the reparations to be exacted from Germany. With her background in the German economy and knowledge of American-owned businesses in Germany, she would have been a valuable asset to the Angell Commission. Philip, on the other hand, as the libraries officer—which is what his job was to become—was to try to establish a modern library system in Japan. Recruited to represent their government abroad, they had no reason to think that they were under suspicion.[3]

Apparently it was not until December 1945—with both already at their overseas posts—that the FBI furnished the State Department with information on Mary Jane and Philip from their 1942 and 1943 investigations. The timing was not coincidental. On November 17, 1945, as a result of the hours of information Elizabeth Bentley provided the FBI, the Silver-masters were put under surveillance. Among the guests observed at their home was Philip Olin Keeney.[4]

Greg Silvermaster, Joseph Bernstein, and Sergey Kurnakov all encour-aged the Keeneys to go abroad, articulating a belief that Philip and Mary Jane would be able to mine useful information from overseas missions. According to Harvey Klehr and Ronald Radosh, as the KGB reevaluated its intelligence gaps after it took control of the Golos/Bentley groups, it may have needed to find ways to gain more information from State De-partment sources.[5] Using the Keeneys may have been one attempt to fill those gaps.

Mary Jane initially was enthusiastic and prepared to take risks to ac-complish the task of gleaning information from the reparations group. Less than a month after her arrival in Paris, on November 22, 1945, she wrote the following in her diary:

> Thanksgiving day. A strange one 3,000 miles from home. Work in the A.M. As we hear nothing about the projected half holiday, leave stuff out in office when we go up to hotel for lunch. [Name blacked out] and I return; she goes to the senate and I decide to seize the chance to read the cable book. Release the covers and am reading absorbedly when a voice says "who has the cable book?" It was Angell at my elbow. I feel his suspicion and realize that circumstances are suspicious—here I am alone reading secret cables! Well, I sit out the situation and read them all anyway.[6]

Not only did Mary Jane write about this incident in her diary, she also described it in a letter to Philip, adding "to me it is important to know what is going on so long as I can accomplish nothing else at least at the moment." Soon after, she wrote, "[Y]ou will remember that I said that if I could observe and report at least that would be something."[7]

While Mary Jane looked over the code books, Philip prepared for his trip. He was a reluctant traveler. The trip to Japan was more suited to Mary Jane, he thought, but their "friends, including Thomas, have made it clear that there is a job to do and it falls to my lot to do it. On this basis, there is nothing for me to do but do it and I am game to deliver according to my best judgment." Although no one in the group was "strictly 'ko-sher,'" he said, there were some good people, so he would "caution care and mind my P's and Q's."[8]

Exercising caution did not extend to the letters Philip and Mary Jane exchanged, however, even though Kurnakov had warned that American mail coming out of Europe was getting the once-over by U.S. censors.

Philip went so far as to include this caution in a letter to Mary Jane while she was in Paris, but neither of the Keeneys did anything to temper the content of their correspondence. In fact, though Mary Jane's cable reading may not have resulted in something she could report to Bernstein or Kurnakov, it did make it into her FBI files. As was its practice, the FBI revealed little about its sources but reported that "An anonymous informant, of known reliability, advised" that Mary Jane had "surreptitiously secured temporary possession of a secret cable book which she succeeded in partly reading."[9] Ultimately, through the surreptitious work of a known FBI agent who read their mail and copied her diary, the "reliable informant" was Mary Jane Keeney; there is no evidence that Angell reported her. In fact, in June 1946, after the mission's end, Angell forwarded to Mary Jane a letter of gratitude from Secretary of State Acheson and added, "I want to thank you again for your own very effective part in what we accomplished."[10]

Philip met with Col. Thomas/Kurnakov several times before leaving for Japan, each time coming away with a greater sense of responsibility and urgency in spite of his own misgivings. He felt Mary Jane's absence keenly: "It all adds up to how very badly I need you at this very moment." He reported that "Everyone says the Keeneys are carrying out tremendous assignments," and that the sum of the work they were doing would be greater than the parts in a world that "has reached that boiling point."[11]

Within a few weeks, however, Mary Jane had concluded that she would be able to observe little of importance; she had vastly overestimated opportunities to gather any valuable intelligence on her European tour. On December 13, 1945, she wrote to Philip:

> You know the truth about my accomplishment—nothing. Aside from seeing a good bit of Paris and a sizable section of France this last week and from experiencing certain historical moments of French history I have precious little to show for these six weeks I have been away. So it is more than a little ironic to read of all the confidence imposed in me by our friends. I predicted accurately when I said that at worst I should be able to observe and report. I can't even observe at first hand but only those written minutes of meetings, cables, etc. and of course cannot take notes on any of these. Hence, accurate reporting is out of the question.[12]

The following day's letter to Philip encouraged him to do better than she was doing. "The Colonel's confidence in us in so far as it is placed in me," she wrote, "is actually what sent me into the doldrums last night. I deserve it so little. I hope you will be able to and it is a satisfaction that you have a good chance to do so if you go to Japan."[13]

Philip tried to reassure Mary Jane that her work was indispensable and continued to send her the good wishes of their friends. He did not want her to feel that her trip had been a "complete fizzle." He hoped that she would hear from Col. Thomas, who was returning to Russia, when she reached Berlin.[14]

When they were not sharing frustrations about their failures to gather intelligence, they went on at length about their innermost thoughts and spare time activities. Often as not, those thoughts and activities were political in nature. Soon after Thanksgiving, Mary Jane sent Philip a letter in which she described a Paris meeting of the Women's International Democratic Federation, an organization with ties to the Soviet Union. At the meeting a film was shown of the Victory Day celebration in Red Square that was witnessed by Gen. Dwight Eisenhower and Stalin (whom she called "Pal Joey"). The meeting featured as well an address by Dolores Ibarruri, the former head of the Spanish Communist Party, who had fled to Russia after the Civil War. Mary Jane heaped praise on the Russian delegates to the WIDF meeting calling them "magnificent . . . some of them in uniforms resplendent with medals."[15]

Philip, in turn, wrote her about the rough treatment that the Soviet Union was getting from the other Allies in the division of postwar power. He further speculated that America's recent involvement in China would be a foreign policy blunder "and to save face, we will shoot our way out." Even if he was correct about the debacle that the United States would create with its foreign policy regarding China, where the United States opposed the Communists, Philip's openness was risky given the possibility that his mail was being read. His indifference to that possibility was further borne out in his written comments to Mary Jane that the Communist Party would provide the best form of government for Czechoslovakia and in his notes to her about his social engagements. On one occasion he had shared lunch with Morris U. Schappes, recently fired from his job at the City College of New York because of his openly leftist philosophy. Another time, Philip was eating out and noticed conservative Sen. John E. Rankin of Mississippi seated in the dining room: This "nearly voided my appetite."[16]

As he prepared to go to Japan, Philip brazenly wrote to Mary Jane concerning his hope that they would someday go to the Soviet Union, "that great land," together.[17] He became even more optimistic about this prospect when he learned that Col. Thomas had been recalled to Russia. With Stalin's purges well known, many people might have been worried for Kurnakov's safety, but not Philip. He believed that his friend was going back to a utopian society. On Christmas Eve he wrote Mary Jane to share the pleasure, as he had earlier shared it with the Silvermasters and Dave Wahl. "It makes me green with envy," he said. "When our chance comes we will have a real friend at court."[18] After returning to Russia, Kurnakov contacted Philip just once before his death in 1952.

Although Mary Jane was dissatisfied with the information she gathered while working with the Angell Commission, she did make a few contacts that later would find their way into her FBI file. She managed to find Teresa Andres, the Spanish librarian the PLC had attempted to help. She visited with Greta Kuckhoff, whose husband had been executed by Hitler because of his activities as a member of the anti-Nazi "Red Orchestra" resistance group, and she connected with the Silvermasters' housemate William Ludwig Ullman.[19] She also was able to secure for Joe Bernstein a much-desired copy of the statement French Communist resistance fighter Gabriel Péri made before his execution. It was Bernstein's intention to translate it into English, and Mary Jane delivered the Péri to him as soon as she returned early from Europe, suffering from an ear abscess.[20]

With Mary Jane now at home, Philip continued to write her from Japan about his efforts to acquire useful information and his sense of loneliness. In February 1946, he wondered to Mary Jane whether he would want to stay in Japan if there was something worthwhile for him to do. "I have the feeling at any rate that we are both on call now which is more than I have felt for months past," he wrote. "We have done everything in our power and that is all we can do."[21] With Kurnakov back in Russia, Bernstein served as Philip's main contact, but the Keeneys remained in touch with Silvermaster and his wife. It was from them that Mary Jane received yet another warning about communicating openly regarding their sentiments and activities.

In March 1946, soon after returning from Europe to Washington, D.C., Mary Jane paid the Silvermasters a social call at their home, only to be cautioned upon entering the house not to speak. They had been visited by FBI agents and were concerned that their home might be bugged. "[T]hey put a note in my hands the moment I entered as a warning against mentioning certain things in conversation," Mary Jane wrote. "It was a shock, I assure you, and led to a most uncomfortable evening." They instructed Mary Jane to warn Philip if she could have a letter to Philip hand delivered by a friend going to Japan. Clearly Mary Jane trusted this individual, still unknown, but the FBI managed to acquire the letter, possibly from the bearer but just as possibly from Philip's lodgings. In it, she told Philip about the frightening visit to the Silvermasters and warned him to be careful about what he wrote to her and to several of their friends in case there was any tampering with their mail. Joe Bernstein had told her to be "on the lookout," she said, and optimistically concluded, "There is no reason for alarm on your part or mine, only it is well to remember that it's better to be safe than sorry."[22]

Curiously, even after this warning, Philip continued to send Mary Jane detailed descriptions of his interest in the Japanese Communist Party.

Still in Tokyo, under date of April 13, 1946, Philip wrote to Mary Jane:

'. . .Probably I might not have come to Japan had it not been for my serious confabs with Colonel Thomas. Now that I am here, it seemed as if I were repeating the long, dry spell that twice occurred while we were part of Joe B's plans (Joseph Milton Bernstein). I should have followed Greg's (Nathan Gregory Silvermaster) advice and relaxed. . .'

'Under date of March 28, 1946, Mary Jane directed the following letter to Philip Keeney. It was not sent through the mail but delivered to Philip by a mutual acquaintance who was proceeding from Washington, D.C., to Japan. The letter is set forth as follows:

'Dearest Love,

'The main thing I want to tell you in this letter, which is to be delivered by safe hand, is to be very careful of what you write in letters to our friends on 30th Street, N.W. (Nathan Gregory Silvermaster), Langdrum Lane (Laurence Tood of Tass News Agency) and R Street (Jack Marsalka). The first mentioned have much reason to believe that mail is tampered with and also that at home they are subjected to the same sort of scrutiny that the Colonel was. The day I went out there they put a note in my hand the moment I entered as a warning against mentioning certain things in conversation. It was a shock, I assure you, and led to a most uncomfortable evening. Later, Helen (Silvermaster) and I had lunch together where we could talk a little more freely and at that time she suggested that I had better get this message to you if I had any way of having it delivered personally.

'Whether the other two families are aware of the same thing, I don't know. There was no indication of anything more untoward than usual in the menage on R Street the night I was there for dinner, and actually evidence that things were looking up. As for the third party, I haven't seen them by themselves but am to have dinner with them next Tuesday.

'It is hard to tell whether this is something real or not but it is of a piece with the general temper I found on my return (from Europe). Joe (Bernstein) told me to be on the lookout as well as several others in New York. There is no reason for alarm on your part or mine only it is well to remember that it's better to be safe than sorry. . .'

- 5 -   487

This page of the Keeneys' FBI file, 101-467-187, p. 487, includes the letter to Philip in which Mary Jane shares her shock when the Silvermasters warned her their home was bugged.

On May 1, 1946, Philip wrote her that he had attended a May Day parade in Tokyo in which many Japanese Communists had participated. He was impressed by the number of young people, several of them women, who also marched. More curious still, Mary Jane failed to follow her own advice. On May 5 she wrote Philip a letter in which she described the New York May Day parade. She was thrilled to report that some 65,000 people marched under union and party banners, many of them men in military uniforms.[23]

Philip was, however, also writing—both to Mary Jane and to Mark Orr, his superior in the Civil Information and Education Section (CIE)—regarding what was needed to restore, democratize, and upgrade Japanese libraries. Described by Orr as looking much older than his 54 years, "frail in appearance," but apparently "strong and energetic,"[24] Philip first traveled to various parts of the country to assess the conditions of buildings and collections, as well as the initiative and provision of service by Japanese librarians.[25] Modeling his proposals on the ideas for larger units of service being promoted in the United States and practiced in California, he began to lay the groundwork for modern library service in Japan.[26] He brought together the country's leading librarians to rejuvenate their professional association, helped to develop library laws, laid groundwork for the development of modern library education, and worked to get buildings rebuilt or refurbished.[27]

Philip found the work difficult. He had to use his powers of persuasion to move the entrenched and rather autocratic librarians to see the virtues of open access and resource sharing, and he felt alone in his political philosophy. In August 1946 he wrote to Bernstein about a conference of librarians he had organized. During the conference he had hosted a hugely successful dinner party in a private dining room for his Japanese guests, who would not normally have been allowed to dine with Americans in the hotel's main dining room. By according them this respect, he had won their allegiance. "The librarians present will follow me through mud, filth and corruption, now, and spread the word of my interest in their problems." But he was not sure if his investment of energy was worthwhile. He was taking a week's vacation to consider whether his work was "worth another couple of years of partial separation from my beloved wife."[28] He would soon have to decide whether to return to Japan after his forty-five-day leave, and he was weighing whether this work was as valuable as something he could do at home. If the United States were to stay in Japan for ten years, he told Bernstein, he "would not hesitate," but he thought a shorter time to make Japanese libraries "a thoroughly democratic tool" would be "a big laugh." And it would take years, without additional help, to "weave into the fabric of

Japanese life the importance of the J[apanese] C[ommunist] P[arty]."[29] By the time he took a furlough in November and December 1946, Philip had decided he would return to Japan and planned to commit another year or two to the effort.

While Philip was on leave in the United States, he and Mary Jane made the rounds, visiting their friends in Washington and New York, including the Silvermasters, the Laurence Todds, Stanley Graze (a KGB contact) and his wife Mildred, and any number of others whose activities the FBI was following closely. They shared Thanksgiving dinner with David and Edith Wahl. Arrangements for these visits were carefully recorded through "technical surveillance," that is, wiretaps on the Keeneys' telephone.[30] The visits themselves were often recorded by FBI agents tailing them or keeping surveillance on their home and those of the people they visited.

In early December, having had his leave extended so that he could attend the ALA's midwinter meeting in Chicago late in the month, Philip addressed a meeting of the Institute for Pacific Relations (IPR), an organization to which he and Mary Jane may have belonged since the early 1940s. The IPR was suspect because, among other things, it distrusted the Chiang Kai-shek government and had a close relationship with the journal *Amerasia,* whose editor, Philip Jaffe, had been arrested in May 1945 for unauthorized possession of classified documents and accused of spying. The Keeneys' contact, Joseph Bernstein, would also have been arrested had not the wiretap transcription of his name been inaccurate.[31]

Their Chicago ALA visit was watched closely as well. While there, Philip and Mary Jane apparently met rather secretively with Leon Carnovsky of the University of Chicago's Graduate Library School, who had traveled to Japan in March 1946 as part of the U.S. Mission. They also met for more than an hour in the room of Charles Brown, the librarian who had spoken so ill of Philip ten years previously, when he was fighting for his job. Brown shared information with the Keeneys about plans being made for library information centers in key cities of Japan. A confidential FBI informant reported that Brown seemed to be offering Philip a role in continuing to shape Japanese libraries. In addition, Keeney and Brown spoke about the need for more materials for Japanese libraries, ones less strictly limited by the Trading with Enemies Act.[32] Philip went back to Japan just before the turn of the year, and Mary Jane returned to their Washington apartment to celebrate the New Year with friends and begin the process of preparing to join Philip in Japan.

The New Year brought another shock, however—one that should have been a portent of things to come. The election of 1946 had dealt the Democrats a fifty-four-seat loss in the House of Representatives. Facing a new session of Congress—and a turnover of committee leadership— Ernest Adamson, staff counsel of HUAC, on December 23, 1946, released without authorization a report prepared under the direction of its outgoing chairman, John S. Wood (D-GA). Issuing this report, which was recalled and not widely available until Sen. Joseph McCarthy entered it into the *Congressional Record* of October 20, 1950, cost Adamson his job. It also placed the names of individuals associated with radio station WQQW (a new enterprise in which Mary Jane was a stockholder) and the Washington Bookshop (with which the Keeneys had been long associated) in the Washington spotlight as people believed to be spreading Communist propaganda at best and engaging in espionage at worst.[33]

According to her later written statement, Mary Jane saw the report that she deemed "actionable for libel" at a cocktail party on January 1, 1947. Allan Rosenberg, an attorney and "former associate" at the BEW told her about the report. He believed that she and Owen Lattimore, another stockholder in WQQW, should sue over the allegations. "He warned that if we did not take advantage of this fortuitous opportunity, that we ourselves might be more heavily attacked later," she recalled, adding parenthetically, "how truly he predicted!"[34] In fact, in a December 26 conversation with Carl Green, an associate of WQQW and the Keeneys, Rosenberg had commented on those named, including Mary Jane and David Wahl, "all of the nice people," and added, "It's on." With regard to a lawsuit, while Wahl had said they ought to sue, Green had commented that "those people are hard to sue."[35]

Mary Jane agreed to file suit only if Lattimore and Metropolitan Broadcasting (WQQW's company) would join, and if Philip, deeply engaged in his work in Japan, would consent. Both knew that a suit would end his work there. Although Philip did ask her "to consider well the great promise of his library program" for strengthening Japanese libraries, he did not preclude her suit, but no one else was eager to join the suit since the copies of the report were withdrawn.[36]

Allan Rosenberg's words were indeed prophetic, and Mary Jane's conversations made it quite plain that she was aware that, withdrawn or not, the effect of the report would linger.[37] And linger it did. On February 19, Mary Jane received a travel authorization from the military to join Philip, with an April departure date. She prepared to leave—arranging to sell their furniture and car, and to ship their dog to a friend—and applied for a passport. As Philip wrote on March 11, 1947, "There is no reason why [your passport] should be held up after your diplomatic entrée into Europe. You have done nothing untoward since your return, hence you should be ready to give up our apartment which has been our real home longer than any other in our life together."[38] As departure time drew near, and her friends feted her in New York and Washington, however, she still had no passport. On March 24, she wrote Philip that "Everyone is now notified who should be of my failure to depart and the uncertainty of my plans."[39] Finally, an April 1, 1947, letter from Ruth B. Shipley, chief of the Passport Division, informed Mary Jane that the State Department "in the exercise of discretion conferred upon it by law, declines to issue you a passport at this time."[40]

A few days later, Mary Jane wrote to Dave Wahl that she had seen Shipley, "and she tells me this is a security matter, i.e., that it is in the best interests of the United States that I not go to Japan." When Mary Jane had insisted that she "should have an opportunity to know what this security matter was comprised of," Shipley agreed, but said she had not been given permission to discuss it. No clearance had been requested when Mary Jane had gone to Europe, Shipley reported. "I asked her if the security of this nation could possibly be promoted by omitting to check on people who represented the government, and then precluding the movements of those same people in the capacity of private citizens," Mary Jane wrote Wahl. "She giggled slightly at this."[41]

Mary Jane consulted Allan Rosenberg and prepared extensive memos for Senators Charles W. Tobey, Wayne Morse, and James E. Murray, whom she believed might be sympathetic, and others she thought might be of assistance.[42] Apparently Senator Murray did inquire, for on May 5, 1947, he received a written response from Hamilton Robinson, director of the Office of Controls, writing at the request of John Peurifoy, the assistant secretary of state charged with loyalty matters. Mary Jane had been denied clearance—and a passport—because of her "known connection with an organization which the Attorney General has characterized as having been penetrated by or under the control of subversive elements." In addition, he wrote, Mary Jane "may have connections with other groups and individuals whose interests are in conflict with the welfare and national security of this country." Exactly what that meant could not be disclosed to her.[43]

A subsequent paragraph confirmed information Mary Jane had received by cable from Philip: "Mr. Keeney has left Tokyo and is now enroute to this country. This fact may change Mrs. Keeney's desire to obtain a passport for travel to Japan."[44] Philip's terse "TRIED TO CALL MY PAPER COLLECTED KEEP CHIN UP," summed up his situation.[45]

Mark Orr, Philip's superior, writing some years later, recalled what occurred:

> One night I returned late to my office and saw a light burning at Mr. Keeney's desk. I dropped by to speak to him and, instead, encountered an unknown American in civilian clothes searching through the items in Mr. Keeney's desk. We had a brief confrontation when he demanded my identification and I responded by asking for his credentials. He said the desk search had the approval of the Chief of CIE and it concerned a security matter he could not discuss with me. Fortunately, Col. Nugent was in his office when I called and confirmed the Army counterintelligence agent's story.
>
> A short time later, without any publicity or further explanation, Mr. Keeney returned to the United States.[46]

Indeed, Philip's departure was so sudden as to be inexplicable to his Japanese colleagues, who wrote him in "the sorrow of parting," to thank him for the seeds he had sown in the Japanese library world. If Japanese libraries were to advance, they said, it would mean that the work he had done had "come into flower and borne fruit."[47] Later Philip would tell his friend Bowen Smith that "everyone he knew in Japan was non-plussed" by his sudden departure under a cloud; "it knocked them for a loop."[48]

Orr and five of Philip's colleagues in the CIE wrote letters that compli-mented Keeney and affirmed his loyalty. Orr wrote that, largely due to Philip's efforts, "library work in Japan is undergoing a complete change of direction. It is becoming a public service field with professional standards."[49] His five colleagues wrote that they had "never known him to speak or behave in a manner inconsistent with the expressed purposes of the Occupation." He had "consistently upheld the ideas of democracy."[50] Although he left Japan without a passport, and certainly would never find federal employment again, he was headed back to his beloved Mary Jane, leaving a legacy of Japanese library development that is still ap-preciated in the twenty-first century.

While Philip had "consistently upheld the ideas of democracy" in rela-tion to his colleagues, his and Mary Jane's notions of "democracy"—for they certainly never accepted the picture of the Soviet Union as a brutal dictatorship—were betrayed by their correspondence. Philip's letters to Mary Jane and Joseph Bernstein revealed his thoughts and his intentions to aid the cause of Communism. So blatant was their disregard for sur-veillance that it almost appears they wanted to be caught. Perhaps Philip and Mary Jane were ambivalent about what they were doing for, although they believed that a better world awaited them in the Soviet Union, the Keeneys loved the liberties afforded them in the United States. Hence, it is not impossible that, though they were concerned about the rising anti-Communist fervor, they retained their trust in the guarantee of civil liberties in a democratic society, and never truly believed that their mail would be opened or their phones tapped. Or perhaps they—and especially Mary Jane—had, instead, a belief in their own rightness and invincibility and a strong desire to have meaning in the world. They certainly could not have known how several events beyond their control and hidden from their view would affect their lives or how acquaintance with Philip and Mary Jane Keeney would come to affect others.

CHAPTER 8

Caught in the Web

Balding, bespectacled, and stoop-shouldered, nearly six feet tall and pencil thin, Philip Olin Keeney was hardly the spy of melodrama or Cold War film. Nor was Mary Jane—just over five feet tall and quite bow-legged, with short, graying, straight hair—an espionage femme fatale. Bit players in the great unfolding drama of espionage and counterespionage, their relationships to those with larger parts placed them squarely center stage in the view of investigators trying to puzzle out the depth and breadth of Soviet spying, even if those relationships failed to clarify the exact nature of the Keeneys' roles. Separate investigations would provide glimpses into the Keeneys' connections—social and political—with accused spies and would expose their deep interest in the Soviet Union, making their lives far more difficult.

It was in the summer and fall of 1945 that Elizabeth Bentley—angry and afraid both of the Russians, who were trying to wrest the remnants of Jacob Golos's espionage network from her, and of the FBI, which had begun to look closely at United States Service and Shipping—decided to take matters into her own hands. She first approached the FBI in August but delayed following through until Igor Gouzenko, a Russian code clerk attached to the Soviet embassy in Ottawa, defected in September and began to talk, followed in early October by the defection of Louis Budenz. Although she had no direct connection with the Canadian group, she knew that Budenz could identify her. Thus on November 7, 1945, a week after Mary Jane left for Paris to work on details of reparations over the recently ended war, Bentley walked into the New York FBI offices and began describing in detail an espionage network so extensive that the agents who listened to her were incredulous.

In a series of interviews she identified scores of government employees who were active in the Communist Party, involved in espionage, or both. She claimed to have dealt directly with many of these people, personally receiving classified documents they had taken from the offices where they worked and then passing on the material to her superiors in the spy network. Bentley said she did not believe the American government workers who gave her these documents were necessarily traitors to their country; she was troubled by the idea that they might face criminal prosecution as a result of her confession. Most of them had no idea that the information they gave her was bound for a foreign power, she said. Instead, they thought that it was going to Earl Browder to be used for improving the position of the American Communist Party. Much of the information did go to Browder, she confirmed, but he then forwarded it to Moscow.[1]

In her 1951 book, *Out of Bondage*, Bentley asserted that she was naïve and had been lured into the Columbia University unit of the Communist Party in 1935 by people who were either as innocent as she or deceptively kind. Like many of her generation, Bentley was deeply troubled by the rise of Fascism in Europe and was personally affected by the economic privations of the Great Depression. A Vassar graduate, she eked out a living at one poorly paid job after another. At party meetings she found an inspiring mood of egalitarianism and concern for the underclass. This generosity of spirit flourished despite the fact that many people attending these meetings were, like her, well educated but underemployed; they cared deeply about people who were worse off than themselves. She was gratified to find that they carried their principles into the conduct of their own organization. To her amazement, the elected leader of the Columbia unit of the party was a cafeteria worker with little formal education.

During Bentley's first three years in the party, she seems to have done little more than pay her dues, attend meetings, and elude the eccentrics and lechers she later concluded were part of the Russian secret police. In 1938, however, she was offered a secretarial job at the Italian Library of Information in New York, a propaganda organization for the Mussolini regime. Recognizing an opportunity to infiltrate a Fascist organization, she asked fellow party members to put her in touch with someone who might be interested in what she could learn. After several attempts, she made contact with a man who, she was told, "was a leading agent of the Communist International, that I could trust him implicitly, and that I should follow his orders without question."[2]

That man, introduced to Bentley as "Timmy," told her that while she was working at the Italian Library she would have to cease participation in all open Communist activities. This meant that she could no longer attend meetings of the Columbia unit and that she would have to jettison her relationships with members of the open party, even at the risk of being mistaken as a traitor to the Revolution. Middle-aged, stocky, and rumpled, Timmy did not exude the authority that might have been expected from a leading agent of the Comintern, but Bentley followed his instructions without hesitation. She cut herself off from her friends and moved from the Columbia area to Greenwich Village, where she was less likely to be recognized.

Within months, Bentley and Timmy became lovers. She found him kind and self-effacing, a tireless worker who risked his own health for the sake of the international revolution. But it would be six months before Bentley would learn, quite by accident, that "Timmy" was actually Jacob Golos. Her surprise at this discovery was exceeded only by his astonishment that she did not know who he really was. Although it is hard to believe that a grown woman would have a lengthy affair with someone she knew only by a first name, Bentley indicated that during this period she also had no idea of where he lived or how he supported himself. Gradually, though, Golos took her into his confidence.

She learned that he was a major underground operative who since 1927 had run World Tourists, a travel agency that subsidized the work of the CPUSA and provided Golos cover for his spying.[3] His cover was nearly blown in 1939, when the Justice Department raided World Tourists.

During the raid they found evidence that CPUSA President Earl Browder had traveled to and from Moscow on a false passport supplied by World Tourists. Browder went to federal prison; Golos was indicted and pled guilty to failing to register the business as an agent of a foreign power. Although he got off with a suspended sentence and a $500 fine, World Tourists no longer provided the necessary cover—and Golos was aware he was being watched.[4]

Golos recovered his footing, however, with a new business financed by the CPUSA. United States Service and Shipping Corporation served the same purpose as World Tourists, but for packages instead of people. To make the new firm more palatable to the American government, John Hazard Reynolds, a wealthy New Yorker, was made titular head of the organization. He knew that Golos and Bentley were Communists and cheerfully agreed to let Bentley run the business from day to day as its vice president, while Golos retained ties to World Tourists.[5] It is not clear, however, that Hazard knew the company served as part of an espionage network.

Golos became increasingly ill, suffering his first heart attack in 1941. His health problems were exacerbated by his escalating struggle to control his network of spies as new Russian KGB operatives attempted to gain control over them.[6] As his health worsened he gave Bentley more responsibility for managing the day-to-day operations of United States Service and Shipping and directed her to meet with members of his espionage network. Bentley's description of those meetings contains the stock clichés of spy novels, complete with code names, attaché cases exchanged in darkened theaters, and passwords: "Carefully, I was given written instructions which I was to memorize and destroy; I was to be in front of a drugstore on Ninth Avenue in the fifties at twelve noon; a man carrying a copy of *Life* magazine would walk up to me and say 'I am sorry to have kept you waiting,' and I was to reply: 'No, I haven't been waiting long.' "[7]

That same year Golos told Bentley that he had made contact with a group of Communists in Washington, D.C., led by Silvermaster, an old friend of Earl Browder. Golos told her that Silvermaster had been a Communist since 1920 and had assisted Browder in California in the 1930s. He had come to Washington, as had many others, to work in the burgeoning Roosevelt administration. Now, said Golos, Silvermaster was gathering a group of government employees who were willing to supply sensitive information for the Soviets, a U.S. ally in the war against the Axis powers.

Bentley's job was to travel from New York to Washington, D.C., every two weeks to advise Silvermaster on what information was needed and to pick up documents that his group had obtained. The breadth of material that the Russians desired was vast. They wanted military and political information, of course, but they also cared passionately about matters shedding light on their place as a world power. They were concerned about the attitude among powerful American officials toward the Soviet Union, partly because it could affect the ability to broker influence and partly because of nationalistic pride.

Elizabeth Bentley's twice monthly meetings with the Silvermaster household began in August 1941. After an awkward beginning, they met usually at the couple's Chevy Chase, Maryland, home, where Ullman at some point set up a photo lab in the basement. The photo lab became crucial in Bentley's operation once the documents the Silvermasters provided—courtesy of many whose names Bentley knew, although she never met most of them—became too voluminous to tote off in her knitting bag. Ullman photographed the material so that she could carry it in the form of undeveloped film—as much as forty rolls at one time.

She would take the film to Golos, and he would send it to Moscow where it was printed.[8]

As long as Golos supervised her, Bentley was relatively comfortable with her job as a courier and handler, but after he died in 1943, things began to get much more tense. She was ordered to work with a succession of cantankerous or nervous agents appointed by Moscow. In 1945, she was instructed to turn her sources over to one of those agents, who was still trying to assume supervision of Golos's contacts and cut her out of the picture. She found this prospect appalling, as had Golos. She had become friendly with some of her contacts, including the Silvermasters, even though this was a violation of the tenets of spycraft. Because she saw her Russian counterparts as sadistic thugs she could not bear the idea that they would assume authority over the sources she had cultivated. In a convoluted leap of logic, she saved her friends from the Soviet Union by betraying them to the FBI.

To Bentley's detractors (and they are legion), Bentley's altruistic explanation of why she gave herself up to the FBI rings false. It is much more likely that Bentley thought that by telling her story—and naming her sources—she would gain protection from her Soviet KGB bosses who might well have killed her, while at the same time mitigating the penalties she believed awaited her at the hands of the FBI. Once she got started naming names, it seemed that she could not stop. The people implicated by Bentley, including the Silvermasters—many of whom were already in their files but to whom the Bureau had paid little attention—soon became objects of intense FBI surveillance.

The Keeneys, however, were not among those she named. In fact, she variously claimed not to know them—and later did not identify a picture of Philip—or claimed that they had been rejected for service because they either were not important enough or were a bit unbalanced.[9] Nevertheless, once the Bureau began surveillance of the Silvermasters, it really did not matter that Bentley had not named them. On December 7, 1945, the Washington Field Office advised the Bureau that agents watching the Silvermasters' home reported that a 1940 De Soto sedan, D.C. tags 112-556 listed to Philip Olin Keeney, 215 B St., N.E., was parked in front of the Silvermaster residence.[10]

From that first notation about the Keeneys' car, Philip and Mary Jane were in the FBI's spotlight. Although the FBI's method of information gathering and reporting often makes it difficult to know when they gleaned any particular piece of information, it is clear they began keeping their eyes on the Keeneys shortly after their car was identified. When Mary Jane discovered and reported to Philip the Silvermasters' visit from the FBI and their concern that their home had been bugged, she should have realized that their association with the Silvermasters increased their vulnerability to FBI discovery. Although "shocked," she appears not to have altered her own behavior in any way.[11]

When she first returned to the United States from her work with the Angell Commission in March 1946, however, she would not yet have had reason to guess that the FBI already had their eyes on her as a result of Philip's visit to the Silvermasters the previous fall. When she docked in New York she was met by her friend Jules Korchien, a member of the Communist Party, and taken by him to the apartment of her friend Ursula Wasserman. The following day, Mary Jane met Joseph Bernstein and delivered to him a French edition of the last statement of Gabriel Péri, a French Communist Resistance fighter who had been executed by the Nazis. Bernstein intended to translate it into English, and he in turn delivered the brown manila envelope that Mary Jane had given him to Communist publisher Alexander Trachtenberg. This transaction—carried out over consecutive days under the watchful eyes of FBI agents—earned Mary Jane the title of "courier" for Communist spies in her FBI file.[12] This episode would become central in the Keeneys' 1949 encounter with HUAC.

The FBI's scrutiny of Mary Jane was intensified by her meeting with Joseph Bernstein, who was subject to surveillance as a result of another case that began in the summer of 1945 and would contribute to the debate over the government's loyalty program and to the development of McCarthyism.[13] Known as the *Amerasia* case, it involved the pro-Communist journal of that name, of which Philip Jaffe was the editor and Bernstein a former employee. In June 1945, an OSS analyst recognized in the journal material from a secret report he had written. OSS security officers investigated and found hundreds of classified documents in the journal's offices. They arrested a number of people involved with the journal and with the State Department on charges of conspiring to commit espionage. Among them were Jaffe and Kate Mitchell, his co-editor. Also named was John Stewart Service—a Foreign Service officer and one of the "China hands," whose distrust of Chiang Kai-shek and disapproval of the administration's China policy brought charges that the China experts were infiltrated by Communists and had "lost" China. A wiretap that had been placed in Jaffe's hotel room caught Jaffe and one of his confederates discussing the fact that Jaffe had been approached to spy by someone the FBI suspected to be Joseph Bernstein. However a transcriptionist, working from an unclear primitive recording, typed his name as "Bursley" and the Keeneys' friend escaped arrest—but not the gaze of the FBI.[14]

Although the *Amerasia* prosecution suffered many problems—among them the illegal entry into the magazine's offices and unauthorized wiretaps—and resulted only in fines, it stoked fears of Communist espionage, especially because of the physical and intellectual closeness of *Amerasia* and the Institute for Pacific Relations (IPR), an organization of scholars who were experts on the Far East. IPR included the "China hands" and the Keeneys.[15]

"[T]he concerted pressure plus the inner difficulty of being out of contact" brought about by *Amerasia* and the Gouzenko Canadian spy case had Bernstein feeling low, Mary Jane told Philip immediately after she saw their old contact upon her return. The winter had been very hard on him, she reported. In May she wrote again that "the Canadian affair will have a very lingering effect."[16] Strangely enough, Bernstein's meeting with Mary Jane had an immediate effect: it not only put Mary Jane more directly under the FBI microscope but also spurred the Bureau to tap Bernstein's home and office phones. The wiretaps provided evidence that, though it could not be used in court, confirmed the FBI's suspicions that Bernstein was the person who had approached Jaffe. And if he had approached Jaffe to spy, his visits to the Keeneys every two weeks or so for years—a pattern the FBI discovered by breaking into the Keeneys' residence and surreptitiously copying Mary Jane's diary—could hardly have been for any purpose other than espionage, they believed. Thus Mary Jane, bearing the Péri "testament" in the brown manila envelope, unwittingly gained more unwanted attention.[17]

While all the activity around *Amerasia*, Gouzenko, and Budenz had already put the FBI on high alert, it was the enormity of the Bentley case—labeled the "Gregory" case by the FBI—that provided the Bureau with the impetus to grow in numbers and power. The end of World War II did not mean a decrease in counterespionage; just the opposite. With the Fascists defeated, attention focused rapidly on the Communists, many of them home grown, and the FBI vastly increased its counterespionage efforts. It certainly required a large number of people to keep tabs on the Silvermasters and their numerous friends; at least two FBI agents—the names that appear most often are Courtland J. Jones in Washington and Francis D. O'Brien in New York—reported regularly on the Keeneys' activities.

One might think interest in Mary Jane would have diminished when, later in 1946, she left government employment. Her previous position had disappeared with the end of the war, and she had failed to settle into another government job. Instead she had resigned from the State Department (into which her work area had been folded) when she learned she could get her accrued leave paid at a higher rate than she had been making.[18]

Nevertheless, with Philip still overseas and Mary Jane trying to join him, the FBI kept watch. More than four hundred pages of "technical surveillance," beginning in October 1946, recount Mary Jane's and then Philip's conversations, and then Mary Jane's until June 1947, when Philip returned from Japan, having been relieved of duty. The phone logs in November and December 1946 record the rounds of luncheon and dinner dates, trips to New York, and attendance at the ALA's midwinter meeting in Chicago that constituted the Keeneys' activities during Philip's two-month furlough. Although many of the conversations revolve around arrangements for these events, there is also talk about the 1946 election, in which the Republicans turned out the Democrats to gain an anti-Harry Truman majority in both houses of Congress, and radio station WQQW. Those whom the Keeneys called or who called them are a veritable who's who of those suspects named by Bentley or associates of those suspects.[19]

After Philip returned to Japan and Mary Jane resumed life in Washington, the Adamson report—which alerted Mary Jane to the fact that she might be a target of investigators—her passport problems, and the IPR vie with her social life as topics of conversation in the telephone logs. But other activities claimed her time and appear in the phone logs as well. One extended series of telephone conversations in January 1947 revolves around a request by Louise Rosskam, a friend living in Puerto Rico, to take Inez Muñoz Marin, the wife of the president of the Puerto Rican Senate (later elected governor), to see progressive schools in the Washington, D.C., area.[20] Mary Jane made the arrangements with the help of friends, including Daniel Melcher, son of the *Publisher's Weekly* publishing family, who had already taken Muñoz Marin to the Washington Bookshop; and Bowen Smith, who suggested a visit to the school that his children attended. Mary Jane took her not only to the schools, but also to a party at the home of Mrs. Boyan Athanassov, with whom Mary Jane was spending a good deal of time. Mr. Athanassov was a diplomat from the People's Republic of Bulgaria.[21]

Mary Jane kept Philip apprised of all these activities through daily letters, and he responded with enthusiasm about her diplomatic efforts. "I am very glad you have brought all of these people together," he wrote. "Louise [Rosskam] could never have picked out a more superb person to work with Mme. Muñoz Marin than she did." With regard to the Athanassovs he enthused, "I am ready to go to Bulgaria. That is one place where our ideas would not be hidden under a pint. What say about going to Bulgaria!!!!"[22] While he may well have been referring to their political ideas, Philip may also have been referring to his plans about library propagation and organization, which he had been hammering out in Japan. He had hopes of implementing his program somewhere, and Latin America and the countries of Eastern Europe were among the places he was considering.[23]

By 1947, the countries of Eastern Europe—including Bulgaria—had fallen into the Soviet sphere of influence, behind an "iron curtain," as Winston Churchill had called it just one year earlier. The uneasy wartime alliance with the Soviets had dissolved, and in an uncertain and divided world, the newly elected Republican Congress was intent on making sure that the Democratic administration did not harbor Communists, or, for that matter, those whom they could accuse of Communist tendencies because they favored liberal causes with which the new Congress disagreed. The pressure from Republicans, as well as the information emerging from the recent spy cases, especially that of Elizabeth Bentley, pushed President Harry S. Truman into a program to eliminate any Communists who might be in the federal government. Not only did he hope to silence the critics within the anti-New Deal and anti-Democratic Congress that had just been elected, but some historians believe he wanted to create an atmosphere of urgency that would help him get his unprecedented foreign aid plan passed. On March 21, 1947, as Mary Jane was complaining to her friends because she could neither get her passport nor a reason for its delay, Truman issued Executive Order 9835, the Federal Loyalty Order, which established a program intended to disqualify disloyal persons from employment with the federal government.[24]

The Loyalty Program set up a procedure to check all employees and applicants of the executive branch. First, the Civil Service was to check names against the files of the FBI, military intelligence, HUAC, and any other pertinent agency. If "derogatory" information was found, the FBI began a full field investigation. Each agency set up a board to review dossiers, hold hearings when needed, and recommend action concerning each case to the agency head. An overall Loyalty Review Board would coordinate agency loyalty programs and hear appeals of all dismissals. An employee was to be dismissed if "reasonable grounds" for believing him or her to be disloyal were found. Evidence for disloyalty ranged from sabotage and espionage, through advocacy for the violent overthrow of the government, to "affiliation with or sympathetic association with" any organization designated by the attorney general as "totalitarian, fascist, Communist, or subversive," or seeking to overthrow the government by unconstitutional means.[25] Although Attorney General Tom Clark did not publish his first official list of proscribed organizations until December 1947, the Washington Bookshop was already on HUAC's list, had been mentioned in the Adamson report, and had been of interest to the Civil Service employees who had interviewed Mary Jane years before. Other organizations with which the Keeneys were affiliated—the American Peace Mobilization and the Jefferson School, for example—were also on Clark's list.[26]

When Mary Jane got Mrs. Ruth Shipley's April 1, 1947, letter telling her that she would not get a passport, she may have known why she was denied. The Executive Order was hardly a secret, and Mary Jane had discussed the Loyalty Program with friends, although she did not acknowledge, even privately, that she could possibly merit suspicion. Indignant, she felt it was her request for a passport that shortly caused Philip to lose his passport and his job. She underestimated the FBI and the kind of scrutiny the two of them had already received and refused to accept that there just might be "reasonable grounds" to find her and Philip disloyal.

In fact, an internal FBI memo of April 7, 1947, recapped the status of the Keeney matter for Assistant Director D. M. Ladd. In February the FBI had sent a memorandum to the State Department and the War Department regarding the Keeneys' "activities." It also noted the names of some of those to whom Mary Jane had turned for help in getting the passport decision overturned: "Nathan Gregory Silvermaster; H. Bowen Smith, a former State Department employee; Eric Beecroft, who has connections in the State Department; and David R. Wahl, a suspected Soviet agent presently in charge of the Washington offices of the American Jewish Congress." All of these friends were under suspicion. In addition, the memo indicated, Wahl had advised Mary Jane to contact an attorney, and had recommended Allan Rosenberg, also "a subject in this case"— the "Gregory" (Bentley) case.[27]

More than a year later Mary Jane made a marginal note in the passport denial letter. Next to the words "may have connections with other groups and individuals whose interests are in conflict with the welfare and national security of this country," Mary Jane wrote, "My guess is that certain personal friends were probably referred to—people later named by Elizabeth Bentley." And in 1951, adjacent to the list of references she provided in the 1947 memorandum supporting her efforts to overturn the decision, she penned, "What I didn't realize at the time was that [Philip] Dunaway, [Allan] Rosenberg, and [Bowen] Smith were also under investigation."[28]

What she did realize as she awaited Philip's return from Japan in May was how complicated and difficult their lives had become. Not only had the stresses and strains exacerbated chronic health problems of Mary Jane's, but the Keeneys faced a most uncertain future.[29] Although they were unaware of the grand jury being impaneled in New York to try for indictments in the "Gregory" (Bentley) case, they were aware that the FBI had been interviewing many of their friends, and believed—perhaps rightly, perhaps not—that the questioning was aimed at them.[30] Mary Jane and Clayton Smith (Bowen's wife) talked about the "recent developments" that had "interfered greatly with their peaceable sleeping." Mary Jane had heard that "a good many, many people" had been visited, and, she told Clayton, once she knew "more about the questions, I think it was a shot in the dark, just attempting, you know, a fishing expedition." Nevertheless, someone's answers had angered them both, although they agreed "you never know how you are going to act until things happen to you." Word was clearly out about the Keeneys' difficulties, because Mary Jane had received an unsolicited call from Martin Popper of the National Lawyers' Guild about Philip's case. However, they would not rush into hiring a lawyer, she told her friend, until they knew more about the reasons Philip had been discharged.[31]

With Philip's arrival on May 23, 1947, the Keeneys began to think about next steps. He had not been told the reason for his firing. In Japan the War Department had referred him to the Civil Service; he was told that his Japanese service was "impeccable," Philip told Bowen Smith. "So it all comes back here," Smith replied.[32] Under the provisions of the law, Philip did not have to be given specific reasons for his firing—his Notice of Separation stated that he was fired "by reason of disqualification because of information which, if known, would have disqualified you for appointment initially." Unfortunately for the Keeneys, "The pertinent information is documented as secret material, and this headquarters is not authorized to make this material available to you."[33]

Had Philip been able to get information, he would have heard a litany of suspect activities: membership in the Communist Party and party contacts in the San Francisco area; attendance at specific party meetings including two at which then party president Earl Browder was present; and correspondence with people in Moscow—all details taken from Mary Jane's diaries. The list included his employment at the Library of Congress, "Obtained . . . through contacts in the Communist Party." Also among the charges (none of which Philip saw, so far as one can tell) were his communications "with known Communists in New York"—presumably Bernstein and Kurnakov—and his contacts with Japanese Communist Party members. Used against him were the quotations taken from his letters to Mary Jane about "that great land" of Russia and his exulting in the May Day parade. He also had shared with Mary Jane information about numbers of servicemen in Japan, numbers apparently freely bandied about on shipboard during his return to Japan after his furlough. The most damning of all, however, was the implication that he was not only a Communist, but a hen-pecked one at that: "His wife, who wields considerable influence over the subject, is a known Communist and active in Communist Front operations."[34]

Friendship with Mary Jane had become somewhat of a problem for others as well, apparently. On May 27, Mary Jane received a call from Dorothy Nortman, whose husband, Bernard, had become suspect as a result of the Bentley investigation and their friendship with the Keeneys. Mary Jane told Dorothy she had avoided calling her because she had received "in a round about way" a message from Bernard that they had interrogated about the Keeneys. But despite the risk of the association Dorothy invited the Keeneys to visit them: "I've decided the Devil with them—I mean they're not going to stop us from living." They had no idea what would happen, Dorothy said, "but they know we know you, so what's the point in pretending in some way that we don't." She was not going to turn and run, she asserted, although if "anything drastic" happened she might not "feel so brave."[35]

By mid-June, 1947, with one job possibility for Mary Jane tabled because of their difficulties, the Keeneys had decided they would go to New York City where perhaps they would be able to find some work. They would be following several of their friends who had left federal employment before being fired, or who had been either downsized or eased out of federal service because of suspicions about their loyalty. However, they wanted to consult an attorney first. On June 13, they met with Martin Popper; the next day Mary Jane told her friend Max Weisman that they had not yet decided whether to make another fight like the bruising one in Montana. Philip had not been "charged" except in the letter of dismissal.[36]

According to their phone conversations, the Keeneys had been encouraged to fight Philip's dismissal, not just for themselves, but on behalf of others as well. Mounting such a fight would require a great deal of support, and they did not know whether that support would be forthcoming or whether they were up to it.[37] Acting on Martin Popper's advice, Philip turned to his old union, the United Public Workers of America (UPWA) and its leader, Art Stein. When they finally talked, Stein agreed to have the UPWA attorney meet with Philip and possibly to handle his case, but the plan apparently went nowhere, or Philip decided against the effort.[38]

He certainly was dispirited. When one friend, calling to commiserate, asked "How is Angus?" (referring to Philip by his nickname) Mary Jane confessed that she was "troubled" about him. "[I]t will be a long time before he will give his whole heartedness as he did to the Japanese project," she said. Philip felt as if he had lost the chance of a lifetime; he had begun in Japan something to which he had committed himself completely but which he would be unable to finish. Writing about the project seemed the only thing he could now do.[39] And under stress, Philip seemed to have little sympathy for others; when Bernard Nortman called to say he had also been fired, Philip replied, "So what?" He added, "These things happen." Nortman, too, wanted to try to fight his firing, but Mary Jane responded that under the provisions of the McCarran Rider, the law under which Philip had been fired, the secretary of state had absolute discretion to fire anyone and "there is no hearing and no appeal." "It's so unsportsmanlike," Nortman complained, "so un-American." The Keeneys could only agree.[40]

Although the groundswell of support that Philip needed to mount a fight to regain his job was not forthcoming, the Keeneys hoped that their network of friends could help them in some other ways. And apparently it did. On July 1, they moved into a New York apartment belonging to friends and later moved into a newly renovated apartment on King Street in a building owned by Philip Dunaway, another friend who preceded them to New York. Others, including people who worked for the United Nations, identified possible avenues for employment for one or both. And so they ended their years of federal employment.[41] Philip and Mary Jane Keeney would make a new beginning, or at least a kind of life, in New York. They would not, however, escape the spotlight for long.

CHAPTER 9

The Un-Americans

When the Keeneys headed for New York, they did what many of the people exposed by Elizabeth Bentley had already done—leave the capital city, leave the U.S. federal government service, and appear to leave spying. There was little Soviet apparatus left to report to, and those citizens who lingered in the government's employ would shortly be fired if they had not already been allowed to resign. The Keeneys, as bit players, did not appear to know that Kurnakov's return to Russia had been precipitated by Bentley's defection and the KGB's almost immediate knowledge of that defection through the infamous British mole, Harold "Kim" Philby. By contrast, in early December 1945—not long after the FBI identified the Keeneys' car at the Silvermaster residence—Itzhak Akhmerov, the KGB station chief in New York, personally delivered the word of Bentley's defection to Silvermaster and told him that they would have to "stop our work totally."[1]

And the twelve remaining federal employees named by Bentley—if not alerted by their spy colleagues, then by crackling phone lines and hints at their offices—were very circumspect and close-mouthed. In spite of the increased numbers of agents, the intensive use of tails and wiretaps, the FBI learned nothing on which a real legal case could be made. Nor was the FBI fortunate enough to find another informant who would corroborate Bentley; unlike Whittaker Chambers she had hidden no supporting documents like those Chambers used to help convict Alger Hiss of perjury. The case against the employees would have been difficult to make at best, because the FBI would have had to prove not only "that the accused persons passed confidential information relating to national defense but also that they engaged in these acts with an intent to do injury to the United States to the advantage of another nation."[2] Bentley had said that she believed that many of her contacts did not know where their information was going. Thus for nearly two years, November 1945 to June 1947, the FBI tried to no avail to develop convincing corroborating evidence of the Soviet espionage ring. This is not to say that they were ineffective in disrupting Soviet spying, for the twin defections of Gouzenko in Canada and Bentley in the United States led Moscow to halt its KGB activities in North America. Anatoly Gorsky, Bentley's KGB contact, severed ties with those who knew Bentley, including many friends of the Keeneys: Allan Rosenberg, Maurice Halperin, Charles Kramer, and Donald Wheeler, among others. Joseph Bernstein in March 1946 told Mary Jane that he was out of action for the indefinite future, although he attributed the inactivity to the Gouzenko and *Amerasia* affairs, not Bentley.[3]

Although they had not entirely given up on prosecuting those whom they firmly believed had betrayed their country, the FBI also had other ways of making their suspects pay for the crimes of which they were accused, though not convicted. Memos like the one to the War Department in February 1947 outlining Philip's offenses were sent out to a number of offices, ensuring that those on whom doubt was cast would no longer have access to classified material—or work. Positions were quietly abolished, employees were forced out; some were allowed to resign. Silvermaster ended his federal employment at the Treasury Department in mid-1946, and Victor Perlo and Ullman followed within the year. Halperin, Wheeler, and the Keeneys' friend Harry Magdoff were also among those who, between 1945 and the end of 1947, left government service either willingly or unwillingly. But it was not enough for the investigators. Although the two-year stalemate left the KGB without a viable espionage apparatus in the United States during the early postwar years, it left the FBI fuming.[4]

FBI Director J. Edgar Hoover finally got desperately needed corroboration of Bentley's story when the first few messages of the top-secret Venona project began to reveal cover names of Soviet spies. The project accelerated after uncovering its first few names in 1946, and by 1947 the FBI learned of information that gave credence to Bentley's story. By October 1948, the FBI's Robert Lamphere had begun an active liaison with the project, and a good many espionage cases were opened.[5] As the Venona project ultimately—although not immediately—revealed, not just twenty-seven, but more than 300 people, most of them U.S. citizens, appeared to have covert relationships with Soviet intelligence. Among the 150 that the Venona project was able to identify by the time it ended were a good many of those named by Bentley. The Keeneys were there, too, in decryptions achieved some years later.

Although the Venona decrypts provided substantiation to some of Bentley's claims, the FBI (and the cryptologists at National Security Agency's forerunner, the U.S. Army's Signal Intelligence Service) which had jealously guarded the secret decoding project, had to weigh whether the convictions they might get would be worth revealing the fact that they had broken a closely-held code and knew a great deal about some aspects of Soviet espionage. Also their interception of diplomatic messages would be regarded as a serious breach of diplomatic etiquette. In the end, the FBI decided not to reveal the existence of the Venona files.[6]

Instead, they decided to call a grand jury, which was impaneled in New York in March 1947, during the period in which Mary Jane Keeney was fighting for a passport to join Philip in Japan. Because grand jury testimony is secret, someone who would never confess what he knew in public might give the government enough information for at least a few indictments. Thus, when Mary Jane and her friends were talking about the interrogations of many of their colleagues, they may well have been discussing the questions potential grand jury witnesses were being asked.[7]

Their friend Silvermaster, who had left government service in mid-1946 to become a New Jersey real estate developer, might well have been testifying before the grand jury at about the time the Keeneys made the move to New York City on July 1, 1947, giving up the Washington apartment that had been their home for longer than anywhere else. The Keeneys were living on savings from what had been a comfortable income—about $14,000 annually between them, or about $134,866 in 2008 dollars.[8] At least they were reunited with their dog Marty, previously shipped to friends in Mexico in anticipation of Mary Jane's joining Philip in Japan. Well into middle age, depressed, and having been fired under the loyalty order, Philip seemed unlikely to work again. Mary Jane thought that he might do some writing about his Japanese experience, but she wanted a full-time job.

She would wait for her job for nearly a year. According to the FBI, in April 1948 an informant (identity blacked out) advised the FBI that Julia Older, working for the United Nations (UN) at Lake Placid, New York contacted Mary Jane and offered her a position at the UN effective beginning in June 1948.[9] She became an editor in the Document Control Section, making her of at least passing interest to Grigory Dolbin, the senior KGB officer in the United States at the time. In August 1948, in a message to Moscow, he mentioned that "Cerberus's [Keeney's] wife" had gotten a United Nations job. "She is of interest. Her husband is not."[10]

A month later, her application for a passport to enable her to travel as a UN employee was turned down. Her friend Ursula Wasserman, another UN employee, was also denied a passport. Mary Jane later attributed both denials (probably correctly) to the events of Mary Jane's return from Europe in 1946 and delivery of the Péri testament to Joseph Bernstein—the " 'Communist courier' charge," she called it. She also believed it to be part of a more general attack on the United Nations.[11]

Although Philip appeared to the FBI to busy himself at home in a "literary" way, he too was headed for passport problems.[12] He had spent much of 1947 developing his "library plan" for efficient and effective library service based on his work in Japan. He shopped it and his services around to various countries, anywhere he "thought there might be an opportunity to have this project put to use." He particularly approached countries in the Soviet bloc and South America, trying to build on the relationships he and Mary Jane had cultivated among the diplomatic set in Washington.[13] He got an indication of interest from Czechoslovakia, he reported. Early in October he tried to get a passport, ostensibly to make a trip to complete research on the book he and Mary Jane had begun long before on the history of libraries, but he had been denied. In December, desperate to find meaningful employment and implement his plan, he attempted, without success, to export his work and himself without benefit of passport on the Polish ship, the *Batory*. This incident made him even more suspect.

And things went from bad to worse. On March 4, 1949, Judith Coplon, a Justice Department employee who had been identified through the decoding of the Venona files, was arrested while apparently attempting to pass information to her Soviet contact, a UN employee named Valentin Gubitchev. In her possession were a number of data slips of FBI files, including that of Joseph Bernstein, with its several references to the Keeneys. Much to the dismay of the FBI, which certainly did not want its methods exposed, Coplon's wily attorney insisted that the entirety of the files represented by the slips in her possession be entered into the trial record. In his decision to release the files, Judge Albert L. Reeves disagreed that making them public would endanger national security; rather "they could only produce irritations and maybe endanger individual lives."[15] Indeed, as a *Washington Post* writer concluded, "No trial in memory has reached down into the lives of so many persons, little and great," as Coplon's, by publishing as much raw and sometimes unverified information as the FBI files contained.[16]

As their HUAC questioning would soon reveal, the Keeneys were among those whose lives were "reached." They had been subpoenaed to appear before HUAC in late May 1949, about a month after Coplon's trial began, but before the judge's June 7 decision to release the files.[17] Philip initially claimed an illness that prevented him from traveling in May, and so both Keeneys appeared with attorney Clifford Durr on June 9, 1949. The questions that the committee counsel Frank Tavenner asked reveal that the committee had access to much if not all of the information contained in their FBI files, including excerpts from the diaries and letters. In the hearings Mary Jane admitted knowing Silvermaster and spy Gerhard Eisler; Philip, though confessing to having tried to leave the country on the same ship and with the advice of the same legal firm as Eisler, took the Fifth Amendment as to knowing either Silvermaster or Eisler or being a Communist. (Eisler had managed to stow away on the *Batory* a few months after Philip's attempted departure.)[18]

When Tavenner asked Mary Jane if she was or had ever been a member of the Communist Party, she denied it under oath. However, she appended to her denial a statement that echoed the one she had made years earlier to the Civil Service investigators who asked her if their investigation had been fair. Over protest from Chairman John S. Wood (D-GA) she insisted that her statement was necessary:

> Were I appearing before this committee solely in my capacity as a citizen of the United States [referring to her UN employment] I should refuse to answer that question on the grounds that it is a violation of my rights under the first and fifth amendments to the Constitution. I believe that the Bill of Rights is the most precious heritage of American citizens and that it constitutes the unique contribution of this Nation to the practice of government. I also believe these constitutional guaranties [sic] if they are to endure must be exercised and reaffirmed by each new generation. Consequently I feel a deep responsibility as a citizen to uphold these rights.[19]

She also responded sharply to an inquiry about whether she had discussed "Communist principles" with others. "You must remember," she chided Tavenner, "that I am an intellectual, that I am interested in ideas, that I of course discuss ideas with people."[20]

During the hearing Mary Jane was also asked who helped her to get her position at the UN. She believed that HUAC was trying to find evidence that "Eastern European delegations" had influenced her appointment, rather than her being hired on the "basis of competence."[21] Relying, she said, on instructions from the UN that employees were not allowed to discuss internal UN matters, she declined to answer. Although HUAC did not press this subject further, the Senate Internal Security Subcommittee (SISS) would later remember that she had never answered the question.[22]

One additional question—whether she had brought anything from Europe for anyone other than a family member—foreshadowed the difficulties still to come. Although the Keeneys' testimony ended in June, HUAC published the hearing on July 23. In the Background Statement section—which the Keeneys would not have seen at the time of their testimony—appeared a chronology of Mary Jane's delivery of the Péri edition to Joseph Bernstein, taken from an FBI report introduced in the Coplon trial. It concluded with the summary statement that Mary Jane had "placed herself in the category of a courier for the Communist Party."[23]

"All hell has broken loose," Mary Jane said, as the July 26 *New York Times* carried the headline "UN Aide Accused as a Red Courier." Mary Jane now understood how her delivery of the Péri testament to Bernstein upon her return from Europe—and his subsequent delivery of the document to Alexander Trachtenberg—was viewed by the U.S. government.[24]

The same *New York Times* also reported that the UN staff organization had "unanimously resolved" that the "unsubstantiated charges" against Mary Jane and "the manner in which they were publicized" caused great damage to the "United Nations in general and the Secretariat in particular."[25] Accusations of Soviet spies in the UN were not new, and Gubitchev's arrest with Coplon had confirmed their presence. It had also strengthened the suspicions of those who disliked the idea of the UN and feared that the United States was relinquishing too much power to a world government.

Trachtenberg himself responded to the *Times* story, "full of innuendo and mystification," by explaining—in a letter to the editor of the *New York Times* that appeared in the August 3, 1949, edition—that he had been trying for some time to acquire a copy of "the text of a brief autobiography which Gabriel Péri, a Communist member of the French Chamber of Deputies and foreign editor of the newspaper 'L'Humanite' wrote before he was executed by the Nazis." The war had made the acquisition difficult, but Bernstein had succeeded in getting, through Mary Jane, a copy that had been published by Editions de Minuit, the publishing house of the French Resistance. Bernstein, a translator, had subsequently prepared the edition for publication by International Publishers, of which Trachtenberg was an editor. It had appeared as *Forward Singing Tomorrows: The Last Testament of Gabriel Péri* in October of 1946.[26]

Although his explanation may or may not have helped (he was, after all, a known Communist), Mary Jane continued to cling to her job. Throughout 1949 and 1950 she refused to resign in spite of what she called the UN administration's "wish to 'unload'" her as a "source of embarrassment"; if the UN had "placed the slightest credence in this slander," she insisted, "MJK should and would have been summarily dismissed for misconduct" (emphasis in the original). She believed she had become a "sort of symbol of the independence of the Secretariat," and that if she had resigned quietly, others would also have lost their jobs. [27]

She may have exaggerated her importance to the Secretariat, which had been and would continue to be under attack, but she had certainly become a symbol—although not in the way she would have liked. Although Mary Jane considered his attack "fortuitous" rather than part of a coordinated effort to remove her from her UN position, the pressure for her removal was heightened by Sen. Joseph McCarthy's (R-WI) addition to the growing roster of Communist fighters in Congress who accused the Truman administration of having harbored "individuals with Communist connections," especially in the State Department. In his famous February 9, 1950, Presidents' Day speech to the Republican Women's Club in Wheeling, West Virginia, McCarthy provided specific examples of people who, upon leaving the State Department under suspicion, had gone on to work at the United Nations. "Mrs. Mary Jane Kenny [sic]," McCarthy declared, "was named in an FBI report and in a House committee report as a courier for the Communist Party while working for the government. And where do you think Mrs. Kenny is— she is now an editor in the United Nations Document Bureau."[28] The State Department, eager to ensure that disloyal people were not taking refuge in the UN, and equally eager to protect itself from Republican charges that it had harbored people who were undermining the United States from within, continued to push the UN to fire those deemed unsuitable. McCarthy added to the pressure by inserting a version of the recalled 1946 Adamson report in an October 1950 *Congressional Record*.[29]

In December 1950, Mary Jane was suspended from her UN position. In March 1951, nearly a year and a half after the "Communist courier" charge, she was fired. In "The Persecution of Philip O. and Mary Jane Keeney" she called it "a miracle" that she had "survived so long as a member of the Secretariat." Its failure to fire her earlier, she claimed, was "conclusive proof" that it was only the pressure of the State Department and FBI, not any lack of ability or "suitability" on her part, that caused her dismissal. With her usual detail and zeal, she immediately prepared an appeal.[30]

In July 1951, closed hearings began for Mary Jane; her friend Benedict Alper, who had worked for the UN for four years; and three other colleagues. Open hearings began a week later. A brief written by leftist labor attorney Frank Donner alleged that the five had been discharged "because of their activities in the staff association or because of their Leftist views." Telford Taylor, who had been chief prosecutor at the

Nuremberg war crimes trials, represented the staff members before the Administrative Tribunal because his position was seen as less radical than Donner's and thus more likely to be heeded. In the open hearings, Taylor accused the Secretariat of concealing or suppressing the reasons for the employees' termination, and Donner said the fired staff members were "victims of a purge."[31]

By August 1951, the Tribunal had ruled that the staff members had a right to appeal and to know the reasons for their firing, both items that the Secretariat had contested. On September 5, the Tribunal ordered Mary Jane's reinstatement because she had not been given a "specific reason" for her firing and thus had no opportunity to refute the charges. If the Secretariat chose not to reinstate her, the Tribunal said, it would have to pay an indemnity.[32] A few weeks later, indemnities were denied. Mary Jane and Raja J. Howrani of Syria, the fired head of the Arab desk, asked for an additional hearing to force the issue. In November, a Paris hearing awarded each of them a fraction of the damages they had requested. Mary Jane's $6,250 was not quite four percent of the total she felt was coming to her. Howrani fared only marginally better.[33]

Now both the Keeneys were out of work. Featured—along with Alger Hiss, Judith Coplon, the Silvermaster–Perlo groups and others—in a year-end HUAC report, *The Shameful Years: Thirty Years of Soviet Espionage in the United States*, there was not much point in trying to find the kinds of jobs they were accustomed to doing.[34] Perhaps remembering their positive experience with the Washington Bookshop, by early 1952 they had used her settlement, and possibly some insurance money of Philip's, and had launched Club Cinema, an art film house, at 430 Sixth Avenue. Mary Jane sold and Philip collected tickets for the films they screened.[35] Club Cinema hosted folk singers, provided space for rallies, and employed the wives of imprisoned Communists, Carl Marzani and Leon Josephson.[36] Full membership in the club entitled members to admission to Friday, Saturday, and Sunday films for $1.00 and a social evening where new films were screened and film trends discussed on the first Thursday of every month. It had a capacity of about 200.[37]

The FBI visited Club Cinema as customers at approximately six-month intervals, noting who was working, what films were showing, and how big the crowd was. Although it was not as focused on the Keeneys now that they no longer worked for the federal government, the FBI still regarded them as dangerous enough to keep an eye on. And according to "reliable informants," the Keeneys maintained almost continuous contact with persons who were suspected of espionage activities. The Bureau's efforts changed in quality as well as quantity, however. No longer did the agents read all their mail; they did, however, note the names and addresses of their correspondents and on occasion make pretext telephone calls to the Keeney residence. The FBI was also tracking others' mail, for on occasion the FBI noted who had received mail from Club Cinema.[38]

Just because the FBI expended less effort on them did not mean that the Keeneys were free to settle into a routine. In February 1952, shortly after their purchase of Club Cinema, they were called to testify before the relatively new SISS.[39] The SISS had in 1951 begun looking into the IPR; Mary Jane had been a member and Philip had spoken to it. Not only did the SISS apparently remember that Mary Jane had declined to answer two years previously a HUAC question about her UN employment, but it may have been interested in the Bernstein relationship. Bernstein was suspected as the espionage contact of *Amerasia*'s Philip Jaffe, who had acquired so many secret documents, and the IPR was closely related, both geographically and intellectually, with *Amerasia*. In addition, the Keeneys were known to have been associates of the Communist Frederick Vanderbilt Field, a principal officer and financial supporter of the IPR.[40] Committee members suspected that the IPR had brought Communist influence to bear on China policy. Philip was involved with the Committee for Democratic Far Eastern Policy (CDFEP), which shared officers and interests with the IPR. According to the March 1949 masthead of its journal, the *Far East Spotlight*, he had for a time been its treasurer; two old friends, Fred Field and former Congressman Hugh DeLacy were on the executive committee. CDFEP, which was conducting a nation-wide campaign for "friendship, trade and recognition of new China," was also on the attorney general's list of suspect organizations.[41]

The Keeneys appeared before the SISS on February 18, 1952. Despite her earlier denial to HUAC, this time Mary Jane refused to answer any questions about the Communist Party or whether she had been associated with the IPR. She willingly rehearsed her federal employment but again refused to answer questions about whether anyone in the State Department had influenced her UN employment, saying that the rules of the UN forbade her to do so. She refused "at her peril," Committee Counsel J. G. Sourwine reminded her.[42] On the other hand, Philip refused to answer anything but the merest details about his federal employment, claiming his Constitutional right to avoid self-incrimination. The committee gave up on him.[43] But it would not stand for Mary Jane's refusal to answer. Within the week, the Senate Judiciary Committee, at the SISS's request, voted to ask the Senate to charge her with contempt.[44]

There was great tension and suspicion regarding the young UN among some members of Congress (and the general public). As Michigan

Congressman Paul Shafer wrote as the Senate was considering the contempt charge, "Does International Big Government—in the form of the United Nations—impose obligations and loyalties upon American citizens which override their obligations and loyalties to the United States?" Shafer cited Mary Jane's refusal to respond to the question as proof that "Americans of doubtful loyalty" could hide behind the UN regulations and "defy the authority" of Congress. This was "one more evidence of the menacing encroachment" of the UN and the need to safeguard "American sovereignty" against it.[45]

On March 17, 1952, the whole Senate embraced the recommendation of the Judiciary Committee, charged Mary Jane with contempt, and handed the charge to the prosecutor. This was not just a way to teach her a lesson but also a challenge to the UN. By that time the UN had told Mary Jane that she could answer, and she did so in a sworn statement "that no one in or out of the State Department advised her or suggested to her that she make application for U.N. employment." But "this showed only a desire on Mrs. Keeney's part to set up the United Nations as superior to the Senate," asserted Sen. Pat McCarran, chairman of the Judiciary Committee and SISS.[46] As her attorney moved to quash the contempt charge, to which she had pled not guilty, Mary Jane issued another statement accusing the SISS of "fabricating a 'spy scare' and using it to disrupt the United Nations."[47] Her publicity campaign was useless; by November 1952, with her legal maneuvering ineffective, her trial was set for January 28, 1953, in the Federal District Court in Washington, D.C. A year had passed since her SISS appearance, and about two years since her UN job ended. As she awaited trial, the UN fired others she knew. A *New York Times* article listed, in addition to Benedict Alper (spared earlier), Stanley Graze, Julia Older, and Ursula Wasserman, among others.[48]

The jury in her delayed March 1953 contempt trial deliberated only half an hour before coming back with a verdict of guilty.[49] Prior to the trial, Mary Jane got permission to address the question that had led to her contempt charge. According to press coverage, facing a possible prison term of a year and a $1,000 fine, "Mrs. Keeney attempted to purge herself of contempt by saying she didn't know who might have recommended her." She was handed a $250 fine and a suspended sentence.[50] She appealed the judgment.

More than a year later, in August 1954, her conviction was set aside because the trial judge had improperly allowed the introduction of highly prejudicial information before the jury, when he alone should have heard testimony pertaining to the pertinence of the question to the subject of the committee inquiry. In this case, the appeals judge wrote, "From the

Mary Jane Keeney as she was pictured in the *New York Times* during her contempt trials. [*New York Times*, courtesy of Redux Pictures]

very outset the jury heard the appellant linked to a nefarious, worldwide Communist movement, with her associates numbered among those performing acts of espionage and sabotage even as they purloined secrets of the United States in favor of the Russian Government." Mary Jane was "naturally gratified" by the reversal. "No citizen, devoted to the institutions of this Republic, can wish to be found in contempt of its legislative body," she added.[51] The government would try her again. A small article announced her April 1, 1955, retrial, four and a half years after the UN fired her. "The case is viewed," the article said, "as a test between the powers of the Senate and the United Nations."[52] In a trial held without a jury, Mary Jane was acquitted.[53]

Even during the time that Mary Jane's job was threatened and her contempt case moved slowly through the courts, the Keeneys never gave up participating in causes they believed in or associating with people who might elicit more surveillance. Perhaps they lacked discretion, perhaps they decided it hardly mattered any more, or perhaps they were simply defiantly determined to assert their beliefs. For example, Philip marched in the 1951 May Day Parade carrying a banner reading "Free the Communist eleven."[54]

The FBI continued to visit Club Cinema from time to time, "cover" their mail, and to identify their acquaintances—repeatedly and in excruciating detail—in the FBI files. The weekend films, advertised in the Communist *Daily Worker*, were listed and their availability investigated to see if the Keeneys were in violation of the Registration Act for bringing foreign propaganda into the United States.[55] They were not.

The FBI watched and waited and kept tabs on the Keeneys, going back to their files to see if any additional leads could be picked up—other information that would tell them something new. It described them as of August 1954, as the Keeneys fought the contempt conviction. It must have been quite a pair: Mary Jane petite and bow-legged, and Philip tall and scrawny with shoulders and mustache both drooping. They both were graying and wore glasses.[56] The FBI noted their visits—with the Stanley Grazes, the Victor Perlos, and others.[57]

In July 1958, the Club Cinema closed, and the building was demolished. Pretext phone calls to the Keeney residence revealed that Philip did not intend to seek new employment; he was enjoying a rest. The FBI closed Philip's file but noted that, as Philip remained a possible security threat, it would check on him every six months.[58] It did not have to check on him for long: he died "swiftly and mercifully" of a massive cerebral hemorrhage at the age of 71 on December 19, 1962.[59]

Mary Jane memorialized her "Angus" with a pamphlet she sent to friends. "Most of us yearn to die in this way," she wrote, "and few deserved so much as he to have death come as a friend." In what was as much her valedictory as his, she wrote, "And so a long chapter in my life has been closed, a chapter of thirty-three years of great struggle for principles we believed in, of many triumphs, and of more than a little tragedy. Neither of us has ever regretted that we engaged in these struggles for justice, to vindicate ourselves though even more to establish an abstract principle of right applicable to many of our countrymen."[60]

Mary Jane, some years younger than Philip, retired in June 1963 as a copy editor of Physicians News Service.[61] Days later, she left the Brooklyn apartment to which she and Philip had relocated in September 1961 and moved into one with two politically sympathetic friends, Anne Florant (a member of the Congress of American Women) and Melba Phillips (a physicist who lost her New York City teaching job after asserting her right against self-incrimination before the SISS). Mary Jane planned to move to England (and got a passport to do so) or to California.[62] After nearly a year of England's damp weather, however, she returned to

New York City, where she lived on another five years under the intermit-
tently watchful eye of the FBI.[63]

At her death at 72 in 1969, she donated her body to medical research
and her selected records of the "The Persecution of Philip and Mary Jane
Keeney" to the Bancroft Library at Berkeley. She distributed gifts to
those who shared her beliefs or supported her in her struggles. Her books
of French Resistance literature, including an edition of Péri, which were
"close to my heart because they cost me dear," to Mildred and Stanley
Graze, "stalwart friends through fair weather and foul," themselves
named in the Keeney file and identified in Venona. To "old and dear
friends" Ethel and Ben Alper, Mary Jane gave "two books about events
that once concerned Ben and me," their firing at the UN; one was Ursula
Wasserman's I Was an American, recounting how Mary Jane's friend
renounced her U.S. citizenship and became an Israeli citizen after feeling
she had become a victim of an American witch hunt. She left the remain-
der of her property to Anne Florant and Melba Phillips in gratitude for
their friendship, while requesting that all her personal files except for
those designated for the University of California at Berkeley be destroyed.[64]

Mary Jane and Philip Keeney's world ended with a whimper, when they
would much have preferred a bang. Mary Jane claimed that they had not
followed the principles of Communism or Socialism, but that they had
tried to defend "an abstract principle of right" that applied to all citizens. Aware that she and Philip had been caught in a web woven by their
government, the fraying threads of the Soviet espionage network, and
their own doing, Mary Jane even in death sought to preserve her version
of the life she and Philip had led.

CHAPTER 10

Guilt and Association

The threat to liberal democracies from Soviet Communism was real, as history has now demonstrated, and the United States had every right and duty to defend its constitutional form of government and the rights and liberties it embodies against harm from its enemies. At times of great national stress, however, the threat to a government may come, wittingly or unwittingly, from the very efforts taken to defend it. The peril is that the government, through its secrecy, its investigatory and punitive processes, and actions of its elected and appointed officials, accomplish the work of the enemy by subverting the very constitutional values it would protect. It gets tangled in its own web. The tension between security and liberty is fraught with ambiguity and ambivalence, as this case exemplifies.

The phenomenon called McCarthyism has at its core the process of attributing guilt by association. Because the tactics of McCarthy and his ilk have long been discredited, there is an assumption today that those to whom guilt was imputed were innocent, but that was surely not always true—and assuredly not true in the case of Philip and Mary Jane Keeney. Grigory Dolbin, in August 1948, referred to Mary Jane as "our agent."[1] However, the case of the "Librarian Spies," as they are dubbed in John Earl Haynes and Harvey Klehr's *Venona: Decoding Soviet Espionage in America*,[2] illustrates the phenomenon at work. Page after page of the Keeneys' FBI file lists persons "associated with," "contacted by," "invited by," "close friend of," "met with," "acquainted with," "known to," "called by," "correspondent of," Philip or Mary Jane. Some were called to testify about their knowledge of the Keeneys; associates were forced to defend themselves against charges of disloyalty only because of their relationship with the Keeneys, however casual. Some never knew their contact with the Keeneys had brought them under suspicion. In Mary Jane's first contempt trial, what led to her conviction was a list of people under suspicion with whom she had associated, not anything she herself had done. This use of associations was repeated over and over again, if not to convict in court then to damn in the court of public opinion.

When the FBI first became seriously interested in the Keeneys in 1945, their file identified their relationships with people named by Elizabeth Bentley—although Bentley did not name the Keeneys and said she did not know them. It then used those relationships as the reason they were suspect and objects of investigation themselves. From the break-ins at the Keeneys that yielded material such as contacts from their telephone book and dates and events from Mary Jane's diary, interception of mail, physical surveillance, and telephone taps they added more relationships. Eventually, building on the strong circumstantial evidence of their regular meetings with Bernstein and repeated contacts with Kurnakov; the content of Philip's letters from Japan; and their meetings and conversations with friends, the FBI dubbed them "well known Communists" and prime espionage suspects.

Then the language of the files changed subtly; the words of early wiretaps were repeated or paraphrased and attributed to a "confidential informant"; the label of "well known Communists" was repeated. It is unclear, however, to whom the Keeneys were well known as Communists other than their circle of friends and handlers and the FBI, until the FBI shared the Keeneys' file in the hearings that brought them to the public's attention. Finally, others' relationships with the Keeneys, regardless of proximity, began to call those others into question and put them in jeopardy. This chaining of relationships as a way of identifying people who were alleged to be disloyal proved devastating not only to the Keeneys, who we now know were guilty, but also to others who were either casual acquaintances or who knew one or the other Keeney only through their workplaces, and who likely had no interest in espionage.

In the files she compiled to send to the University of California at Berkeley, Mary Jane listed those government employees for whom she was certain association with her had become a problem—a small fraction, no doubt, since she was extremely social. "In each case," she wrote, "the association was in connection with some friendly act on my part." Sylvia Braslow lived in the Keeneys' apartment building and carpooled to work with them. Mary Jane recommended Alice Demerjian for a position in the State Department that Mary Jane had turned down. John Flynn's Communist wife Hulda had been a friend of Mary Jane's for ten years, but she knew John less well. Dan Levin's wife was also a friend of Mary Jane's and had visited her in the hospital in 1947. All four of these were exonerated.[3]

The fifth, Bernard Nortman, was not so lucky. His case became the fodder for Bert Andrews's *Washington Witch Hunt*[4] after he lost his State Department job partly at least because of his friendship with the Keeneys. "When I heard, sometime in the early winter of 1947," Mary Jane wrote, "that he was under investigation as to 'suitability,' I refrained from calling him lest the reference to me in the Adamson report . . . be used to embarrass him." In addition, she stated, "The transcript of the telephone conversation with his wife on 27 May 1947 (a month before he was summarily dismissed) is entirely accurate—I recall the portions quoted." The transcript was, she averred, "direct evidence of illegal wiretapping." Indeed it was evidence of wiretapping, so at that time it was inadmissible in court; the wiretapping itself may well have been illegal under restrictions imposed by various U.S. attorneys general. Ultimately Nortman was allowed to resign.[5]

Although she did not list him in her papers, Abraham Feingold, a New York City Manual Training High School teacher, was tried in 1950 for insubordination for refusing to indicate whether he was a Communist. During his trial, it appeared that a visit from Mary Jane Keeney, which had been noted in her FBI file, was used against him.[6]

There were others, though. Of those who came into contact with the Keeneys perhaps no one suffered a more bewildering and devastating impact than Beatrice Braude. Braude was a young linguist with the U.S. Information Agency (USIA), who contacted Mary Jane in 1946 to deliver a message from a woman in Germany. The woman requested clothing and supplies for Greta Kuckhoff, a German Communist Mary Jane had met while in Germany with the Angell Commission.[7] Braude did not know Kuckhoff and believed she was on an errand of mercy. She had, at most, two additional fleeting contacts with Mary Jane and a short-lived social acquaintance with Judith Coplon, both of which had been satisfactorily explained to the Loyalty Security Board in 1951. In December 1953, however, a day after being praised for her work, she was dismissed allegedly because funding for the USIA had been cut, according to Stanley I. Kutler's 1982 study of her case in *The American Inquisition: Justice and Injustice in the Cold War*. It may well be that the timing of her dismissal had to do with the new Eisenhower loyalty-security program initiated in April of that year. Or it may have had to do with McCarthy's attack on the USIA, which occurred in the spring of 1953.[8]

Although she was assured that her termination was due strictly to the agency's reduced budget, Braude never again was able to find work in the federal government, nor was she able to discover why she was black-listed until 1974, when she requested her files through the Freedom of Information Act. It took Senate action in 1997 and 1998 by Sen. Daniel Patrick Moynihan and Sen. Alfonse D'Amato to spur the court into examining the wrong done Braude, to clear her name posthumously, and to provide monetary damages to her survivors to compensate for her blacklisting and the secrecy that made it impossible for her to know and answer the charges against her.[9] It was this secrecy, lack of due process and a fair hearing that made the government's tactics in fighting problems of loyalty and security so contrary to traditional American values.

Another person who was permanently marked by his association with the Keeneys and the examination that followed was Paul Boswell, a Library of Congress employee. An informant called him "one of the closest associates of Philip O. Keeney while he was at the Library of Congress."[10] When he was suspended in 1948 by the library's loyalty panel, he went to its chair, Chief Assistant Librarian Verner Clapp, to appeal his suspension. With a wife and child to support, he was naturally worried about losing his job. Clapp did not lift the suspension but tried to "expedite" hearings and locate counsel for Boswell. In his daily report, Clapp recounted their exchange: "Says he, 'How does one prove one isn't a Communist?' I wished I could tell him." Although he was eventually cleared, Boswell declined to discuss his experience even years after his retirement. All he would say was that he worked for the Library of Congress for thirty years.[11]

Donald and Alice Dozer also found that having a "social acquaintance" with the Keeneys and Alice's working as Keeney's secretary at the Library of Congress from July 1940 to September 1941 had been held against them. In July 1949, Donald, then working at the State Department, wrote Professor Jesse Shera of the Graduate Library School at the University of Chicago to tell him he would have the "'opportunity' of defending" himself, and to enlist Shera's help to document his loyalty. The Dozers' attorney, Thurman Arnold of Arnold, Fortas, and Porter, a firm which argued a good many loyalty cases, thought that, though there were other factors to be addressed, "these charges are directed mainly at my OSS record [where he worked with Maurice Halperin and Woodrow Borah, named in the Bentley file] and of course Alice's association with Keeney. He says that because of this association she is as deeply involved as I am." Although he thought he would be able to keep his job, he knew the fight would be a hard one. He requested that Shera add his notarized statement on the Dozers' behalf. Shera did so.[12]

Shera's role in helping refute charges of disloyalty that stemmed in part from a colleague's association with Keeney makes the total silence of the librarian community with regard to the Keeneys' strange career even more remarkable. Shera had not only been a defender of Philip's when he was fired in Montana, but had also belonged to the PLC for a time. Shera had known—and formed a negative opinion of—Philip when the two worked together at the Library of Congress, the Coordinator of Information, and OSS. But neither Shera, who by the late 1940s had become quite prominent, nor any other librarian lifted an audible voice to comment either positively or negatively about the events that befell the Keeneys. The library press was totally silent on the subject.

Although Philip and Mary Jane had done nothing to endear themselves to the leadership of the ALA and in fact had aggravated it considerably with the PLC, during this period the ALA was very much concerned about postwar planning for Japanese libraries and intellectual freedom. Both of these were topics that might have elicited comment—pro or con—about the Keeneys from librarians. They do not appear to have done so, even though the Keeneys' confrontations with various entities of the federal government were widely published.[13]

As the first libraries officer in Japan, Philip would have been expected to exert considerable influence on the direction of postwar library development in Japan, and in fact did so. He is still held in high regard in Japan. Other far better known librarians, Charles Brown and Leon Carnovsky, visited Japan to help establish ties with the ALA and to develop library education. Both of them briefly and very inconspicuously consulted Philip during the ALA midwinter conference in 1946, and Brown, in spite of having told others that Philip was "no good," either thought highly enough of Keeney's work in Japan to appear to encourage him to participate in the activities Brown was organizing, or perhaps he knew in advance there was no danger of Philip's staying in Japan, and thus made the offer hypocritically.[14] A subsequent attempt at a meeting Brown requested with Mary Jane before he traveled to Japan was rebuffed; she did not trust him.[15] And except for the articles Keeney himself submitted regarding the status of libraries in Japan,[16] nothing appeared in the library literature about his accomplishments; he got no credit for his achievements from the library establishment. Nor was there any comment on his recall from Japan or his highly publicized attempt to leave the country to market his "Library Plan" to Czechoslovakia.

As a librarian who had earlier been embroiled in a controversial tenure case that also involved principles of intellectual freedom, and who was now accused of disloyalty, Philip Keeney might have elicited a response from the ALA because of the charges leveled against him and Mary Jane. In 1948 the ALA adopted the Library Bill of Rights, which decried the imposition of a single standard of "Americanism" and called on librarians to join forces with other groups to fight censorship. It protested the removal of the *Nation* from the shelves of New York City Schools, and fought against labeling books to indicate possible "red" content or authors.[17]

From June 1948, following the implementation of the Truman Loyalty Program and its state imitators, until June 1950, as the Cold War became hot in Korea, the ALA Council argued over a Resolution on Loyalty Investigations in Libraries. Influential federal librarians such as Verner Clapp urged adoption of a resolution opposing "abuse," whereas others, particularly David Berninghausen, chairman of the Intellectual Freedom Committee, argued for a resolution opposing "use" of such investigations. It was clear that for federal employees, having their professional association oppose the loyalty probes, which in Clapp's opinion gave them an opportunity to clear themselves, placed their employment in jeopardy. Although opposing factions finally came to an agreement on a carefully worded resolution, the ALA's record of support for any librarian fired for refusal to sign a loyalty oath or because of some derogatory information was very poor: not even Quaker librarians who refused to sign oaths as a matter of conscience got support.[18] Perhaps the Keeneys' difficulties, surfacing in the press during this time, made the debaters even more uncomfortable; perhaps acknowledging the Keeneys' relationship to librarianship would further complicate an already sticky argument. Of course, the ALA was not alone in failing to protest against uses or abuses of loyalty probes, even the ACLU expelled board members with a history of membership in the still-legal Communist Party.

In fact, even before their public problems, the library community appeared to be assiduously avoiding the Keeneys. Likely this stemmed from the PLC's aggressive stance toward the ALA leadership, but also from the PLC's, and especially the Keeneys' leftist tilt at a time when being seen as too far left became increasingly dangerous. The Sheras of the PLC—and there had been any number of later library leaders who briefly joined the short-lived group—had come through the war years and moved into positions of greater responsibility. Some were tasked with administering loyalty oaths or presiding over loyalty investigations. They may have been much less likely to combat the pervasive pressure for "loyalty." After all, the ALA had yet to learn how to fight censorship effectively without jeopardizing its slight status by associating with the Keeneys.

The vast majority of the ALA leadership tended to be centrist or conservative and bureaucratic, solidly anti-Communist while decrying anti-

Communism's excesses, which harmed libraries. In fact, the ALA's attitude toward Communism or signs of disloyalty by members, at least the attitude of the leadership or those who published in the prominent journals, seems to have been simply to ignore them into oblivion. Rather than either to support the Keeneys as people who were being subjected to a great deal of negative publicity without any provable charges, or to condemn the Keeneys as people who were harming the profession and their country through their alleged espionage, the association and its members acted as if they—or any threat from Communism—simply did not exist.[19]

Most books about spying today pay about as much attention to the Keeneys as the ALA did; they do not even appear in the indexes. Clearly the Keeneys are today seen as relatively insignificant, which is how Elizabeth Bentley regarded them. The Silvermasters had mentioned the Keeneys "as possible contacts" who were not used. Unlike many of their associates, the Keeneys were not called to give grand jury testimony.[20]

The Keeneys did not want to be insignificant, however, and they certainly wanted to be used. Through Philip they repeatedly sought contacts with the Soviet espionage apparatus: Wahl, Golos, Silvermaster, Kurnakov, and Bernstein. Ultimately, however, it was Mary Jane who remained of interest as an agent, and appears to have been the driving force behind the couple's efforts; she did, indeed, "wear the pants" and influence Philip. If one can believe the completeness of the FBI files, the Keeneys rarely associated with anyone who did not share their views, and nearly all of their associates show up today in lists of people identified by Venona or the KGB archives or some other source as having been Communists, "contacts" of the Soviets, or outright spies. Their friends, the George Wheelers, kept in touch with the Keeneys from Czechoslovakia, Philip's December 1948 destination, to which they had defected.[21] The Keeneys themselves show up in several decrypts, in each one appearing to be "approached," "entrusted" to an agent, or seeking a reconnection.

The Venona decrypts cover a minuscule portion of Soviet intelligence and include few GRU cables, and thus are hardly definitive about the Keeneys' accomplishments. The Keeneys' letters, however, seem to speak of frustration and failure to produce anything useful in the way of information. As Mary Jane's own writings reveal, she wanted badly to be a significant participant in history, and she brought the phlegmatic Philip with her. Their conversations and writings—especially Mary Jane's, whose voice we hear most frequently in the wiretaps and in testimony—have more than a tinge of righteous indignation that they should be suspected of wrongdoing. Mary Jane casts them as principled and misunderstood martyrs to a cause.

There is no longer a question about whether they were spies. Spies take secret government information and give it to another country with the intent or reason to believe that it will advantage that country over one's own. Although the Keeneys may not have intended directly to harm the United States, they certainly did intend to help the Soviet Union. They seem to have believed the USSR was being treated unfairly, and that they could help level the playing field. And it is quite likely that many kinds of information to which they had access would give the Soviet Union an advantage over the United States.

Did they provide the Soviet Union with any valuable information? They certainly wanted to do so, but neither the FBI nor the various investigating committees had any evidence of their having given their KGB or GRU handlers anything. Despite Venona and the brief opening of the KGB Archives, we have no evidence yet of what the Keeneys may have produced comparable to the evidence we have regarding Nathan Gregory Silvermaster, whose deliveries are spelled out in detail in some of the Venona decrypts, and who received high honors from the Soviets for his work. In spite of their apparent aspirations, the Keeneys got only trouble for their trouble.

Even if the Venona cables concerning the Keeneys had been decoded earlier, and even if the FBI had been willing to use them as evidence in a trial against the Keeneys, what did they prove? If the FBI wiretaps had been legal as evidence, what usable evidence did they really provide? A prosecutor could bring a strong circumstantial case that the Keeneys attempted to aid the Soviet Union. A defense attorney could provide a strong rebuttal that they were ineffectual aspirants who sought martyrdom for a cause, but that the only people they harmed were themselves.

Through this process of sifting and winnowing, of struggling with ambiguities and ambivalence, the historian begins to have an uncomfortable realization of her own use of the Keeneys' associations. Their closest colleagues show up in Bentley's now-substantiated narrative or in the Venona files or both. Of course, some people who show up in both were approached as possible spies and turned down the opportunities. Not the Keeneys. As librarians their job was to provide access to information, but in government and in private industry, often their more important role is to protect it. Mary Jane and Philip sought the chance to provide information or to create a hospitable environment for the Communist ideas they warmly embraced. They wanted to be useful and were miserable when they felt they had failed. They acted as if they could not possibly have done anything to merit suspicion, but they never removed themselves from suspicious activities or associations. If guilt can be proven by association, the Keeneys had plenty of both.

The historian tries to find the bits of significant evidence in activities and associations and expose them for all to see and judge. She pieces together a meaningful narrative out of disparate pieces of information. She selects from that information to paint the picture she believes is closest to the reality she has discovered. She aims for transparency. She tries to account for missing information—to understand what is left out or not recorded. She tries to expose the trail she has followed.

The government, on the other hand, hid everything it could. Philip never knew the "charges" against him when he returned from Japan and so could never try to answer them. Mary Jane was initially found guilty of contempt because of whom she knew, not because of the question she failed to answer. When the Keeneys took the Fifth Amendment did they "hide behind" a U.S. citizen's cherished civil liberties? Could there have been a better way than suspect wiretaps and break-ins, the use of unverified information in FBI files leaked to investigating committees or given to the press, to handle individuals suspected of disloyalty?

No doubt the government's tactics were effective in removing possible spies from the sources of valued information. One could argue that blacklisting suspicious actors from government work was better than imprisoning them, although deprivation of livelihood is surely a genuine punishment; citizens of the United States are not supposed to be deprived of life, liberty, or property (including livelihood) without due process. Citizens of the United States are supposed to be able to know the charges against them and to have an opportunity to face their accusers. The Keeneys were never really given that opportunity, and their punishment was real.

One could also argue, however, that the costs of secrecy and suspect investigative methods, as well as the use of hearings and letters full of circumstantial or sometimes unverified information to discredit an individual, go beyond the very real damage to the individual who is the subject of the probe. In abrogating democratic values such as due process and the right to fair hearing, the tactics undermine "our Constitutional form of government" that such actions are taken allegedly to protect. Not only do they place all the power in the hands of the investigator and reduce the individual to a case file or a target, but they erode the necessary trust between citizens and government.

As a result of that erosion at least a large part of one generation grew up skeptical of the Federal government's stories about Communist spies. We never had any corroboration of the "Blond Spy Queen's" story, and until the last decade, large numbers of people were unconvinced of the guilt of the Rosenbergs and of Alger Hiss—and some still are. Because information was gathered illegally, it could not be used in trials, and spies like Judith Coplon, who came to trial, were acquitted because evidence against them was gathered illegally. So missed opportunities to capture and prosecute spies were another effect of the FBI's illegal tactics. And the inability to catch and prosecute spies added to the lack of credibility and left the government with only headlines and hearings as tools to quell the espionage trade and to try to unite the country against the "enemy within."

What to make of all this? Information is powerful. It is valuable and can be dangerous. It can be especially dangerous if one is irretrievably convinced one is right, is wedded without exception to his or her own vision of the truth. Then information can become not a tool of liberation, but a weapon of destruction and oppression. And when government acts outside the law, or behind a veil of secrecy, it harms its own interests. Not only can it not use the legal avenues to which it has recourse, but it creates an unbridgeable gulf between itself and the people it is supposed to serve.

There is surely a necessity for the United States or any nation to be able to protect itself from espionage. There is just as surely a necessity to guard jealously the foundational principles on which the nation is founded. Today we face a similar thorny problem: how to detect and prevent attacks from terrorists. In protecting our homeland we have again run the risks of destroying that which we seek to preserve. We do not want to be caught in our own web.

NOTES

INTRODUCTION

1. Joseph R. McCarthy, "Communists in the State Department." *Congressional Record*, 81st Congress, 2nd Session, pp. 1952–1957. Reprinted in *Annals of America*: *1950*: 16–21.

2. United States. Congress House. Committee on Un-American Activities. "Testimony of Philip O. Keeney and Mary Jane Keeney and Statement Regarding Their Background." 81st Congress, 1st Session. May 24, 25, June 9, 1949.

3. Over a period of years, Mary Jane Keeney compiled a file of documents that she titled "The Political Persecution of Philip and Mary Jane Keeney." They were accompanied by a narrative in which she spelled out how she and her husband had been targeted. The papers are in Box 2 of the Philip Olin Keeney Papers at the Bancroft Library in Berkeley, California. The full citation for the papers is Philip Olin Keeney Papers 71/157, hereafter cited as Keeney Papers [Bancroft, Box 2].

4. Extension of Remarks of Hon. Joseph R. McCarthy of Wisconsin in the Senate of the United States, Saturday, September 23 (legislative day of Friday, September 22), 1950. "The Metropolitan Broadcasting Corp.—the Report Which Was Never Released." *Congressional Record—Appendix*, October 20, 1950, pp. A7679–7692; "Institute of Pacific Relations," United States Senate, Subcommittee to Investigate the Administration of the Internal Security Act and Other Internal Security Laws of the Committee on the Judiciary. Washington D.C., February 18, 1952 (Washington, D.C.: GPO, 1952): 2773–2780; "Mrs. Keeney Faces a Contempt Action," *New York Times* (Feb. 26, 1952), p. 15.

CHAPTER 1—PHILIP

1. In "The Political Persecution of Philip and Mary Jane Keeney," Mary Jane claimed that Philip had received a firm offer of a job from the Czech government prior to his attempt to board the *Batory*. Keeney Papers [Bancroft, Box 2].

2. The description of the *Batory* incident is based on background information preceding the transcript of the Keeneys' testimony before the House Un-American Activities Committee on May 24, 25, and June 9, 1949. The fact that Keeney tried to leave the country on the *Batory* was further sensationalized when a few months later Gerhart Eisler, touted as a Communist "master spy" succeeded in leaving the United States without a passport as a stowaway on the same ship.

3. For a volume that traces the entire history of U.S.–U.S.S.R. relations from the 1917 until the death of McCarthy and beyond, including how spy rings such as the Silvermasters' operated, see Ted Morgan, *Reds: McCarthyism in Twentieth-Century America* (New York: Random House, 2003).

4. This idea of the motives of many spies during this time period has been widely discussed. Many spies wanted to level the intelligence playing field for a war ally who they felt was being excluded from valuable information.

5. The CIA's forerunner was the World War II Office of Strategic Services (OSS); the Bureau of Investigation was founded in 1908, but did not become known as the FBI until later.

6. The terms *Soviets* and *Russians*, as well as the *Soviet Union* and *Russia*, are used interchangeably in this book. Technically, this is incorrect because the former Soviet Union comprised several nationalities, of whom Russians were just one. Throughout its existence, however, the Soviet Union was commonly referred to as Russia.

7. Nicholas Dozenberg, quoted in Earl Latham, *The Communist Controversy in Washington* (Cambridge, MA: Harvard University Press, 1966), 82.

8. Latham, *The Communist Controversy in Washington*, 76. Other books echo this point.

9. Two thoughtful accounts of the ex-Communist witness phenomenon written around the time it occurred are Murray Kempton's *Part of our Time: Some Ruins and Monuments of the Thirties* (New York: Simon and Schuster, 1955), and Herbert Packer, *Ex-communist Witnesses: Four Studies in Fact Finding* (Stanford, CA: Stanford University Press, 1962). Recent books about Bentley include Kathryn S. Olmsted, *Red Spy Queen: A Biography of Elizabeth Bentley* (Chapel Hill: University of North Carolina Press, 2002); and Lauren Kessler, *Clever Girl: Elizabeth Bentley, the Spy Who Ushered in the McCarthy Era* (New York: HarperCollins, 2003). Chambers actually informed on Hiss and others as early as 1939, but for some reason the information he provided was not taken seriously.

10. Although the Keeneys may not have been named directly by Bentley, the FBI's scrutiny of the group led to FBI scrutiny of the Keeneys.

11. The authors want to express appreciation to J. S. Kronick of the Rockville, Connecticut, Public Library who provided information about the Keeneys from the Rockville city directories from 1879–1920. In addition, Ms. Kronick

also located data about Keeney residences from the Connecticut Historical Commission's Historic Resources Inventory, as well as photographs from the *Vernon Rockville Sesquicentennial Photo Record, 1808–1958*.

12. Philip O. Keeney to C. H. Clapp, July 3, 1931. Philip Keeney Personnel File. K. Ross Toole Archives, University of Montana, Missoula; referenced hereafter as [Montana].

13. Charles Clarence Williamson, *Training for Library Service: A Report Prepared for the Carnegie Corporation of New York* (New York: The Corporation, 1923), 142. Not everyone was convinced that the profession's problems would be solved by recruiting more men to librarianship. In fact, the "woman question" has been the subject of controversy among librarians since the late 1800s. During the 1930s, it came to a head with what became known as the "Soft Shoulders" debate in which men and women squared off in the pages of the professional literature to argue their cases about abilities as librarians based on gender. In the 1970s, female librarians expressed a great deal of concern about disparities in salaries based on gender.

CHAPTER 2—MARY JANE

1. Mary Jane Keeney, "The Making of a Radical: An Experience in American Education," *Black & White* 1 (Sept. 1939): 16. The Philip Olin Keeney Papers include two biographical sketches that Mary Jane wrote. One is an unpublished draft titled "Biography of Mary Jane Keeney" and includes much of the materials that she used for the article published in *Black & White*, a publication of the League of American Writers. The biographies are not identical, however, and are cited variously.

2. "Biography of Mary Jane Keeney": 1 [Bancroft, Box 2].

3. "Biography of Mary Jane Keeney": 2 [Bancroft, Box 2].

4. A good description of the Pullman Strike may be found in Ray Ginger, *The Bending Cross: A Biography of Eugene Victor Debs* (New Brunswick, NJ: Rutgers University Press, 1949), 108–183.

5. *Letters of Eugene V. Debs, V.1, 1874–1912*, Ed. J. Robert Constantine (Urbana: University of Illinois Press, 1990).

6. "The Making of a Radical": 16.

7. "The Biography of Mary Jane Keeney": 3 [Bancroft, Box 2].

8. Gilkey is listed as a board member in the Chicago Chapter in the League for Industrial Democracy according to Elizabeth Dilling's 1934 self-published *Red Network; Who's Who and Handbook of Radicalism for Patriots*, 185–187, which tarred many groups with the red brush, whether or not they deserved it. Frederick Vanderbilt Field, a Communist scion of the wealthy Vanderbilt family, was a member of the national board and Washington, D.C., friend of the Keeneys.

9. "The Making of a Radical": 17.

10. "The Biography of Mary Jane Keeney": 4 [Bancroft, Box 2].

11. "The Making of a Radical": 17. Unfortunately, she does not mention which periodicals they were.

12. "The Making of a Radical": 17.

13. Ibid.

14. Years later Mary Jane would experience considerable grief over this article when she was questioned about it during the course of her testimony before the House Committee on Un-American Activities. United States Congress. House Committee on Un-American Activities. "Testimony of Philip O. Keeney and Mary Jane Keeney and Statement Regarding Their Background." 81st Congress, 1st Session. May 24, 25, June 9, 1949: 262. According to Allen Weinstein in the introduction to *The Haunted Wood: Soviet Espionage in America—the Stalin Era* (New York: The Modern Library, 1999): xix, an autobiography was part of the process of becoming a spy. However, they were normally not published. It is not surprising that Mary Jane would deny being a member of the Communist Party, because anyone entering the underground spying apparatus avoided membership in the party.

15. "The Making of a Radical": 17.

16. Harvey Klehr, *The American Communist Movement: Storming Heaven Itself* (New York: Twayne, 1992), 25. Harvey A. Levenstein, *Communism, AntiCommunism and the CIO* (Westport, CT: Greenwood Press, 1981), 5.

17. Klehr, *The American Communist Movement*, 56.

18. Ibid.

19. "The Biography of Mary Jane Keeney": 4 [Bancroft, Box 2].

20. Interview of Melba Phillips and Ann Florant by Rosalee McReynolds, May 18, 1995, New York City.

21. William Stephens (Legare George), *Standard Forgings: Collected Poems 1919–1950* (Ann Arbor, MI: Ardis, 1978). Selden Rodman, ed. *A New Anthology of Modern Poetry* (New York: The Modern Library, 1936), 347–349.

22. According to her brief biography in the finding aid in the Iowa Women's Archive, it was Margaret Thomsen Raymond, whom Legare George married in Chicago in 1944, who edited and published his posthumous collection of poetry. See http://sdrc.lib.uiowa.edu/iwa/findingaids/html/RaymondMargaret.htm (accessed April 4, 2007).

23. The California Junior Republic continues to operate in Chino Hills. We are indebted to Max Scott, the current executive director, for providing information about Legare George.

24. Jack Holl, *Juvenile Reform in the Progressive Era; William R. George and the Junior Republic Movement* (Ithaca, NY: Cornell University Press, 1971), 31–32.

25. "Biographical Note" in William Stephens, *Standard Forgings: Collected Poems, 1919–1950* (Ann Arbor, MI: Ardis, 1974), 111.

26. "No song" in *Standard Forgings*, 65. The poem was written in 1928 and published by *Coronet* in 1940.

27. *Poetry Magazine* Papers, 1912–1936. [Box 8, folder 23], The University of Chicago Library, Department of Special Collections. The letter is signed with an indecipherable first name, along with the last name of George. The first name bears no resemblance to Mary Jane, but the handwriting is identical to hers.

28. Legare George, *Standard Forgings*, 111.

29. The AFL had traditionally represented skilled workers. The AFL and the CIO united in 1955. By that point, anti-Communists had gained the upper hand in the CIO.

CHAPTER 3—THE LIBRARIANS

1. Mary Jane Keeney, "The Making of a Radical," *Black & White* 1 (Sept. 1939): 18.

2. Theodore Draper, *American Communism and Soviet Russia* (New York: Viking Press, 1960), chapter 1.

3. The Workers Party was formed in 1922, the CPUSA in 1929.

4. In fact, when an individual or group opposed or encouraged U.S. entrance into World War II became a test of whether that person or group was Communist or at least a fellow traveler.

5. Harvey Klehr, *The American Communist Movement: Storming Heaven Itself* (New York: Twayne, 1992); Allen Weinstein and Alexander Vassiliev, *The Haunted Wood: Soviet Espionage in America—The Stalin Era* (New York: The Modern Library, 2000); John Earl Haynes and Harvey Klehr, *Venona: Decoding Soviet Espionage in America* (New Haven, CT: Yale University Press, 2000).

6. A sample of the many responses to the books produced by the researchers who used the Russian archives can be found in the following reviews: Guenter Lewy, "The Secret World of American Communism," *Society* 34 (Nov./Dec. 1996): 101–102; David Plotke, "The Secret World of American Communism," *Political Science Quarterly* 111 (Winter 1996/97): 730–732; Edward P. Johanningsmeier, "The Soviet World of American Communism," *The Historian* 62 (Winter 2000): 412; Athan G. Theoharis, "The Soviet World of American Communism," *American Political Science Review* 93 (June 1999): 489–490.

7. For the Venona cables themselves and the story of their decoding, see the National Security Agency Website: www.nsa.gov/venona/ (accessed April 5, 2007).

8. Albert May Todd in *Who Was Who in America*, 1 (Chicago: A.N. Marquis, 1943), 1243.

9. Todd joined and unjoined any number of organizations during his lifetime, as evidenced in entries within *Who's Who in America* from 1914 to 1929. Among other organizations, he belonged to the National Direct Legislation League, the National Municipal League, the National Child Labor Committee, and the Debs Memorial Radio Fund. Joseph S. Czestochowski, *The Legacy of Albert May Todd* (Kalamazoo, MI: Kalamazoo Historic Conservancy for the Preservation of Art, 2000).

10. Todd's and Gilkey's membership in the LID also offended Elizabeth Dilling, a career anti-Communist, who named them in her 1934 self-published book *Red Network; Who's Who and Handbook of Radicalism for Patriots*. At the time the book was published, Todd had been dead for three years.

11. "Biography of Mary Jane Keeney": 6 [Bancroft, Box 2].

12. Laurence Todd, *Correspondent on the Left: The Memoirs of Laurence Todd, 1882–1957* (Anchorage, AK: privately published, 1996).

13. Interview with Lucille Speer, retired Montana State University librarian, 1981 [Montana].

14. Philip Keeney, "Flexibility of Library Organization," *Library Journal 59* (April 1, 1934): 312–313; "Democratic Aids to Staff Responsibility," *Library Journal 59* (April 15, 1934): 361.

15. "The Making of a Radical": 18.

16. During the 1920s, some leftists refused to participate in what they considered to be a corrupt electoral process, but Philip's failure to vote can most likely be attributed to apathy.

17. "The Making of a Radical": 18.

18. Ibid., 19.

19. Jesse H. Shera to Joe W. Kraus, October 3, 1972, Charles Brown Papers, Iowa State University, Ames, Iowa, hereafter [Brown].

20. Alice I. Bryan, *The Public Librarian* (New York: Columbia University Press, 1948). See also "Gender Issues in Librarianship," *Encyclopedia of Library History*, edited by Wayne A. Wiegand and Donald G. Davis. Jr. (New York: Garland Publishing, 1994), 227–232.

21. According to a letter from Jesse Shera to Edith C. Lawrence, May 4, 1938, [Brown], Keeney did not receive a fellowship he wanted in part because he was never seriously considered, because Bishop had reported to Charles Brown, the arbiter of the fellowships, that Keeney's performance at Michigan had been poor.

22. Now called the University of Montana.

23. Sidney Mitchell to Charles Clapp, July 1, 1931 [Montana].

24. Mitchell to Clapp, July 1, 1931; Theodore Norton to Clapp, August 8, 1931; F.L.D. Goodrich to Clapp, August 10, 1931 [Montana].

25. Interview with Lucille Speer [Montana].

26. "Charges Made against Professor Keeney by President Simmons to Members of Investigating Committee of A.S.U. [American Student Union], Sat., May 15, 1937," apparently written by Philip [Bancroft, Box 2]; G. Finlay Simmons, interview with Helen Duncan, Library Secretary, September 15, 1939, authors' personal file, provided by George F. Simmons, son of G. Finlay Simmons.

27. "Reasons for Failure to Issue New Contract to Philip O. Keeney," unsigned and undated memo [Montana] mentions Keeney's delegating the teaching of classes while taking most of the salary for the job; "Academic Freedom and Tenure: Montana State University," *Bulletin of the American Association of University Professors* 24 (1938): 343–346.

28. [Mary Jane Keeney], "Interview with Civil Service Investigators, 810 18th St., N.W., Friday, Sept. 10, 1943, 1:00–4:30 p.m.," p. 2. This is not an official transcript, but rather Mary Jane's dramatization of the interview based on her memory [Bancroft, Box 2]. The FBI later refers to it as "satiric."

29. Ibid., p. 3.

30. "Biography of Mary Jane Keeney": 8–9 [Bancroft, Box 2].

31. "Charges Made against Professor Keeney by President Simmons to Members of Investigating Committee of A.S.U. [American Student Union], Sat., May 15, 1937," apparently written by Philip [Bancroft, Box 2].

32. "Biography of Mary Jane Keeney": 9 [Bancroft, Box 2].

33. "Charges Made against Professor Keeney . . . ," 1–2, recapitulates the items that appeared on President Clapp's memo, as does the AAUP report.

34. "Open Shelf" [list of books on Montana State Library Open Shelf], [Bancroft, Box 2].

35. George Finlay Simmons to Carl Moore, April 17, 1936 [Montana].

36. H. H. Swain to Philip O. Keeney, December 10, 1935 [Bancroft, Scrapbook].

37. Keeney to Montana State Board of Education, September 20, 1935 [Bancroft, Scrapbook].

38. In the opinion of legal scholar William W. Van Alstyne, the case that significantly broadened the right of teachers in public institutions to openly differ from their employers was *Pickering v. Board of Education of Township High School*, 399 U.S. 563 (1968). The U.S. Supreme Court found on behalf of a high school teacher who was fired after the local newspaper published his letter to the editor criticizing the local school board for its method of raising revenues. Van Alstyne, "Academic Freedom and the First Amendment," *Law and Contemporary Problems* 53 (Summer 1990): 94.

39. Stephenson Smith, "To the Members of the Montana State Board of Education" [n.d.] [Bancroft, Scrapbook].

40. H. H. Swain to Philip O. Keeney, December 10, 1935 [Bancroft, Scrapbook].

41. George Finlay Simmons, *Who Was Who in America*, 3 (Chicago: A.N. Marquis, 1960): 787.

42. *State of Montana ex rel Philip O. Keeney v. Roy Ayers et al* (1st Cir, 1938). Reprinted in Transcript of the Record on Appeal, 69, *W.S. Davidson et al v. State of Montana ex rel Philip O. Keeney*. From a facsimile copy in the Philip Olin Keeney Papers at the Bancroft Library.

43. Harry Clements and Charles McKinley, "Draft of a Report on the University of Montana Tenure Inquiry," 24 [AAUP].

44. Stephenson Smith to Simmons, December 20, 1935 [Bancroft, Scrapbook].

45. Simmons to Smith, February 22, 1936 [Bancroft, Scrapbook].

46. Ibid.

47. James R. Steele, "Hire Learning in Montana," *Pacific Weekly* (March 16, 1936): 131–132.

48. "'J. Ryan' of 'Progressive League' not Graduate," *Montana Kaiman* (April 10, 1936): 1:5; 4:5.

49. Clements and McKinley, "Draft of a Report," 3.

50. Simmons to Keeney, July 8, 1936 [Montana].

51. Resolution of the Montana Board of Education, April 14, 1936; this quotation is taken from an undated, handwritten copy of the resolution in the Montana archives; in a letter that Simmons wrote to Keeney two days later he refers to the resolution and informs Keeney that it was passed at the board's April 14, meeting (Simmons to Keeney, April 16, 1936). [Montana].

52. Ibid.

53. "Statement of Philip O. Keeney," I, 8 [Bancroft, Box 1].

54. Herbert R. Ranson to Keeney, January 14, 1937; Keeney to Ranson, January 16, 1937 [Bancroft, Scrapbook].

55. "Statement of Philip O. Keeney," I, 10 [Bancroft, Box 1].

56. Simmons to Keeney, April 6, 1937 [Montana]. The AFT representative was Hugh DeLacy, a 27-year-old teaching assistant at the University of Washington English Department, and a Communist organizer. See "Communism in Washington State: History and Memory Project" at http://faculty.washington. edu/gregoryj/cpproject/phipps.htm (accessed April 6, 2007). He was later a congressman and a Washington, D.C., social friend of the Keeneys.

57. Clements and McKinley, "Draft of a Report," 4.

58. "Dr. Simmons Is Given Contract for 3 Years," *Daily Missoulian* (14 April 1937).

59. Evelyn Geller, *Forbidden Books in American Public Libraries, 1876–1939: A Study in Cultural Change* (Westport, CT: Greenwood Press, 1984), xv. The relationship of the Keeney case with the development of ALA's intellectual freedom position is outlined in Louise S. Robbins, *Censorship and the American Library: The American Library Association's Response to Threats to Intellectual Freedom, 1939–1969* (Westport, CT: Greenwood Press, 1996), 12–13.

60. Carl Milam to Keeney, May 13, 1937 [Bancroft, Box 2].

61. Paul North Rice to Keeney, June 7, 1937 [Bancroft, Box 2].

62. Simmons to R. E. Himstead, May 17, 1937 [Montana]; Keeney knew that the letter to Himstead had been sent to Hazel Timmerman, staff to the Committee on Salaries, Staff and Service, and shared with the committee by way of a letter from Paul North Rice, July 13, 1937 [Bancroft, Box 2].

63. Milton Ferguson, "A Case for Careful Investigation," *Library Journal* 62 (15 June 1937): 512. Stephen Karetsky, in *Not Seeing Red: American Librarianship and the Soviet Union, 1917–1960* (Lanham, MD: University Press of America, 2002), alleges that ALA has always been too tolerant of Communism. In his editorial Ferguson reveals the suspicion of anything smacking of radicalism in U.S. librarianship that marked ALA leadership during most, if not all, of the period covered in Karetsky's book.

64. *Library Journal* had been the ALA official publication when the association was founded in 1876. The *Bulletin of the American Library Association*, now *American Libraries*, became the official organ of ALA in 1906.

65. Keeney to Milton Ferguson, June 25, 1937 [Bancroft, Box 2].

66. Ferguson to Keeney, July 21, 1937 [Bancroft, Box 2].

67. Bertine Weston to Keeney, September 22, 1937; Paul North Rice to Keeney, July 13, 1937 [Bancroft, Box 2].

68. Geller, *Forbidden Books*, 171.

69. Nathan Glazer, *The Social Basis of American Communism* (New York: Harcourt, Brace & World, 1961), 141.

70. Ibid., 225. The classic study to which Glazer refers is Alice I. Bryan, *The Public Librarian* (New York: Columbia University Press, 1948). It was one of several studies that made up the Public Library Inquiry.

71. ALA Executive Board Meeting, December 30, 1939. Board on Salaries, Staff and Tenure. (27/34/6), Box 1; Hazel B. Timmerman, chief of the ALA's personnel division, to Bertha Schuman, November 24, 1941 (27/34/6. SST Correspondence, 1941). Attached to the file draft copy of this letter (dated October 14)

is a note to Timmerman from Flora Ludington: "Is there any danger in being asked whether or not we requested funds for a tenure investigation?"

72. A copy of the memo is included in a letter from Amy Winslow to Hazel Timmerman, August 4, 1942 (ALA archives 27/34/6, Box 1).

73. Jesse H. Shera to Joe W. Kraus, October 3, 1972, personal file provided to authors by Mr. Kraus.

74. *The Keeney Case: Big Business, Higher Education, and Organized Labor, Report of an Investigation Made by the National Academic Freedom Committee of the American Federation of Teachers into the Causes of the Recent Dismissal of Professor Philip O. Keeney, Librarian, from Montana State University and the role Played by Certain Business and Political Interests in the Affairs of the University* (Chicago: American Federation of Teachers, 1939). The pamphlet lays out organized labor's perspective. Montana, a mining state, had a long and contentious labor history prior to the Keeney case, in particular in relation to the Anaconda Mining Company. It is highly likely that the labor unions had a good many Communists and fellow travelers, especially because Montana was home to a number of Eastern European ethnic groups and because the Mine, Mill, and Smelter Workers Union had the reputation of having a large number of Communists.

75. "Academic Freedom and Tenure: Montana State University," *Bulletin of the American Association of University Professors* 24 (1938): 343–346.

76. Record on Appeal, 15, *W.S. Davidson et al v. State of Montana ex rel Philip O. Keeney.* From a facsimile copy in the Philip Olin Keeney Papers [Bancroft].

77. Charles W. Hope to Simmons, August 10, 1937 [Montana].

78. "Charges Made against Professor Keeney . . . ," 1–2.

CHAPTER 4—STRUGGLE

1. Victor Wolfgang Von Hagen, *Ecuador the Unknown; Two and a Half Years' Travels in the Republic of Ecuador and Galápagos Islands* (New York: Oxford University Press, 1940).

2. FBI File of Philip Olin and Mary Jane Keeney, 101-467, Section 1-30, p. 7. [Hereafter cited as FBI File, #, page #.]

3. "Biography of Mary Jane Keeney": p. 13 [Bancroft, Box 2].

4. Wayne L. Morse to John Studebaker, October 20, 1937 [Bancroft, Box 2].

5. He was also elected to Congress in 1944 and associated with the Keeneys in Washington, D.C. According to James Gregory's "Toward a History of Communism in Washington State," http://faculty.washington.edu/gregoryj/cpproject/gregory.htm (accessed February 4, 2006), DeLacy was a Communist. The essay is part of *Communism in Washington State—History and Memory Project.* This site is one of the Pacific Northwest Labor History Projects directed by Prof. James Gregory and sponsored by the Harry Bridges Center for Labor Studies at the University of Washington.

6. DeLacy to Philip and Mary Jane Keeney [n.d.] [Bancroft, Box 2].

7. "Dismissal of Philip O. Keeney," *American Library Association Bulletin* 32 (October 15, 1938): 771.

8. FBI File 101-467, Section 1-8, p. 6; Section 1-30, p. 7. Wahl was formerly employed by the New York Public Library. In fact, notations in the Silvermaster file quote Mary Jane's diary as saying that David Wahl was trying to get the job of Librarian of Congress for Philip. FBI File 65-56402-2260, p. 114.

9. Silvermaster FBI File 65-56402-234, p. 4 [63].

10. FBI File 101-467, Section 1-30, p. 7.

11. FBI File 101-467, Section 1-30, p. 8.

12. Earl Latham, *The Communist Controversy in Washington* (Cambridge, MA: Harvard University Press, 1966), 95.

13. FBI File 101-467-187, p. 895.

14. John Earl Haynes and Harvey Klehr, *Venona: Decoding Soviet Espionage in America* (New Haven, CT: Yale University Press, 1999). The Keeneys were observed with Chevalier as late as January 5, 1941 in New York City. FBI File 101-467-187, p. 555.

15. Haynes and Klehr, *Venona*, 328.

16. Although it does not appear that the Keeneys were even acquainted with Oppenheimer, Mary Jane took a deep interest in his fall from grace. She kept an extensive clipping file on him, with the intention of writing about him. McReynolds' interview with Melba Philips and Ann Florant, May 18, 1995.

17. Mary Jane Keeney, "Farewell to Montana." Typescript, 3 [Bancroft, Box 2].

18. Ibid., p. 4.

19. Ibid.

20. Ibid.

21. G. Finlay Simmons to H. H. Swain, March 30, 1940 [Montana].

22. Swain to Simmons, April 2, 1940 [Montana].

23. Simmons to Keeney, April 1, 1940 [Montana].

CHAPTER 5—PROGRESSIVE LIBRARIANS' COUNCIL

1. Philip Keeney to Arnold Shukotoff, July 5, 1938 [Bancroft, Box 2].

2. *PLC Bulletin* 1, no. 1 (September 1939): 1.

3. Philip Keeney to Ralph Munn, June 30, 1939 [Bancroft, Box 2].

4. Schuman was also the membership chairman, or at least received the memberships. *PLC Bulletin* 1, no. 2 (October 1939): 5.

5. PLC's approval of MacLeish was voiced in its first issue, *PLC Bulletin* 1, no. 1 (September 1939): 3; See Louise Robbins, *Censorship and the American Library: The American Library Association Responds to Threats to Intellectual Freedom, 1939–1969* (Westport, CT: Greenwood, 1996), 10 for a brief summary of the event, which librarians took as a devaluing of the profession; see also Frederick Stielow, "Librarian Warriors and Rapprochement: Carl Milam, Archibald MacLeish, and World War II," *Libraries and Culture* 25 (Fall 1990): 513–533.

6. Peggy Sullivan, *Carl H. Milam and the American Library Association* (New York: H.W. Wilson, 1976), 172; Scott Donaldson, *Archibald MacLeish: An American Life* (Boston: Houghton Mifflin, 1992), 296; "Library, Librarian," *Time* (June 19, 1939); "Panned Poet," *Newsweek* (June 19, 1939).

7. Scott Donaldson, *Archibald MacLeish*, 154–156.

8. "F. D. Roosevelt to Felix Frankfurter, May 3, 1939." Reprinted in *American Libraries*, 79 (1995): 408.

9. Ibid.

10. Ibid.

11. Donaldson, *Archibald MacLeish*, 300.

12. Ibid., 24; 98.

13. Ibid., 36–38.

14. FBI File 101-467, Section 1-8, p. 3.

15. Application for Federal Employment, 11/19/45, in Philip Keeney, General Personnel Records, United States Office of Personnel Management. This file is a compilation of Philip's government employment records.

16. *PLC Bulletin* 2, no. 1 (August 1940): 1.

17. For a picture of the issues of most concern to the PLC, see Joe W. Kraus, "The Progressive Librarians' Council," *Library Journal* 97 (July 1972): 2351–2354.

18. "Report of the Committee on Racial Discrimination," typewritten (Chicago: 1936), ALA Archives. Quoted in Dennis Thomison, *A History of the American Library Association, 1876–1972* (Chicago: American Library Association, 1978), 132. As Thomison points out, holding conferences in northern cities was no guarantee of equal treatment for Blacks. In Chicago, they were denied the same accommodations available to Whites by the Palmer House and Drake Hotels.

19. *PLC Bulletin* 1, no. 4 (January 1940): 3.

20. "Where to Stay in Cincinnati," *ALA Bulletin* 34 (March 1940): 195.

21. *PLC Bulletin*, 2, no. 1 (August 1940): p. 1.

22. Sullivan, *Carl H. Milam and the American Library Association*, 135.

23. Protecting librarians from firings and other job discrimination is an area where the ALA has never made a firm commitment. In 1992, John N. Berry III, editor of *Library Journal*, suggested that "ALA is so dominated by library bosses that employment disputes are deemed 'none of ALA's business.'" *Library Journal* 117 (February 15, 1992): 100.

24. "The American Library Association Library's Bill of Rights," *American Library Association Bulletin* 33 (October 15, 1939): 60–61.

25. Attacks on *The Grapes of Wrath* were discussed in "Truth Goes Marching On," *PLC Bulletin* 1, no. 1 (September 1939): 4; for the development of ALA's intellectual freedom positions, see Robbins, *Censorship and the American Library*.

26. For ALA and World War II, see Patti Clayton Becker, *Books and Libraries in American Society during World War II: Weapons in the War of Ideas* (New York: Routledge, 2005).

27. *PLC Bulletin* 2, no. 1 (August 1940): 3. The telegram went on to say: "We believe that our grave unemployment problem will be solved by increasing opportunities for peaceful employment rather than by employing our people to produce materials which can mean only further destruction. We urge you,

therefore, to keep America out of war and to protect the cultural achievements and civil liberties of the American people by ending loans and credits to warring nations and by solving our domestic problems constructively."

28. Thomison, 143.

29. "Report for 1940–41," *PLC Bulletin* 3, no. 1 (August 1941): 5, shows 235 members in 1940, 114 new 1940–1941 members, but only 235 members in good standing in 1941.

30. "Biography of Mary Jane Keeney": 15 [Bancroft, Box 2].

31. Russell Munn to Joe Kraus, April 21, 1972 [Kraus File].

32. Archibald MacLeish, *The Irresponsibles* (New York: Duell, Sloan and Pearce, 1940). In this essay, MacLeish takes librarians and other intellectuals to task for failing to actively oppose fascism.

33. Fred Stielow, "Librarian Warriors and Rapprochement: Carl Milam, Archibald MacLeish, and World War II," *Libraries and Culture* 25 (1990): 521.

34. "Breakfast in Honor of Archibald MacLeish," *PLC Bulletin* 2, no. 1 (August 1940): 4.

35. Donaldson, *Archibald MacLeish,* relates the numerous insults hurled upon MacLeish by Ernest Hemingway, insults which MacLeish forgave almost to a fault.

36. *Library of Congress Newsletter* (Local 28, United Public Workers of America, CIO) 4, no. 8, (August 1941): 4.

37. "Editorials," *PLC Bulletin* 3, no. 1 (August 1941): 1.

38. "On the Role of the Librarian in the War," *PLC Bulletin* 3, no. 4 (March 1942): 1–2.

CHAPTER 6—THE SPIES AT HOME

1. Venona #1234, KGB New York to Moscow, August 29, 1944. Philip is also the subject of cable #325, May 17, 1942, and cable #726–729, May 22, 1942, and with the cover name "Cerberus" almost certainly the subject of cable #32, January 18, 1945. The NKVD was the forerunner of the KGB, the Soviet Secret Police. KGB will be used in this book. Almost all the decoded cables were sent to the KGB. Very few military intelligence, or GRU, cables were decoded, which may explain why so few dealt with the Keeneys, who apparently worked first or perhaps exclusively for the GRU. Proper names, especially cover names, were usually all caps in the Venona decrypts.

2. Sometimes spelled *Kournakoff* or *Kournakov*. *Sergey* is sometimes *Sergei*.

3. This educated guess is based on a number of factors: Wahl's recruitment of Keeney to work at the Library of Congress; his continued close contact with Keeney throughout his Washington government career; his later encouragement of Keeney to go to Japan; and his own identification by Elizabeth Bentley as one of the people who provided information to the Nathan Gregory Silvermaster group. Indeed Wahl, not Mary Jane Keeney, was the contact person Keeney listed when he went to Japan. To add weight to this evidence, handwritten archival KGB materials covering the 1930s to the 1950s contain an unidentified source, cover name Pink, who is described as working for the Bureau of Economic Warfare/

Foreign Economic Administration during the war and after the war for the American Jewish Conference and Americans for Haganah, which matches Wahl's career path. Thanks to email communication of July 26, 2007, to Louise Robbins from John Early Haynes, who with Harvey Klehr was in the midst of this archival translation in 2007–2008.

4. Following the indictment involving World Tourists, Golos opened a second business, United States Service and Shipping. See Haynes and Klehr, *Venona: Decoding Soviet Espionage in America*, 93–97. The life of Jacob Golos and his relationship with Bentley is described in Bentley's own autobiography, *Out of Bondage: The Story of Elizabeth Bentley* (New York: Devin-Adair, 1951) and discussed in Lauren Kessler, *Clever Girl: Elizabeth Bentley, the Spy Who Ushered in the McCarthy Era* (New York: HarperCollins, 2003), 61–65; See also Allen Weinstein and Alexander Vassiliev, *The Haunted Wood: Soviet Espionage in America—the Stalin Era* (New York: Modern Library, 2000); Kathryn S. Olmsted, *Red Spy Queen: A Biography of Elizabeth Bentley* (Chapel Hill: University of North Carolina Press, 2002).

5. Sergei Kournakoff [Sergey Kurnakov], *Savage Squadrons* (Boston: Hale, Cushman & Flint, 1935).

6. Pavel Sudoplatov, *Special Tasks: The Memoirs of an Unwanted Witness—A Soviet Spymaster* (Boston: Little Brown, 1994).

7. See Haynes and Klehr, *Venona*, 225–226; *Venona Historical Monograph #3: The 1944–45 New York and Washington—Moscow KGB Messages* found at www.theblackvault.com/documents/nsa/venona/monographs/monograph-3.html (accessed July 28, 2008); The conflict is also discussed in Kessler, *Clever Girl;* Weinstein and Vassiliev, 85–94.

8. Igor Gouzenko also defected in Canada at about this same time.

9. Venona Cable #1469, October 17, 1944; Information about areas on which Mary Jane Keeney did research and editing can be found in her personnel file, released from the United States Office of Personnel Management, St. Louis Area Office, November 1988.

10. FBI File 101-467-178, p. 53.

11. I have had little luck finding information about George Faxon, except that he was a teacher at the Boston Latin School who was asked to answer whether he had ever been a Communist before the Senate Internal Security Subcommittee in early 1953 according to "The Witnesses (Cont'd)," *Time* (April 6, 1953), Time Archive www.time.com/time/magazine/article/0,9171,818137,00.html?promoid=googlep (accessed January 21, 2008).

12. FBI File 101-467-187, p. 356. The FBI got their information from patterns in Mary Jane's diary, which they secured from a "confidential informant," an FBI euphemism for an illegal break-in of their apartment or "black bag job."

13. Venona #39, January 18, 1945. The cable identifies Cerberus as working in Peak's office at that time. Peak was Frank Coe, assistant administrator of the Foreign Economic Administration, where Keeney worked. In newly translated documents, Cerberus and his wife are characterized as ex-GRU agents in touch with the KGB. They are the only known people who fit these varied criteria.

14. Robin Winks, *Cloak and Gown: Scholars in the Secret War, 1939–1961* (New York: William Morrow, 1987), 336. Winks's book describes in detail the relationship between Yale and the American Intelligence service.

15. According to John Earl Haynes, "Espionage agencies, for very good reasons, find that sources in positions such as that of a librarian or other record/file keeper for a target organization are in an excellent position to get access to documents and are often treated as a second priority by institutional counter-intelligence staff because of their 'support' rather than 'line role.'" Personal communication with Louise S. Robbins, October 11, 2006.

16. The OSS employees listed by Haynes and Klehr include the following whom the authors refer to as "KGB assets": Horst Baerensprung (OSS consultant on Germany), Jane Foster (OSS Far Eastern and Indonesian section), Maurice Halperin (chief of the Latin American Division of OSS Research and Analysis), Hans Hirschfeld (OSS consultant on Germany), Bella Joseph (motion picture section of OSS), Julius Joseph (OSS Far Eastern section), Duncan Lee (counsel to General Donovan and the OSS's Japanese intelligence section), Helen Tenney (OSS Spanish section), Donald Wheeler (OSS Research and Analysis). GRU "assets" included Thomas Babin (OSS section working with Yugoslav resistance), Philip Keeney (OSS librarian), and Leonard Mins (Russian section of OSS Research and Analysis). They might also have listed Samuel Bloomfield (Eastern European Section) (See Venona cable #726–729).

17. Jesse Shera to Joe W. Kraus, October 3, 1972, Kraus file in possession of the authors.

18. Ibid.

19. "Recommendation to the Personnel Officer," September 22, 1943; "Application for Federal Employment," November 19, 1945; In Philip O. Keeney's government personnel file, released from the U.S. Office of Personnel Management, St. Louis Area Office, November 1988.

20. Mary Jane Keeney's government personnel file, released from the U.S. Office of Personnel Management, St. Louis Area Office, November 1988.

21. Mario P. Canaipi to U.S. Civil Service Commission, August 18, 1945. In Mary Jane Keeney's government personnel file.

22. Mark Riebling, *Wedge: The Secret War between the FBI and CIA* (New York: Alfred A. Knopf, 1994), 29; Phillip Jaffe, *The Amerasia Case from 1945 to the Present* (New York: Philip J. Jaffe, 1979), 21–23.

23. For an account of the Smith Act trials see Michael R. Belknap, *Cold War Political Justice: The Smith Act, the Communist Party, and American Civil Liberties* (Westport, CT: Greenwood Press, 1977).

24. Paul Buhle and Dan Georgakas, "Communist Party, USA" in *Encyclopedia of the American Left*, p. 151; Irving Howe and Lewis Coser, *The American Communist Party: A Critical History (1919–1957)* (Boston: Beacon Press, 1957), 328.

25. Howe and Coser, 424.

26. Selma R. Williams, *Red-Listed: Haunted by the Washington Witch Hunt* (Reading, MA: Addison-Wesley, 1993), 212.

27. Ibid., 214–215.

28. Ibid., 209–210. It should be noted that Wilkerson was a Communist.

29. Angus McDonald to Gene [last name unknown], November 15, 1942, Keeney file [Bancroft, Box 2].

30. The Bookshop was ultimately listed as a subversive organization, and anyone who had frequented the shop, no matter what his politics, was likely to be suspect.

31. FBI File 101-467, Section 1, p. 8.

32. FBI File 101-467, Section 1-8, p. 3.

33. Ibid., p. 1.

34. FBI File 101-467, Section 1-8, p. 6; Silvermaster FBI File 65-56402-367, p. 3.

35. FBI File 101-467, Section 1-8, p. 5; FBI File 65-56402-367, p. 3; there is nothing to indicate that Shera was among those interviewed.

36. FBI File 101-467, Section 1-8, pp. 8-10.

37. Ibid.

38. Verner W. Clapp to Philip O. Keeney, December 7, 1942 [Bancroft, Box 2].

39. FBI File 101-467, Section 1-30, p. 20.

40. "Interview with Civil Service Investigators, 810 18th St., N.W., Friday, Sept. 10, 1943. 1:00–4:30 P.M." Keeney File [Bancroft, Box 2].

41. Ibid.

42. FBI File 101-467-187, pp. 357–360.

43. It is worth noting, but perhaps of no consequence, that Philip applied for a job in the Department of Agriculture in 1938 when he was living in Berkeley and awaiting the outcome of the Montana case. His efforts to get the job were unsuccessful for the simple reason that his civil service scores were not high enough.

44. Elizabeth Bentley became an FBI informant, but many of her stories were disbelieved until the release of the Venona files. The FBI learned of the Keeneys in several ways, but one way was by their surveillance of the Silvermasters.

45. Mrs. Wheeler (George or Donald), Silvermaster File 65-56402-673, p. 97.

46. Harvey Klehr, "The Strange Case of Roosevelt's 'Secret Agent': Frauds Fools, & Fantasies," *Encounter* 59, no. 6 (Dec. 1982): 84–91.

47. *Investigation of Un-American Propaganda Activities in the United States. Report of the Special Committee on Un-American Activities House of Representatives. Seventy-Eighth Congress, Second Session on H. Res. 282 to Investigate (1) the Extent, Character, and Objects of Un-American Propaganda Activities in the United States, (2) the Diffusion within the United States of Subversive and Un-American Propaganda that is Instigated from Foreign Countries or of a Domestic Origin and Attacks the Principle of the form of Government as Guaranteed by our Constitution, and (3) All Other Questions in Relation thereto That Would Aid Congress in Any Necessary Remedial Legislation* (Washington, D.C.: Government Printing Office, 1944), 651–652.

48. Harvey Klehr, "The Strange Case of Roosevelt's 'Secret Agent'," 84–91.

49. FBI File 101-467, Section 1-30, pp. 20 and 21.

50. Dennis Thomison, *A History of the American Library Association, 1876–1972* (Chicago: American Library Association, 1978), 161.

51. FBI File 101-467-187, p. 356.

52. FBI File 101-467, Section 1-30, p. 22.

53. Quoted in Klehr, "The Strange Case of Roosevelt's 'Secret Agent'," 88.

54. Ibid., 87.

55. Quoted in James G. Ryan, *Earl Browder: The Failure of American Communism* (Tuscaloosa: The University of Alabama Press, 1997), 215. One can only assume that Green's quotation from Browder was not exact since Ryan interviewed Green in 1992, some fifty years after the conversation.

56. Ryan, 246–253.

57. FBI File 101-467-187, p. 352.

58. Ryan, 263.

59. Guenter Lewy, *The Cause that Failed: Communism in American Political Life* (New York: Oxford University Press, 1990), 307–308. Lewy lists projected Party membership statistics from 1919 to 1998.

CHAPTER 7—THE SPIES ABROAD

1. J. H. Hildring to Bowen Smith, 14 November 1945 [Bancroft, Box 2].

2. FBI File 101-467-187, p. 220; Silvermaster FBI File 65-56402-1655, pp. 5, 13; see also Mary Jane and Philip O. Keeney's personnel files.

3. FBI File 101-467-187, p. 116.

4. FBI File 65-56402, Section 2a, p. 45.

5. Harvey Klehr and Ronald Radosh, *The Amerasia Spy Case: Prelude to McCarthyism* (Chapel Hill: University of North Carolina Press, 1996), 71. Bernstein was apparently charged to help fill that gap.

6. FBI File 101-467-30, Section 1, p. 23.

7. Ibid., pp. 23–24.

8. FBI File 101-467-187, p. 351.

9. Ibid., p. 109.

10. James W. Angell to Mary Jane Keeney, June 1, 1946 [Bancroft, Box 2].

11. FBI File 101-467-187, p. 353.

12. FBI File 101-467-30, Section 1, p. 36.

13. Ibid.

14. FBI File 101-467-187, p. 354.

15. Ibid., p. 411.

16. FBI File 65-56402-1655, pp. 48–54.

17. FBI File 101-467-178, p. 587.

18. FBI File 101-467-187, pp. 223–224. It is likely that Kurnakov's recall to the USSR was occasioned by the defection of Bentley. The Soviets would have moved to try to protect their assets. The cause of Kurnakov's death is not known, but apparently he died of natural causes.

19. FBI File 101-467-187, pp. 388, 453–456.

20. Ibid., p. 149.

21. Ibid., p. 486.

22. Ibid., pp. 487–488. Of course, it is not a foregone conclusion that the FBI secured the contents of the letter from the person entrusted with the delivery.

It might well have been copied without that person's knowledge while in transit or later during a break-in at Keeney's Tokyo residence or office.

23. FBI File 101-467-30, p. 26.

24. Mark T. Orr, personal communication with Rosalee McReynolds, July 6, 1989, file in possession of Louise Robbins.

25. Copies of several reports summarizing Keeney's findings, mainly from April 1946, just a few months into his stint, are found in the Keeney file [Bancroft].

26. Akira Nemoto, Taro Miura, Yuriko Nakamura, and Takashi Noga, "Library Policies of the Civil Information and Education Division, GHQ/SCAP in Japan, 1945–1952; an Analysis of the Policy Statements," *Bulletin of the School of Education, University of Tokyo* (1999): 459–461, 473–474.

27. There are several sources for this information. Among the most interesting are the letters of thanks written by the Japanese librarians and the letter of commendation written by Mark T. Orr, Chief, Education Division, CIE, to Keeney on April 29, 1947, several days after Keeney was separated from the CIE [Bancroft, Box 2]. See also Yuriko Nakamura, Taro Miura, and Akira Nemoto, "American Library Officers in the Occupied Japan," unpublished paper presented at the American Library Association conference, July 9, 2000.

28. According to medical records dated May 1946 in his personnel file, Keeney's loneliness must have led him to seek sex with an unknown person, as he presented to medical personnel with "penile lesions" and reported that he had had sex ten days before. The doctor concluded that the lesions were "venereal." Personnel File of Philip O. Keeney.

29. FBI File 65-56402-2477, pp. 57–58.

30. The Technical Surveillance Logs pertaining to the Keeneys all appear to be pulled from the Silvermaster FBI File 65-56402-1. They are numbered in the Keeney File as part of 101-467-187, consecutively paged. The invitation to Thanksgiving dinner is in 65-56402-1-988, p. 1128. Stanley Graze is identified by "Alexander Vassiliev's Notes on Anatoly Gorsky's December 1948 Memo on Compromised American Sources and Networks (Annotated)." Annotated by John Earl Haynes, Translated by Ronald Bachman and Harold Leich, assisted by John Earl Haynes, Additional assistance provided by Alexander Vassiliev. Revised October 2005. www.johnearlhaynes.org/page44.html#_ftnref46 (accessed March 2, 2008).

31. FBI File 65-56402-1-988, p. 1127. Klehr and Radosh, *The Amerasia Spy Case: Prelude to McCarthyism* (Chapel Hill: University of North Carolina Press, 1996), 84–86.

32. FBI File 65-56402-1920, pp. 4–6, 12–13.

33. "The Metropolitan Broadcasting Corp—The Report Which Was Never Released." Extension of Remarks by Hon. Joseph R. McCarthy of Wisconsin, September 23, 1950. *Congressional Record* October 20, 1950. Mary Jane Keeney placed a written statement about the report in her "Persecution of Philip and Mary Jane Keeney" file [Bancroft, Box 2].

34. Ibid.

35. Technical Surveillance Log FBI File 65-56402-1-1164; FBI File 101-467-187, p. 1166.

36. "The Metropolitan Broadcasting Corp—The Report Which Was Never Released." Mary Jane Keeney placed a written statement about the report in her "Persecution of Philip and Mary Jane Keeney" file [Bancroft, Box 2].

37. Technical Surveillance Log FBI File 65-56402-1-1131, FBI File 101-467-187, p. 1170.

38. FBI File 65-56402-2601, p. 32.

39. Ibid., p. 33.

40. R. B. Shipley to Mary Jane Keeney, April 1, 1947 [Bancroft, Box 2] and also FBI File 65-56402-2601, p. 34.

41. FBI File 65-56402-2601, p. 35.

42. Ibid., p. 45.

43. Hamillton Robinson to Honorable James E. Murray, May 5, 1947 [Bancroft, Box 2].

44. Ibid.

45. FBI File 65-56402-2601, p. 47.

46. Mark T. Orr, Comments Concerning Philip O. Keeney, file in possession of Louise Robbins.

47. Toshie Eto, director-in-chief, Japan Library Association, to Philip O. Keeney, April 28, 1947 [Bancroft, Box 2].

48. FBI File 101-467-187, p. 1418; Technical Surveillance Log FBI File 65-56402-1-1659.

49. Mark T. Orr to Philip O. Keeney, April 29, 1947 [Bancroft, Box 2].

50. Howard M. Bell, Helen Heffernan, Louis O. Moss, Kenneth M. Harkness, and Franklin B. Judson to To Whom It May Concern, May 5, 1947 [Bancroft, Box 2].

CHAPTER 8—CAUGHT IN THE WEB

1. Elizabeth Bentley, *Out of Bondage: The Story of Elizabeth Bentley* (New York: Devin-Adair, 1951); Lauren Kessler, *Clever Girl: Elizabeth Bentley, the Spy Who Ushered in the McCarthy Era* (New York: HarperCollins, 2003); Kathryn S. Olmsted, *Red Spy Queen: A Biography of Elizabeth Bentley* (Chapel Hill: University of North Carolina Press, 2002).

2. Bentley, *Out of Bondage*, 64; Kessler, *Clever Girl*, 53.

3. Haynes and Klehr, *Venona*, 95.

4. Ibid., 85, 97; Bentley, *Out of Bondage*, 102.

5. Haynes and Klehr, *Venona*, 96–97.

6. Kessler, *Clever Girl*, 76.

7. Bentley, *Out of Bondage*, 102.

8. Kessler, *Clever Girl*, 85–88.

9. FBI File 101-467-178, p. 53.

10. FBI File 65-56402-367, p. 50.

11. FBI File 101-467-187, pp. 487–488.

12. Gabriel Péri was "the former editor of 'L'Humanite' newspaper, Communist organ in Paris. He was executed by shooting at Mont-Val Erien, on December

15, 1941, presumably by the Germans," according to FBI File 101-467-187, p. 360; also p. 486.

13. Harvey Klehr and Ronald Radosh, *The Amerasia Spy Case: Prelude to McCarthyism* (Chapel Hill: University of North Carolina Press, 1996), 9.

14. Ibid., 64–68. A grand jury refused to indict Service based on the evidence it had, but Service was subject to numerous loyalty investigations and his career in the State Department was ended. He ultimately won reinstatement after a suit but resigned when it became clear he would not have any significant work to do.

15. Klehr and Radosh, *The Amerasia Spy Case.*

16. FBI File 101-467-187, pp. 360, 361.

17. Ibid., pp. 68–71.

18. "Exhibit II, C, 1, The Political Persecution of Philip O and Mary Jane Keeney" [Bancroft, Box 2].

19. FBI Technical Surveillance Logs, Silvermaster File 65-56402-1, various locations; or 101-467-187, pp. 1101–1467 various locations.

20. FBI Technical Surveillance Logs, Silvermaster File 65-56402-1, or 101-467-187, pp. 1188–1189, 1193–1195, 1198. The request had been made by a friend, Louise Rosskam, who knew the Muñoz Marins in Puerto Rico, where her husband was working with the government.

21. FBI Technical Surveillance Logs, Silvermaster File 65-56402-1, or 101-467-187, pp. 1188–1189, 1193. Daniel Melcher was moving to New York to rejoin his family's publishing firm, Bowker, after being dismissed as the first director of the National Committee on Atomic Information. The Melcher and Bowker names are legendary in librarianship and publishing. Daniel Melcher was instrumental in the U.S. adoption of the International Standard Book Number (ISBN) and launched *Books in Print*, an annual listing of books by title and author, according to the *Supplement to the Dictionary of American Library Biography*, ed. Wayne A. Wiegand (Englewood, CO: Libraries Unlimited, 1990), 75–78. His father, Frederic, established the Newbery and Caldecott Awards, and Daniel continued the funding after his father died.

22. FBI File 65-56402-2326, p. 84.

23. FBI File 101-467-187, pp. 639 and 654.

24. There are a good many books on the loyalty program. See Eleanor Bontecou, *The Federal Loyalty-Security Program* (Ithaca, NY: Cornell University Press, 1953); for Truman's motives see David McCullough, *Truman* (New York: Simon & Schuster, 1992), 551–553, as well as Athan Theoharis, *Seeds of Repression: Harry S. Truman and the Origins of McCarthyism* (Chicago: Quadrangle Books, 1971) and Richard M. Freeland, *The Truman Doctrine and the Origins of McCarthyism: Foreign Policy, Domestic Politics, and Internal Security* (New York: Knopf, 1972).

25. Bontecou, 275–281.

26. Lewis Wood, "Ninety Groups, Schools Named on U.S. List as Being Disloyal," *New York Times* (December 5, 1947).

27. FBI File 65-56402-1-1454; FBI File 65-56402-2242, pp. 1, 2. The internal memo even tells us that Mary Jane received the letter on April 3, 1947.

28. R. B. Shipley to Mary Jane Keeney, April 1, 1947 [Bancroft, Box 2] and also FBI File 65-56402-2601, p. 34; Hamillton Robinson to Honorable James E. Murray, May 5, 1947 [Bancroft, Box 2]; Memorandum: Denial of Passport to Mrs. Mary Jane Keeney to join her husband in Japan, April 10, 1947 [Bancroft, Box 2]. All of these men were close colleagues of the Keeneys, and all were and are suspected of espionage.

29. Mary Jane was hospitalized in May 1947, apparently for a severe case of the flu, but she also suffered from chronic sinusitis and other ailments; FBI File 101-467-187, p. 1397.

30. Kessler, *Clever Girl*, pp. 152–155. There is more on the grand jury in chapter 9. Of course, there probably were specific questions about the Keeneys, since they emerged from the Bentley case through Silvermaster.

31. FBI File 101-467-187, p. 1408.

32. Ibid., p. 1419.

33. Notice of Separation to Philip O. Keeney from E. M. Conner, April 24, 1947 [Bancroft, Box 2].

34. FBI File 101-467-178, p. 587.

35. FBI File 101-467-187, p. 1427. Technical Surveillance Log. (These logs tend to have multiple paginations, making them confusing to identify. All the omitted pages on either side of this page have Keeney file numbers. In some cases the logs themselves, titled "HT Summary" have Silvermaster file numbers. This one labeled 65-56402-1-1678.)

36. FBI File 101-467-187, pp. 1429, 1435, 1438 (Technical Surveillance Log).

37. Ibid., p. 1439 (Technical Surveillance Log).

38. Ibid., pp. 1446, 1452 (Technical Surveillance Log).

39. Ibid., p. 1439 (Technical Surveillance Log).

40. Ibid., p. 1452 (Technical Surveillance Log). The McCarran Rider was the focus of the suit of John Stewart Service of *Amerasia* fame, who succeeded in having his firing declared invalid because the McCarran Rider was used instead of the regulations that bound the Secretary. *Service v. Dulles*, 354 U.S. 363 (1957).

41. FBI File 101-467-187, p. 1441.

CHAPTER 9—THE UN-AMERICANS

1. KGB archives File 35112, Vol. 9, p. 145 as cited in Allen Weinstein and Alexander Vassiliev, *The Haunted Wood: Soviet Espionage in America—the Stalin Era* (New York: Modern Library, 2000), 17; Kessler, *Clever Girl*, 140.

2. According to FBI File 65-56402-1862, twenty-seven government employees had been named by Bentley, but fifteen had left the government by October 1946; however, one additional federal employee suspect developed through the case was still in government service in October—presumably Philip Keeney. The conditions for being charged for spying as cited in Kessler, p. 141. See also the Espionage Act of 1917, www.staff.uiuc.edu/~rcunning/espact.htm (accessed June 11, 2008).

3. Kessler, *Clever Girl*, 141; FBI File 101-467-187, pp. 360, 361.

4. Kessler, 138–143.

5. VENONA Chronology, National Security Agency Website, www.nsa.gov/venona/venon00127.cfm (accessed June 11, 2008).

6. Kessler, *Clever Girl*, 144–147; for more on Venona, see John Earl Haynes and Harvey Klehr, *Venona: Decoding Soviet Espionage in America* (New Haven, CT: Yale Nota Bene, 2000).

7. Kessler, 152–155.

8. Bureau of Labor Statistics, CPI Inflation Calculator, www.bls.gov/ (accessed and calculated on June 11, 2008).

9. FBI File 101-467-268, p. 27.

10. Grigory to Center, August 19, 1948, KGB file 43173 v. 4, p. 369, Alexander Vassiliev, *Black Notebook [2007 Translation into English]*, trans. Philip Redko (1993–96), 71. Thanks to John Earl Haynes and Alexander Vassiliev for sharing this translation prior to the publication of *Spies: The Rise and Fall of the KGB in America* (forthcoming 2009).

11. "The Political Persecution of Philip O. and Mary Jane Keeney. Note on the Organization of the Material in this File" [Bancroft, Box 2], 5.

12. FBI File 101-467-99, p. 1.

13. "Testimony of Philip O. Keeney and Mary Jane Keeney and Statement Regarding Their Backgrounds." Hearings before the Committee on Un-American Activities. House of Representatives. 81st Congress, 1st Session, May 24, 25; June 9, 1949 (Washington, D.C.: Government Printing Office, 1949), 246.

14. "Testimony of Philip O. Keeney and Mary Jane Keeney . . . ," 246–250; FBI File 101-467-114, pp. 2–3.

15. Thomas and Marcia Mitchell, *The Spy Who Seduced America: Lies and Betrayal in the Heat of the Cold War—The Judith Coplon Story* (Montpelier, VT: Invisible Cities Press, 2002), 104 and various pages. According to the Mitchells entire files were read in court.

16. As cited in Mitchell, 105.

17. The HUAC "Statement Regarding Background of Mary Jane and Philip O. Keeney" in "Testimony of Philip O. Keeney and Mary Jane Keeney . . . ," 221–225, draws heavily on material found in the Keeneys' or in Bernstein's FBI file and is cited as coming from various locations in *U.S.A. v. Judith Coplon*.

18. "Testimony of Philip O. Keeney and Mary Jane Keeney . . . ," 246–250; Thomas and Marcia Mitchell, *The Spy Who Seduced America*, various pages; FBI File 101-467-114.

19. "Testimony of Philip O. Keeney and Mary Jane Keeney . . . ," 262.

20. Ibid., 264.

21. "The Political Persecution of Philip O. and Mary Jane Keeney. Note on the Organization of the Material in this File" [Bancroft, Box 2], 6.

22. "Testimony of Philip O. Keeney and Mary Jane Keeney . . . ," 272.

23. "Testimony," 224–225, includes the statement "With further reference to Mrs. Keeney's Communist activities, the following FBI report was introduced as evidence in the trial of the *U.S.A. v. Judith Coplon*, volume XXXI, pages 5649, 5650, and 5651," followed by a recounting of Mary Jane's delivery of the Péri "will" to Bernstein, and his presentation of it to Trachtenberg. Because this

material appears only in the "Statement Regarding Background of Mary Jane and Philip O. Keeney," published at the head of the hearing transcript, the Keeneys would not have heard the summary allegation in the HUAC statement that Mary Jane had "placed herself in the category of a courier for the Community Party."

24. FBI File 101-467-158, p. 33; "U.N. Aide Accused as a Red Courier," *New York Times*, July 26, 1949.

25. "U.N. Staff Scores 'Spy' Accusations," *New York Times* (July 26, 1949).

26. Alexander Trachtenberg, "Letters to the Times," *New York Times* (August 3, 1949).

27. "The Political Persecution of Philip O. and Mary Jane Keeney. Note on the Organization of the Material in this File" [Bancroft, Box 2], p. 7.

28. "The Political Persecution . . . ," p. 7; Joseph R. McCarthy, "Communists in the State Department," *The Annals of America: 1950*, 19.

29. "The Metropolitan Broadcasting Corp.—The Report Which Was Never Released," *Congressional Record*, October 20, 1950: A7679–A7690.

30. "The Political Persecution of Philip O. and Mary Jane Keeney. Note on the Organization of the Material in this File" [Bancroft, Box 2], 8. Because there is no material in this chronology concerning the conduct of the appeal or its outcome, and because the heading for the last part of the chronology is headed "Fourth and so far successful attempt to get MJK out of the Secretariat, 28 December, 1950," one can assume that the chronology was written after the suspension, but before the appeal.

31. Walter Sullivan, "U.N. Staff's Charges of Bias in Ousters Get Final Hearing," *New York Times* (July 29, 1951); "Ousted U.N. Aides begin Final Fight," *New York Times* (August 7, 1951).

32. "Ousters Revoked by U.N. Tribunal," *New York Times* (September 5, 1951).

33. "New U.N. Hearing Asked," *New York Times* (September 27, 1951); "2 Win Damages from U.N.," *New York Times* (November 14, 1951). Alper lost his job because his four-year contract was up and his firing was deemed a non-renewal.

34. Committee on Un-American Activities, U.S. House of Representatives, *The Shameful Years: Thirty Years of Soviet Espionage in the United States* (Washington, D.C.: GPO, December 30, 1951). Coplon trial transcripts are also cited here.

35. FBI File 101-467-178, p. 32.

36. Carl Marzani was convicted of defrauding the government for failure to acknowledge his previous membership in the Communist Party and for denying under oath that he had ever been called Tony Whales. He served nearly three years in federal prison. His wife, Edith, was employed by the Keeneys. Leon Josephson was convicted of contempt of Congress for refusing to be sworn in to testify before HUAC. Lucy Josephson also worked for the Keeneys.

37. FBI File, 101-467-167, p. 16.

38. FBI File 101-467-132, p. 5.

39. Its official name was the Special Subcommittee to Investigate the Administration of the Internal Security Act and Other Internal Security Laws, and it

was authorized in 1950 to keep tabs on the implementation of the Internal Security Act, or the McCarran Act, according to the Guide to the Records of the U.S. Senate at the National Archives www.archives.gov/legislative/guide/senate/chapter-13-judiciary-1947–1968.html#SISS (accessed July 18, 2008). The investigation of the Institute of Pacific Relations was the first major investigation initiated by the subcommittee.

40. Klehr and Radosh, *The Amerasia Spy Case*; FBI File 100-6470-50, the Institute of Pacific Relations, www.education-research.org/PDFs/IPR02.pdf (accessed July 18, 2008).

41. Institute of Pacific Relations. Hearings. 82nd Congress, 1st Session (Washington, D.C.: G.P.O., 1952): 2789; For information on the Truman Loyalty Program see Eleanor Bontecou, *The Federal Loyalty-Security Program* (Ithaca, NY: Cornell University Press, 1953); Lewis Wood, "Ninety Groups, Schools Named on U.S. List as Being Disloyal," *New York Times* (December 5, 1947).

42. Institute of Pacific Relations. Hearings, 2773–2779.

43. Ibid., 2789–2794.

44. William S. White, "Mrs. Keeney Faces a Contempt Action," *New York Times* (February 26, 1952), 15.

45. Paul Shafer, Statement issued February 25, 1952, found in Keeney file [Bancroft, Box 2]. For more on attitudes toward the United Nations, see for example, Paul Boyer, *When Time Shall Be No More* (Cambridge, MA: Harvard Belknap, 1992).

46. FBI File 101-467-193, p. 41; "U.S. to Test Rules of United Nations," *New York Times* (March 18, 1952).

47. Richard H. Parke, "U.N. Editorial Aide Admits Red Links," *New York Times* (October 25, 1952); FBI File 101-467-193, p. 41.

48. "Contempt Trial Ordered," *New York Times* (November 7, 1952); "11 in U.N. Accused of Communist Ties," *New York Times* (January 2, 1953).

49. "Ex-Aide of U.S. and U.N. Found Guilty of Contempt," *New York Times* (March 18, 1953); FBI File 101-467-205, p. 3. The file cites a number of articles on the case.

50. FBI File 101-467-205, p. 3; "Mrs. Keeney Fined; Answers Job Query," *New York Times* (March 21, 1953). Other newspapers also carried the story.

51. "U.N. Ex-aide Wins Contempt Appeal," *New York Times* (August 27, 1954).

52. "U.N. Aide on Trial Again," *New York Times* (April 1, 1955).

53. "Mrs. Keeney Freed in Contempt Trial," *New York Times* (April 5, 1955).

54. FBI File 101-467-167, p. 7.

55. FBI File 107-467-205, pp. 14–16, 25.

56. FBI File 107-467-223, p. 10.

57. FBI File 101-467-249, p. 2.

58. FBI File 101-467-253, p. 1.

59. "In Memoriam, Philip Olin Keeney ('Angus')," Keeney papers [Bancroft, Box 2].

60. Ibid.

61. FBI File 101-467-269, p. 1.

62. Ibid., p. 1.

63. FBI File 101-467-275, p. 1; 101-467-284, p. 6.

64. Last will and testament of Mary Jane Keeney, Surrogate court, New York City, Sept. 23, 1965; codicil April 14, 1968. The second book was Herbert Steinhouse's *The Time of the Juggernaut* (New York: William Morrow, 1958).

CHAPTER 10—GUILT AND ASSOCIATION

1. Grigory to Center, August 19, 1948, KGB file 43173 v. 4, p. 371, Alexander Vassiliev, *Black Notebook [2007 Translation into English]*, trans. Philip Redko (1993–96), p. 71. Thanks to John Earl Haynes and Alexander Vassiliev for sharing this translation prior to the publication of *Spies: The Rise and Fall of the KGB in America* (forthcoming 2009).

2. Haynes and Klehr, *Venona*, 178.

3. "Statement concerning loyalty cases in which the name of MJK has been mentioned," January 14, 1951, Keeney File [Bancroft, Box 2].

4. Bert Andrews, *Washington Witch Hunt: The Star-Chambers Proceedings of the State Department* (New York: Random House, 1948). Andrews won the Pulitzer Prize for the book.

5. "Statement concerning loyalty cases"; FBI file 101-467-187, p. 1427. Technical Surveillance Log; See Whitfield Diffie and Susan Landau, *Privacy on the Line: The Politics of Wiretapping and Encryption* (Cambridge, MA: The MIT Press, 1998), pp. 156–162.

6. FBI File 101-467-193, p. 23.

7. FBI File 101-467-187, pp. 262, 265, 453–456.

8. See Louise S. Robbins, "U.S. Librarians and Publishers Confront Joseph McCarthy: The Overseas Libraries Controversy and *The Freedom to Read*," *Libraries & Culture* 36 (Winter 2001): 27–39 for an account of McCarthy's attack on the USIA.

9. Stanley I. Kutler, *The American Inquisition; Justice and Injustice in the Cold War* (New York: Hill and Wang, 1982); *Congressional Record—Senate* (January 21, 1997): S537–538; *Congressional Record—Senate* (February 5, 1998): S459–460.

10. FBI File 101-467-187, p. 751.

11. Daily Reports. Chief Assistant Librarian. August 27, 1948. Vol. 8, Record Group 553, Library of Congress Archives. Paul Boswell, telephone communication with Louise S. Robbins, January 12, 1993. See Louise S. Robbins, "The Library of Congress and Federal Loyalty Programs, 1947–1956: No 'Communists or Cocksuckers'," *The Library Quarterly* 64 (October 1994): pp. 365–385.

12. Donald M. Dozer to Jesse Shera, July 5, 1949; Jesse H. Shera to Loyalty Security Board, U.S. Dept. of State, July 11, 1949; both Edward G. Holley File in possession of Louise Robbins. There is no follow-up letter in the file indicating whether Dozer kept his State Department job.

13. In *Library Literature and Information Science Fulltext*, the definitive article database of literature pertaining to libraries and librarians, a search of the

entire retrospective file contains only Philip's brief obituary and two feature length articles about Japanese libraries and librarians by Philip Keeney, both in *Library Journal* in May 1948. Judging from the wide coverage of the Keeneys carried over a number of years and available through *NewspaperArchive.com* in papers as diverse as the *European Stars and Stripes*; the *Ada, Okla. Evening News*; the *North Adams, Mass. Transcript*; the *Las Cruces, N.M. Sun-News*; the *Statesville, N.C. Record*; the *San Antonio, Texas Express;* and the *Long Beach, Calif. Independent*, there could have been few librarians who were unaware of the Keeneys' adventures.

14. FBI File 65-56402-1920, pp. 4–6, 12–13. Unless Brown's room was bugged, it is hard to know who Informant T-1 would be unless it was Brown himself. There is no mention in the FBI file of anyone else being in the room besides Brown and the Keeneys. If the room was bugged, it must have been so with Brown's knowledge.

15. FBI File 101-467-187, p. 1203; Technical Surveillance Log 65-56402-1-1360.

16. Philip O. Keeney, "Meet the Japanese Librarians," *Library Journal* 73 (May 1948): 768–772; "Japanese Libraries Are War-Damaged," *Library Journal* 73 (May 1948): 681–684. Keeney's article that more nearly detailed the plan he implemented in Japan and intended to implement in another country appeared as "Reorganization of the Japanese Library System," *Far Eastern Survey* 17 (January 1948): 19–22.

17. See Louise S. Robbins, *Censorship and the American Library: The American Library Association Responds to Threats to Intellectual Freedom, 1939–1969* (Westport, CT: Greenwood Press, 1996), especially pages 29–68.

18. Louise S. Robbins, "After Brave Words, Silence: American Librarianship Responds to Cold War Loyalty Programs, 1947–1957," *Libraries and Culture* 30 (Fall 1995): 345–365. Several librarians, mostly Quakers who would not sign a loyalty oath for religious reasons, lost their jobs during this time.

19. Although I have not looked at every manuscript page in the voluminous ALA Archives at the University of Illinois Urbana-Champaign, I have looked at all of the file of the Intellectual Freedom Committee for the period of this book, and nowhere in the 1940–1960 is there mention of the Keeneys' loyalty problems. If the committee debated whether or not to take up their cause it would be in this file or the file of David K. Berninghausen at the University of Minnesota, as Berninghausen was chair of the committee much of this time and was regarded as a "young turk," more radical than many of the established leaders. There is no mention of the Keeneys. Nor is there any discussion of the Keeneys in the debate on Loyalty Investigations, a logical place for them to be raised as a specter.

20. FBI File 101-467-178, p. 53. Daniel Melcher, a friend of the Keeneys, joined Bowker, the most prominent publishing house in the history of American librarianship and headed by his father Frederic Melcher, when he lost his position as director of the Committee on Atomic Information for being too close to Communists; this never appears in his biographies along with his impressive list of accomplishments. "The Political Persecution . . ." [Bancroft, Box 2], 3.

21. FBI File 101-467-193, pp. 46 and 47.

BIBLIOGRAPHY

PRIMARY SOURCES

Archival Material

American Association of University Professors Papers. Gelman Library. George Washington University, Washington, D.C.

American Library Association Archives. University of Illinois, Urbana-Champaign.

Charles Brown Papers. Iowa State University, Ames, Iowa.

Federal Bureau of Investigation. Washington, D.C.
> Philip and Mary Jane Keeney File 101-467.
> Nathan Gregory Silvermaster File 65-56402.

Federal Bureau of Investigation File 100-6470-50, the Institute of Pacific Relations, found at www.education-research.org/PDFs/IPR02.pdf (accessed July 18, 2008).

Edward G. Holley File. Personal file on Keeneys in possession of Louise S. Robbins.

Iowa Women's Archive. University of Iowa. http://sdrc.lib.uiowa.edu/iwa/findingaids/html/RaymondMargaret.htm (accessed April 4, 2007).

Mary Jane Keeney. U.S. Government Personnel File. Released from the United States Office of Personnel Management, St. Louis Area Office. November 1988.

Philip Olin Keeney Personnel File. K. Ross Toole Archives, University of Montana, Missoula.

Philip Olin Keeney Papers. Record Group 71/157, the Bancroft Library, University of California at Berkeley. Chiefly Box 2.

Philip Olin Keeney. U.S. Government Personnel File. Released from the United States Office of Personnel Management, St. Louis Area Office. November 1988.

Joe W. Kraus personal file on Progressive Librarians' Council in possession of Louise S. Robbins.

Library of Congress Archives, Record Group 538.

Poetry Magazine Papers, 1912–1936. The University of Chicago Library, Department of Special Collections.

PLC [Progressive Librarians Council] Bulletin. Entire run in the possession of Louise S. Robbins.

Alexander Vassiliev. Summaries and documents from the archive of the Russian Foreign Intelligence Service for the KGB. File 43173, v. 4. *Black Notebook [2007 Translation into English]*, trans. Philip Redko (1993–96). Thanks to John Earl Haynes and Alexander Vassiliev for sharing this translation prior to the publication of *Spies: The Rise and Fall of the KGB in America* (forthcoming 2009).

Venona Files. National Security Agency Website: www.nsa.gov/venona/ (accessed April 5, 2007).

Interview

Melba Phillips and Anne Florant, interviewed by Rosalee McReynolds, New York City, May 18, 1995.

Newspaper Articles

"Contempt Trial Ordered." *New York Times,* November 7, 1952.

"Dr. Simmons Is Given Contract for 3 Years." *Daily Missoulian,* April 14, 1937.

"11 in U.N. Accused of Communist Ties." *New York Times,* January 2, 1953.

"Ex-Aide of U.S. and U.N. Found Guilty of Contempt." *New York Times,* March 18, 1953.

"'J. Ryan' of 'Progressive League' not Graduate." *Montana Kaiman,* April 10, 1936.

"Mrs. Keeney Faces a Contempt Action." *New York Times,* February 26, 1952.

"Mrs. Keeney Fined; Answers Job Query." *New York Times,* March 21, 1953.

"Mrs. Keeney Freed in Contempt Trial." *New York Times,* April 5, 1955.

"New U.N. Hearing Asked." *New York Times,* September 27, 1951.

"Ousted U.N. Aides begin Final Fight." *New York Times,* August 7, 1951.

"Ousters Revoked by U.N. Tribunal." *New York Times,* September 5, 1951.

Parke, Richard H. "U.N. Editorial Aide Admits Red Links." *New York Times,* October 25, 1952.

Sullivan, Walter. "U.N. Staff's Charges of Bias in Ousters Get Final Hearing." *New York Times,* July 29, 1951.

Trachtenberg, Alexander. "Letters to the Times." *New York Times,* August 3, 1949.

"2 Win Damages from U.N." *New York Times,* November 14, 1951.

"U.N. Aide Accused as a Red Courier." *New York Times,* July 26, 1949.

"U.N. Aide on Trial Again." *New York Times*, April 1, 1955.
"U.N. Ex-Aide Wins Contempt Appeal." *New York Times*, August 27, 1954.
"U.N. Staff Scores 'Spy' Accusations." *New York Times*, July 26, 1949.
"U.S. to Test Rules of United Nations." *New York Times*, March 18, 1952.
White, William S. "Mrs. Keeney Faces a Contempt Action." *New York Times*, February 26, 1952.
Wood, Lewis. "Ninety Groups, Schools Named on U.S. List as Being Disloyal." *New York Times*, December 5, 1947.

Other Materials

"Academic Freedom and Tenure: Montana State University." *Bulletin of the American Association of University Professors* 24 (1938): 343–346.
"The American Library Association Library's Bill of Rights." *American Library Association Bulletin* 33 (October 15, 1939): 60–61.
"Breakfast in Honor of Archibald MacLeish." *PLC Bulletin* 2, no. 1 (Aug. 1940): 4.
Committee on Un-American Activities. U.S. House of Representatives. *The Shameful Years: Thirty Years of Soviet Espionage in the United States.* Washington, D.C.: GPO, December 30, 1951.
Diffie, Whitfield and Susan Landau. *Privacy on the Line: The Politics of Wiretapping and Encryption.* Cambridge, MA: The MIT Press, 1998.
"Dismissal of Philip O. Keeney." *American Library Association Bulletin* 32 (October 15, 1938): 771.
"Editorials." *PLC Bulletin* 3, no. 1 (August 1941): 1.
Ferguson, Milton. "A Case for Careful Investigation." *Library Journal* 62 (June 15, 1937): 512.
"Institute of Pacific Relations." United States Senate. Subcommittee to Investigate the Administration of the Internal Security Act and Other Internal Security Laws of the Committee on the Judiciary. February 18, 1952. Washington, D.C.: GPO, 1952.
Investigation of Un-American Propaganda Activities in the United States. Report of the Special Committee on Un-American Activities House of Representatives. Seventy-Eighth Congress. Second Session on H. Res. 282 to Investigate (1) the Extent, Character, and Objects of Un-American Propaganda Activities in the United States, (2) the Diffusion within the United States of Subversive and Un-American Propaganda that is Instigated from Foreign Countries or of a Domestic Origin and Attacks the Principle of the form of Government as Guaranteed by our Constitution, and (3) All Other Questions in Relation thereto That Would Aid Congress in Any Necessary Remedial Legislation. (Washington, D.C.: GPO, 1944), pp. 651–652.
The Keeney Case: Big Business, Higher Education, and Organized Labor, Report of an Investigation Made by the National Academic Freedom Committee of the American Federation of Teachers into the Causes of the Recent Dismissal of Professor Philip O. Keeney, Librarian, from Montana State University and

the role Played by Certain Business and Political Interests in the Affairs of the University. Chicago: American Federation of Teachers, 1939.

Keeney, Mary Jane. "The Making of a Radical: An Experience in American Education." *Black & White* 1 (Sept. 1939): 16–20.

Keeney, Philip. "Flexibility of Library Organization." *Library Journal* 59 (April 1, 1934): 312–313.

Keeney, Philip. "Democratic Aids to Staff Responsibility." *Library Journal* 59 (April 15, 1934): 361.

Keeney, Philip. "Meet the Japanese Librarians." *Library Journal* 73 (May 1948): 768–772.

Keeney, Philip. "Japanese Libraries Are War-Damaged." *Library Journal* 73 (May 1948): 681–684.

Keeney, Philip. "Reorganization of the Japanese Library System." *Far Eastern Survey* 17 (January 1948): 19–22.

"Library, Librarian." *Time* (June 19, 1939), p. 18.

Library of Congress Newsletter (Local 28. United Public Workers of America. CIO) 4, no. 8 (August 1941): 4.

MacLeish, Archibald. *The Irresponsibles.* New York: Duell, Sloan and Pearce, 1940.

McCarthy, Joseph R. "Communists in the State Department." Congressional Record 81st Cong., 2nd Session, pp. 1952–1957. Reprinted in *Annals of America* 17 (1950): 16–21.

McCarthy, Joseph R. "The Metropolitan Broadcasting Corp.—the Report Which was never Released." Extension of Remarks of Hon. Joseph R. McCarthy of Wisconsin in the Senate of the United States. Saturday, September 23 (legislative day of Friday, September 22), 1950. *Congressional Record—Appendix*, October 20, 1950, pp. A7679–7692.

"On the Role of the Librarian in the War." *PLC Bulletin* 3, no. 4 (March 1942): 1–2.

"Panned Poet." *Newsweek* (June 19, 1939), p. 20.

"Peace Letter." *PLC Bulletin* 2, no. 1 (August 1940): 3.

"Report for 1940–41." *PLC Bulletin* 3, no. 1 (August 1941): 5.

State of Montana ex rel Philip O. Keeney v. Roy Ayers et al (1st Cir, 1938). Reprinted in Transcript of the Record on Appeal, 69, *W.S. Davidson et al v. State of Montana ex rel Philip O. Keeney.*

Steele, James R. "Hire Learning in Montana." *Pacific Weekly* (March 16, 1936): 131–132.

"Testimony of Philip O. Keeney and Mary Jane Keeney and Statement Regarding Their Background." United States. Congress. House. Committee on Un-American Activities. 81st Congress. 1st Session. May 24, 25, June 9, 1949.

"Truth Goes Marching On." *PLC Bulletin* 1, no. 1 (September 1939): 4.

"Where to Stay in Cincinnati." *America Library Association Bulletin* 34 (March 1940): 195.

"The Witnesses (Cont'd)." *Time* (April 06, 1953), Time Archive www.time.com/time/magazine/article/0,9171,818137,00.html?promoid=googlep (accessed January 21, 2008).

SECONDARY SOURCES

Encyclopedia Articles

Buhle, Paul and Dan Georgakas. "Communist Party, USA" in *Encyclopedia of the American Left*. Edited by Mari Jo Buhle, Paul Buhle, and Dan Georgakas. New York: Oxford University Press, 1990.

"Daniel Melcher." *Supplement to the Dictionary of American Library Biography*. Edited by Wayne A. Wiegand. Englewood, CO: Libraries Unlimited, 1990, pp. 75–78.

"Todd, Albert May." *Who Was Who in America*, vol. 1. Chicago: A.N. Marquis, 1943, p. 1243.

"Gender Issues in Librarianship." *Encyclopedia of Library History*. Edited by Wayne A. Wiegand and Donald G. Davis. Jr. New York: Garland Publishing, 1994, pp. 227–232.

"Simmons, George Finlay." *Who Was Who in America*, vol. 3. Chicago: A.N. Marquis, 1960, p. 787.

Other Articles

Berry, John N. III, Editorial. *Library Journal* 117 (February 15, 1992): 100.

"F. D. Roosevelt to Felix Frankfurter. May 3, 1939." Reprinted in *American Libraries* 89 (May 1995): 408.

Johanningsmeier, Edward P. "The Soviet World of American Communism." *The Historian* 62 (Winter 2000): 412.

Klehr, Harvey. "The Strange Case of Roosevelt's 'Secret Agent': Frauds, Fools, & Fantasies." *Encounter* 59, no. 6 (Dec. 1982): 84–91.

Kraus, Joe W. "The Progressive Librarians' Council." *Library Journal* 97 (July 1972): 2351–2354.

Lewy, Guenter. "The Secret World of American Communism." *Society* 34 (Nov./ Dec. 1996): 101–102.

Nakamura, Yuriko, Taro Miura, and Akira Nemoto. "American Library Officers in the Occupied Japan." Unpublished paper presented at the American Library Association conference, July 9, 2000, in the possession of the author.

Nemoto, Akira, Taro Miura, Yuriko Nakamura, and Takashi Noga. "Library Policies of the Civil Information and Education Division, GHQ/SCAP in Japan, 1945–1952; an Analysis of the Policy Statements." *Bulletin of the School of Education. University of Tokyo* (1999): 459–461, 473–474. [English translation made of Japanese article made for Louise Robbins by Naomi Shiraishi.]

Plotke, David. "The Secret World of American Communism." *Political Science Quarterly* 111 (Winter 1996/97): 730–732.

Robbins, Louise S. "The Library of Congress and Federal Loyalty Programs, 1947–1956: No 'Communists or Cocksuckers'." *The Library Quarterly* 64 (October 1994): pp. 365–385.

Robbins, Louise S. "U.S. Librarians and Publishers Confront Joseph McCarthy: The Overseas Libraries Controversy and *The Freedom to Read*." *Libraries & Culture* 36 (Winter 2001): 27–39.

Robbins, Louise S. "After Brave Words, Silence: American Librarianship Responds to Cold War Loyalty Programs, 1947–1957." *Libraries and Culture* 30 (Fall 1995): 345–365.

Stielow, Frederick. "Librarian Warriors and Rapprochement: Carl Milam, Archibald MacLeish, and World War II." *Libraries & Culture* 25 (Fall 1990): 513–533.

Theoharis, Athan G. "The Soviet World of American Communism." *American Political Science Review* 93 (June 1999): 489–490.

Van Alstyne, William. "Academic Freedom and the First Amendment." *Law and Contemporary Problems* 53 (Summer 1990): 94.

Books and Other Materials

"Alexander Vassiliev's Notes on Anatoly Gorsky's December 1948 Memo on Compromised American Sources and Networks (Annotated)." Annotated by John Earl Haynes, Translated by Ronald Bachman and Harold Leich, assisted by John Earl Haynes, Additional assistance provided by Alexander Vassiliev. Revised October 2005. www.johnearlhaynes.org/page44.html#_ftnref46 (accessed March 2, 2008).

Andrews, Bert. *Washington Witch Hunt: The Star-Chambers Proceedings of the State Department.* New York: Random House, 1948.

Becker, Patti Clayton. *Books and Libraries in American Society during World War II: Weapons in the War of Ideas.* New York: Routledge, 2005.

Belknap, Michael R. *Cold War Political Justice: The Smith Act, the Communist Party, and American Civil Liberties.* Westport, CT: Greenwood Press, 1977.

Bentley, Elizabeth. *Out of Bondage: The Story of Elizabeth Bentley.* New York: Devin-Adair, 1951.

Bontecou, Eleanor. *The Federal Loyalty-Security Program.* Ithaca, NY: Cornell University Press, 1953.

Boyer, Paul. *When Time Shall Be No More.* Cambridge, MA: Harvard Belknap, 1992.

Bryan, Alice I. *The Public Librarian.* New York: Columbia University Press, 1948.

Bureau of Labor Statistics. CPI Inflation Calculator. www.bls.gov/ (accessed and calculated on June 11, 2008).

"Communism in Washington State: History and Memory Project." http://depts.washington.edu/labhist/cpproject/index.htm (accessed July 28, 2008).

Congressional Record—Senate (January 21, 1997): S537–538.

Congressional Record—Senate (February 5, 1998): S459–460.

Czestochowski, Joseph S. *The Legacy of Albert May Todd.* Kalamazoo, MI: Kalamazoo Historic Conservancy for the Preservation of Art, 2000.

Debs, Eugene V. *Letters of Eugene V. Debs,* vol. 1, *1874–1912.* Edited by J. Robert Constantine. Urbana: University of Illinois Press, 1990.

Dilling, Elizabeth. *Red Network: Who's Who and Handbook of Radicalism for Patriots.* Chicago: Dilling, 1934.

Donaldson, Scott. *Archibald MacLeish: An American Life.* Boston: Houghton Mifflin, 1992.

Draper, Theodore. *American Communism and Soviet Russia*. New York: Viking Press, 1960.

Espionage Act of 1917. www.staff.uiuc.edu/~rcunning/espact.htm (accessed June 11, 2008).

Freeland, Richard M. *The Truman Doctrine and the Origins of McCarthyism: Foreign Policy, Domestic Politics, and Internal Security*. New York: Knopf, 1972.

Geller, Evelyn. *Forbidden Books in American Public Libraries, 1876–1939: A Study in Cultural Change*. Westport, CT: Greenwood Press, 1984.

Ginger, Ray. *The Bending Cross: A Biography of Eugene Victor Debs*. New Brunswick, NJ: Rutgers University Press, 1949.

Glazer, Nathan. *The Social Basis of American Communism*. New York: Harcourt, Brace & World, 1961.

Guide to the Records of the U.S. Senate at the National Archives. www.archives.gov/legislative/guide/senate/chapter-13-judiciary-1947–1968.html#SISS (accessed July 18, 2008).

Haynes, John Earl and Harvey Klehr. *Venona: Decoding Soviet Espionage in America*. New Haven, CT: Yale University Press, 2000.

Holl, Jack. *Juvenile Reform in the Progressive Era; William R. George and the Junior Republic Movement*. Ithaca, NY: Cornell University Press, 1971.

Howe, Irving and Lewis Coser. *The American Communist Party: A Critical History 1919–1957*. Boston: Beacon Press, 1957.

Jaffe, Philip. *Amerasia: The Case from 1945 to the Present*. New York: Philip J. Jaffe, 1979.

Karetsky, Stephen. *Not Seeing Red: American Librarianship and the Soviet Union, 1917–1960*. Lanham, MD: University Press of America, 2002.

Kempton, Murray. *Part of our Time: Some Ruins and Monuments of the Thirties*. New York: Simon & Schuster, 1955.

Kessler, Lauren. *Clever Girl: Elizabeth Bentley, the Spy Who Ushered in the McCarthy Era*. New York: HarperCollins, 2003.

Klehr, Harvey. *The American Communist Movement: Storming Heaven Itself*. New York: Twayne, 1992.

Klehr, Harvey and Ronald Radosh. *The Amerasia Spy Case: Prelude to McCarthyism*. Chapel Hill: University of North Carolina Press, 1996.

Kournakoff, Sergei [Sergey Kurnakov]. *Savage Squadrons*. Boston: Hale, Cushman & Flint, 1935.

Kutler, Stanley I. *The American Inquisition; Justice and Injustice in the Cold War*. New York: Hill and Wang, 1982.

Latham, Earl. *The Communist Controversy in Washington*. Cambridge, MA: Harvard University Press, 1966.

Levenstein, Harvey. *Communism, AntiCommunism and the CIO*. Westport, CT: Greenwood Press, 1981.

Lewy, Guenter. *The Cause that Failed: Communism in American Political Life*. New York: Oxford University Press, 1990.

McCullough, David. *Truman*. New York: Simon & Schuster, 1992.

Mitchell, Thomas and Marcia Mitchell. *The Spy Who Seduced America: Lies and Betrayal in the Heat of the Cold War—The Judith Coplon Story.* Montpelier, VT: Invisible Cities Press, 2002.

Morgan, Ted. *Reds: McCarthyism in Twentieth-Century America.* New York: Random House, 2003.

Olmsted, Kathryn S. *Red Spy Queen: A Biography of Elizabeth Bentley.* Chapel Hill: University of North Carolina Press, 2002.

Packer, Herbert. *Ex-communist Witnesses: Four Studies in Fact Finding.* Stanford, CA: Stanford University Press, 1962.

Riebling, Mark. *Wedge: The Secret War between the FBI and CIA.* New York: Alfred A. Knopf, 1994.

Robbins, Louise S. *Censorship and the American Library: The American Library Association's Response to Threats to Intellectual Freedom, 1939–1969.* Westport, CT: Greenwood Press, 1996.

Rodman, Seldon. Ed. *A New Anthology of Modern Poetry.* New York: The Modern Library, 1938.

Ryan, James G. *Earl Browder: The Failure of American Communism.* Tuscaloosa: The University of Alabama Press, 1997.

Service v. Dulles, 354 U.S. 363 (1957).

Stephens, William [Legare George]. *Standard Forgings: Collected Poems 1919–1950.* Ann Arbor, MI: Ardis, 1978.

Sudoplatov, Pavel. *Special Tasks: The Memoirs of an Unwanted Witness—A Soviet Spymaster.* Boston: Little Brown, 1994.

Sullivan, Peggy. *Carl H. Milam and the American Library Association.* New York: H.W. Wilson, 1976.

Theoharis, Athan. *Seeds of Repression: Harry S. Truman and the Origins of McCarthyism.* Chicago: Quadrangle Books, 1971.

Thomison, Dennis. *A History of the American Library Association, 1876–1972.* Chicago: American Library Association, 1978.

Todd, Laurence. *Correspondent on the Left: The Memoirs of Laurence Todd, 1882–1957.* Anchorage, AK: privately published, 1996.

VENONA Chronology, National Security Agency Website. www.nsa.gov/venona/venon00127.cfm (accessed June 11, 2008).

Weinstein, Allen and Alexander Vassiliev. *The Haunted Wood: Soviet Espionage in America—the Stalin Era.* New York: The Modern Library, 1999.

Williams, Selma R. *Red-Listed: Haunted by the Washington Witch Hunt.* Reading, MA: Addison-Wesley, 1993.

Williamson, Charles Clarence. *Training for Library Service: A Report Prepared for the Carnegie Corporation of New York.* New York: The Corporation, 1923.

Winks, Robin. *Cloak and Gown: Scholars in the Secret War, 1939–1961.* New York: William Morrow, 1987.

INDEX

Figures in *italic* type refer to illustrations.

ABOUT THE AUTHORS

ROSALEE McREYNOLDS was a library historian and Director of Serials and Special Collections at Loyola University in New Orleans.

LOUISE S. ROBBINS is Professor and Director of the School of Library and Information Studies at the University of Madison, Wisconsin, and author of *Censorship and the American Library: The American Library Association Responds to Threats to Intellectual Freedom, 1939–1969* (Westport, CT: Greenwood Press, 1996) and *The Dismissal of Miss Ruth Brown: Civil Rights, Censorship and the American Library* (Norman, OK: The University of Oklahoma Press, 2000).